A Guide to the Contemporary Commonwealth

Also by W. David McIntyre

BACKGROUND TO THE ANZUS PACT

BRITISH DECOLONIZATION

COLONIES INTO COMMONWEALTH

NEW ZEALAND PREPARES FOR WAR

THE COMMONWEALTH OF NATIONS – ORIGINS AND IMPACT

THE IMPERIAL FRONTIER IN THE TROPICS

THE RISE AND FALL OF THE SINGAPORE NAVAL BASE

THE SIGNIFICANCE OF THE COMMONWEALTH

A Guide to the Contemporary Commonwealth

W. David McIntyre
Emeritus Professor of History
University of Canterbury
Christchurch
New Zealand

© W. David McIntyre 2001

First published 2001 by
PALGRAVE
Houndmills, Basingstoke, Hampshire RG21 6XS and
175 Fifth Avenue, New York, N. Y. 10010
Companies and representatives throughout the world

PALGRAVE is the new global academic imprint of
St. Martin's Press LLC Scholarly and Reference Division and
Palgrave Publishers Ltd (formerly Macmillan Press Ltd).

ISBN 0–333–96309–1 hardback
ISBN 0–333–96310–5 paperback

This book is printed on paper suitable for recycling and
made from fully managed and sustained forest sources.

A catalogue record for this book is available
from the British Library.

Library of Congress Cataloging-in-Publication Data
McIntyre, W. David (William David), 1932–
    A guide to the contemporary Commonwealth / W. David
McIntyre.
        p. cm.
    Includes bibliographical references and index.
    ISBN 0–333–96309–1
        1. Commonwealth countries—Handbooks, manuals, etc.
        2. Commonwealth (Organization)—Handbooks, manuals, etc.
    I. Title.

    DA10.5 .M39 2001
    909'.0971241—dc21
                                                    2001031520

10   9   8   7   6   5   4   3   2   1
10   09 08 07 06 05 04 03 02 01

Printed and bound in Great Britain by
Antony Rowe Ltd, Chippenham, Wiltshire

Contents

Part VI   People's Commonwealth – VIPPSOs

19.	Professional Associations	163
20.	Philanthropic Organisations	176
21.	Educational and Cultural Endeavours	185
22.	Sport and the Commonwealth Games	201
23.	Public–Private Partnerships and a Commonwealth Business Culture	211

Conclusion: The Commonwealth and the New Century   221

How to Keep up with the Commonwealth   231

Notes   235

Index   250

List of Tables

Country Codes

Ant	Antigua and Barbuda	Moz	Mozambique
Aus	Australia	Mts	Montserrat
Bah	Bahamas	Nam	Namibia
Ban	Bangladesh	Nfi	Norfolk Island
Bar	Barbados	Nhe	New Hebrides (Vanuatu)
Biz	Belize	Niu	Niue
Bot	Botswana	Nru	Nauru
Brg	British Guiana (Guyana)	Nzl	New Zealand
Bri	Britain	Nig	Nigeria
Bru	Brunei Darussalam	Pak	Pakistan
Bvi	British Virgin Islands	Png	Papua New Guinea
Caf	Central African Federation	Ski	St. Kitts – Nevis
		Slu	St. Lucia
Cmr	Cameroon	Sro	Southern Rhodesia
Can	Canada	Svg	St. Vincent and the Grenadines
Cey	Ceylon (Sri Lanka)		
Cok	Cook Islands	Sam	Samoa
Cyp	Cyprus	Sey	Seychelles
Dca	Dominica	Sle	Sierra Leone
Fij	Fiji	Sin	Singapore
Gam	The Gambia	Sol	Solomon Islands
Gha	Ghana	Rsa	Republic of South Africa
Grn	Grenada	Sri	Sri Lanka
Guy	Guyana	Swa	Swaziland
Ind	India	Tan	Tanzania
Jam	Jamaica	Tga	Tonga
Ken	Kenya	Tok	Tokelau Islands
Kri	Kiribati	Tri	Trinidad and Tobago
Les	Lesotho	Tuv	Tuvalu
Maw	Malawi	Uga	Uganda
Mas	Malaysia	Van	Vanuatu
Mdv	Maldives	Wsi	West Indies
Mlt	Malta	Zam	Zambia
Mri	Mauritius	Zim	Zimbabwe

Source: Derived mainly from Commonwealth Games country codes.

Preface

My intention in this book is to provide a fresh guide to the contemporary Commonwealth. The need for such a book has been a constant refrain in numerous reviews of Commonwealth activities over the past ten years. My main concern is to highlight critical questions of balance that emerged at the start of the new century as between the relative roles of governments and official agencies, voluntary associations and the private business sector.

The first part of the book briefly summarises the evolution of the Commonwealth for those unfamiliar with the background. The main body of the book looks at the association's symbols; political consultations and values; shared inter-governmental agencies; the huge voluntary field of endeavour known as 'the People's Commonwealth' including sport; and the rising expectations now laid on private business.

I started writing the book in Ottawa during 1998 while I held a T. H. B. Symons Fellowship in Commonwealth Studies tenable at Carleton University and I offer grateful thanks to the Association of Commonwealth Universities for this award. Special thanks are due to Anne and Norman Hillmer, who arranged accommodation and computer facilities, and David Farr, who organised introductions, and each of whom in so many ways made the time in Ottawa so pleasant and productive. Affectionate acknowledgements are offered to the ever-helpful staff at the Public Record Office, Kew, London; the National Archives of Canada, Ottawa; the New Zealand Archives, Wellington, and the University of Canterbury Library, Christchurch, New Zealand. The Commonwealth Secretariat, the Commonwealth Foundation, the Commonwealth of Learning, and the former Commonwealth Agricultural Bureaux (now CAB-International, a stand-alone international organisation) have all been extremely generous in granting interviews and supplying documentary material. The same is true for numberless voluntary organisations. My thanks to Ian Catanach and Ian Wards for perceptive criticisms of earlier drafts. For Marcia McIntyre my admiration and gratitude for mastering word processing skills to cope with my secretary-less state, for stylistic suggestions and much else cannot be adequately expressed.

I have had the advantage of observing each of the Commonwealth Heads of Government Meetings since 1987, as special correspondent of the *New Zealand International Review*. This has given me a first-hand feel of the renaissance that the Commonwealth experienced in the 1990s. I have also sensed the significant changes of balance that emerged, more especially since 1995, and some of the problems this is producing. The long-term effect of this changing focus is as yet unclear and gives ground for some disquiet about the future direction of the association. This book is offered as a contribution to the on-going debate.

W. DAVID MCINTYRE

Introduction

The Commonwealth entered the twenty-first century in a mood of historical celebration following a decade of revival and renewal. Yet among significant anxieties about its future, two matters stood out. One was all too well known; the other little appreciated. The first was regret that so little attention was paid to the Commonwealth and so little was generally known about it. Although it is the world's oldest political association of states, an association unique in the width and depth provided by its voluntary, unofficial and non-political life, it is little known except for the symbolic Head, the Queen, and its most popular event, the Commonwealth Games. Report after report during the 1990s deplored this low profile and even lack of up-to-date literature.

The second question is more interesting and urgent. An association that had evolved around political consultations and shared inter-governmental agencies turned increasingly in the 1990s to cherish, and to work through, its wealth of voluntary, non-official organisations. Trumpeted rather grandly as 'the People's Commonwealth', or more recently as 'civil society', these elements came into their own in the 1990s as never before. Yet by the end of the decade a new lodestar had appeared in the optimistic role accorded to the private business sector. There was talk of a 'Commonwealth business culture' and 'public–private partnerships'. Emerging new balances between the political, civil society and business sectors provide the new century's most fascinating unresolved issue. In seeking to provide an up-to-date survey of recent developments, this new guide also highlights this question of the new balances.

The twentieth century closed with some euphoria over historical anniversaries and recent landmarks. In 1997, 500 years after John Cabot's first voyage from Bristol to Newfoundland, the last populous colonial enclave, Hong Kong, was handed back to China after 156 years of British rule. The same year marked the centennial of the second Colonial Conference, held at the time of Queen Victoria's Diamond Jubilee. It was the half-centennial of the ending of the British Raj in the Indian sub-continent – a jubilee marked by a visit to India and Pakistan by Queen Elizabeth, the Head of the Commonwealth. It was also the half-centennial of New Zealand's formal independence. That was an anniversary nobody remembered – even in New Zealand! It was the fortieth anniversary of independence for Ghana and Malaya. It was the year of the Queen's golden wedding and of the first Commonwealth Heads of Government Meetings (now known by the bluff, unmusical acronym, Chogm) to be held in Britain for 20 years. As it could be the last to be held there during her reign, the Queen was invited, for the very first time, to take part in the opening ceremony and to address the association as its Head.

Fiji returned to the fold in 1997 after a lapse of membership lasting ten years. This brought the total membership to 54, though one member, Nigeria, was then under suspension. Applications for membership were received from some very unlikely hopefuls, namely Yemen, Rwanda and the Palestinian Authority. Yet they were not rejected – they were to be kept under review. In the run-up to the Chogm, the first Commonwealth Business Forum was held in London and the first Commonwealth Youth Forum met in Edinburgh. During the Chogm, another 'first' was marked by a large unofficial jamboree called 'Commonwealth Forum' mounted in the wings of the Chogm, where over 80 voluntary organisations mounted displays, ran mini-conferences and gave press briefings.

Two years later, 1999 was quietly celebrated as the jubilee of the modern Commonwealth. Secretariat letterheads incorporated the logo '*50 – The Modern Commonwealth – Celebrating Fifty Years*' to mark the anniversary of the London Declaration of 1949, which had facilitated India's continued membership under its republican constitution and recognition by all the members of the symbolic position of 'Head of the Commonwealth'. In this role, the Queen addressed the Chogm once again in Durban, and concluded by quoting the 1949 Declaration's pledge to cooperation by the 'free and equal members … in the pursuit of peace, liberty, and progress'. All this activity, which is little reported, suggests an active, expansive, association at the official and non-official levels.

Yet euphoria is misplaced. The millennial dawn was overshadowed by a looming 'generation gap'. The Heads of Government were given and approved, in 1997 at Edinburgh, two very significant, though little remembered, reports. One was on Commonwealth Studies at the tertiary level, which concluded that there was a signal paucity of such provision. It pointed to the significant 'generation gap' in sheer knowledge about the Commonwealth and especially a failure to reflect its evolution into 'a truly polycentric association'. The second report, on information services, indicated that public relations was a virtual disaster area. In spite of the myriad of activities around the world – many of considerable intrinsic interest and value – popular perceptions rarely moved beyond the periodic Games or a royal visit or an occasional media-induced 'crisis' during a Chogm once every two years. Indeed, during the launch of a challenging unofficial pamphlet on *Reinventing the Commonwealth* at the time of the Durban Chogm, a young South African journalist said she had no particular attachment to the Commonwealth and declared that the young people running the new South Africa did not feel they needed to know about it. This book represents a modest attempt to tackle the crisis of perception by filling in some of this information and educational gap.

The section on 'Historical Perspectives' is designed as background to indicate how the association reached its present stage. How did a concept first evolved by imperial federalists, who sought the unity of the former British Empire, evolve into something quite the opposite – an association of equal, independent states? How could a grouping which, as recently as the Second World War, acted as one of the Great Powers, turn into what is in effect the world's premier forum for small states? How have the British, who found this evolution at times so disappointing and even offensive, overcome their disillusionment and indifference and have continued to play a prime part?

The bulk of the book – Chapter 7 onwards, for those familiar with the background – analyses certain recent developments, which surprised many people. They amounted to a renaissance of the Commonwealth in the 1990s, but raised the new question of balance.

On the matter of symbolism: why, it may be asked, does an association with an overwhelming majority of republican states, have as chief symbol a monarch, Queen Elizabeth? And why is the state where the symbol was first suggested, Ireland, not a member? One of the supreme ironies of the modern Commonwealth is that the symbolic Headship was first adopted to facilitate India's membership as a republic, but the idea had originated earlier from Eamon de Valera, the Irish revolutionary, whose country left the Commonwealth only nine days before the symbolic Headship was adopted. Looking at political consultation: why are so many heads of government prepared to attend the biennial Chogms? These are the world's oldest, largest and longest meetings of presidents and prime ministers where the leaders of a few multi-million populations sit around the table with a majority of leaders from countries of 1,500,000 or less. How does the organisation manage to prosecute its activities on slender resources? Compared with bureaucracies like the United Nations, the European Union, and the World Bank, the Commonwealth Secretariat is minuscule and its aid-granting arm can provide only a fraction of the sums available from the main international and even national providers. Why, then, are these slender Commonwealth resources so cherished? What values, if any, does the association profess? And what mechanisms are available for policing them?

Turning to the so-called 'People's Commonwealth' and 'civil society': how real are these concepts? Why have so many voluntary, professional, philanthropic and sporting organisations flourished in the Commonwealth? How are they harnessed by the political Commonwealth, or do they find themselves in conflict with it? How far do citizens have any real share in the Commonwealth? And why the recent focus on private business enterprise? What is meant by the Commonwealth business culture? Will the corporate world contribute as much or more than the politicians, the official agencies or the voluntary organisations? Such new questions of balance will dominate the early years of the new century.

The Commonwealth entered the twenty-first century with a sense of quiet confidence that it had found a useful role for itself in the post-imperial, post-Cold War world of international relations. Yet the conviction remained that the association was little understood, and was undervalued; was lacking in focus and public profile; and, above all, powerless to prevent serious violations by undemocratic forces determined to undermine its values. Meanwhile, those involved in its affairs, in politics, administration, civil society and business were trying to come to grips with new balances of influence and focus within the association.

Part I
Historical Perspectives

1
Origins and Meanings

A publisher once told the author that 'Commonwealth' in the title was the kiss of death for a book. One reason for the Commonwealth's low profile in public imagination is that its meaning and symbols are obscure and little understood. During the 1997 Chogm in Edinburgh, Tony Blair, the British prime minister, tried to rectify the deficiency, but only managed to create further obfuscation: 'The word "Commonwealth" has become so familiar that we do not pause often enough to think of its meaning. The very word means commonweal; a shared richness; something to be possessed by all.'[1]

Clearly Blair had not looked beyond the first definition listed in the Oxford English Dictionary. There were five to choose from: 1) general good, public welfare or commonweal; 2) body politic, the body of people constituting a state or nation; 3) a republic, a state with supreme power vested in the people; 4) a body of persons united for some common purpose, like the commonwealth of letters; and 5) the title of certain specific states. This last makes quite a list: Australia, Bahamas, Dominica, Kentucky, Northern Marianas, Massachusetts, Puerto Rico and, not least, England between 1649 and 1660. Then, in 1991, twelve former Soviet Republics joined in the 'Commonwealth of Independent States'. Blair's choice of 'commonweal' may have suited his political purpose of proclaiming New Labour's 'Cool Britannia', but it did less than justice to the origins of the contemporary Commonwealth.

'Commonwealth', in its modern usage, incorporates aspects of most of the dictionary definitions but is, perhaps, best rendered as a 'family of nations' from within the former British Empire. It was first used in this way before the American Revolution in relation to the early colonies and there were also maverick uses in Victorian times. Lord

Carnarvon referred in 1868 to the 'Imperial Commonwealth', and Lord Rosebery in 1884 called the Empire a 'commonwealth of nations'.[2] By the early years of the twentieth century, the labels 'Colony', 'Empire' and 'Imperial' were felt to be too harsh, authoritarian and old-fashioned for those groups of self-governing colonies, which had coalesced into 'nations' in Australia, Canada, New Zealand and South Africa. Commonwealth, in the sense of family, felt better. Alternative suggestions, 'Britannic Alliance or Partnership', very apt for the time, did not catch on.[3]

The other label which came into use at this time was 'Dominion' – the modern meaning of which also became the antithesis of its origins. Originally it signified subordination, from *dominus*, master, lord, and *dominium*, lordship, authority, sovereignty, lands of a feudal lord, territory subject to a ruler. The earliest colonies in the New World were the King's 'Dominions beyond the Seas'. Yet Dominion came to signify complete self-government, then independence.

The pioneers in this transition were Canadians. In 1867, the British North America Act authorised the confederation of the North American Colonies – originally comprising Canada (divided into Ontario and Quebec), Nova Scotia and New Brunswick – as 'one dominion under the name of Canada'. The intended title 'Kingdom of Canada' was dropped to avoid offending the great republic to the south. Credit for the new style is accorded to Leonard Tilley of New Brunswick, who came up with this solution during his daily scripture readings. Psalm 72, verse 8, runs: 'He shall have Dominion also from sea to sea, and from the river unto the ends of the earth.' Was this not suitably symbolic for the new Canada?[4] But the new synonym for kingdom did not alter Canada's legal subordination as part of the 'Dominions beyond the Seas'. Better descriptive labels were sought in the early years of the twentieth century.

It was a Francophone Canadian prime minister, Wilfred Laurier, who complained that vast, self-governing, federal Canada was still lumped together with little places like Trinidad and Barbados. During discussions in 1907 about the make-up of proposed imperial conferences, a formula was sought to mark the distinction. 'Self-governing Colonies' was the prosaic label offered by Sir Joseph Ward of New Zealand. Laurier preferred 'self-governing Dominions beyond the Seas'. Alfred Deakin of Australia went for the constitutionally more precise 'British Dominions possessing responsible government', but his fellow premiers liked the simpler 'self-governing Dominions'. Laurier preferred one word, so Deakin conceded that, as the Dominion of Canada was senior to the Commonwealth of Australia, 'Dominion' had the better claim. Laurier concluded, rather enigmatically, that Dominion was 'a general term which covers many words which it is not possible to define otherwise'.[5] So 'Dominion' became the label for the self-governing colonies – a meaning which, in spirit, was the opposite of that in the original designation 'Dominions beyond the Seas'.

The Dominions became the core of the 'Commonwealth'. Here was the other new usage, which would soon reverse its meaning. Commonwealth, for its leading proponents, embodied considerable idealism. The originators of the style 'British Commonwealth of Nations' at the time of the First World War – Alfred Zimmern, Lionel Curtis and Jan Smuts – had an exalted concept of self-government and citizenship derived largely from classical sources, which seemed to offer a solution in the dangerous predicament Britain discovered itself to be in, as it came to realise that the peak of its power in relation to rivals had passed. The global spread of Empire presented severe and expensive defence liabilities, but it also provided some close allies and potential reinforcements to boost Britain's military and naval power. Yet, if the Dominions were to assist in the defence of the Empire and help to pay for its navy, they would want a voice in policy and decision-making. The solution, in the view of the imperial idealists of *The Round Table*, lay in federation or union. The popularisers of the 'Commonwealth' label were mainly imperial federalists, who adopted the word to symbolise the reality of self-government combined with mutual sharing of burdens. Lionel Curtis, who pressed the logic of these ideas to their extreme, posed the stark choice: federate or disinte-grate.[6] Few could accept his logic and the new style came to apply to the loose, voluntary association, which is the antithesis of federation or union.

This crucial reversal of meaning dates from the very start of the formal usage of the new title. In an attempt to restore peace in Ireland and satisfy the long-standing Irish craving for Home Rule, articles of agreement for a treaty were drawn up in 1921, which provided that Ireland would become the Irish Free State and have the same status as Australia, Canada, New Zealand and South Africa in the 'group of nations forming the British Commonwealth of Nations'.[7] This was the first formal use of the style, which was soon sanctified by its incorpora-tion in the definition of the 'position and mutual relations' of Britain and the Dominions drafted by Lord Balfour in 1926. It was legalised in the Statute of Westminster of 1931, which made the Dominions as independent as they wished to be under a common allegiance to the

Crown. Yet this formal embodiment of the idealists' concept proved short-lived.

'British Commonwealth of Nations', along with 'British Empire', may have been grist for some high-flown Churchillian rhetoric during the Second World War, but, with the independence of India, Pakistan and Ceylon as Dominions in 1947–8, both of these titles became outmoded and inaccurate. In 1948 'British' was dropped from the front of the title and 'Dominions' gave way to 'Commonwealth Members'. The title 'Commonwealth of Nations' had an even shorter life. After a final appearance in the Declaration of Principles adopted in 1971, it faded from the political lexicon leaving the simple 'Commonwealth' of contemporary usage. This signifies a voluntary association of independent states that consult and cooperate in matters of common interest and recognise the Queen as Head of the Commonwealth.

2
Dominion Status and the 1926 Declaration

The Dominions made up the original core of the Commonwealth, but this label would soon disappear from the political dictionary. Ironically, Virginia is still known as the 'Old Dominion', but 'Dominion of Canada' dropped out of common use from the 1920s. Canada joined the United Nations under the style used in the British North America Act – 'Canada' – though it continued to celebrate Dominion Day until 1982. New Zealand joined the United Nations as 'New Zealand', but continued to have Dominion Weather Forecasts until the 1970s. 'Dominions beyond the Seas' was removed from the royal title in 1952 when Queen Elizabeth was proclaimed as 'Queen of this Realm and all Her other Realms and Territories, and Head of the Commonwealth'. Among the few relics of this usage to remain are New Zealand's Dominion Museum and the Inter-Dominion Trotting Championships between Australia and New Zealand.

The original 'Dominions' that chose this distinguishing mark in 1907 were – in order of 'seniority' – Canada, Australia, New Zealand, Newfoundland, Cape Colony, Natal and Transvaal. The last three came together in 1910, along with the Orange Free State (not represented in 1907), to make a single Dominion called the Union of South Africa. When the southern counties of Ireland, as the Irish Free State, became the sixth Dominion in 1922, the seeds of complete transition were sown.

Dominion status was a halfway house between colonial status and independence. It proved short-lived because the six Dominions could not agree about the meaning of their status. Australia and the smallest, most remote, Dominions (New Zealand and Newfoundland) were happy with it and cherished the British Empire. Canada, South Africa and the Irish Free State had their reasons for pressing self-government to its logical conclusion. Canada, with its Francophone population, and South Africa, with the Afrikaners, had domestic reasons for muting the 'Britishness' of the connection. The Irish Free State government fought a civil war with those Irish Nationalists who resented partition of the Ulster counties and wanted an all-Ireland republic. A resolution of the Imperial War Conference of 1917 gave the 'restless' Dominions some hope that the constitution of the Commonwealth of Nations would be ironed out, once and for all, after the war. This never happened. In 1926 a committee on inter-imperial relations, chaired by Lord Balfour, considered the 'position and mutual relations' of Britain and the six.[1] In what Leo Amery called the 'defining sentence' or 'status formula',[2] the first principle of the modern Commonwealth was declared:

> *They are autonomous Communities within the British Empire, equal in status, in no way subordinate one to another in any aspect of their domestic or external affairs, though united by a common allegiance to the Crown and freely associated as members of the British Commonwealth of Nations.*

This formula, the 'Balfour definition', often called 'Balfour declaration', should not be confused with the other 'Balfour declaration' of 1917, announcing the policy of creating a Jewish national home in Palestine.

The 1926 declaration was really only a description of a situation which had evolved over an 80-year period and it embodied some glaring ambiguities. The parties (Britain and the Dominions) were described as 'within the British Empire', but they were 'freely associated' as members of the 'British Commonwealth of Nations'. The report even went on to say that 'equality of status', the root principle of the relationship, did not 'universally extend to function'. The ambiguity was deliberate. Sir Saville Garner, of the Dominions Office, later saw it as only the first of the many 'antiphonal' declarations that would characterise the modern Commonwealth.[3] More significantly, the four-fold doctrines of **autonomy, equality, common allegiance** and **free association** had real political and emotional force at the time.

They were embodied in the preamble of the Statute of Westminster in 1931 by which the Dominions became as independent as they wished. This Act ended the power of the British Parliament over the Dominions unless they made a specific request and consented to it. The constitutional instruments of Canada, Australia and New Zealand were exempted from the Act and the operative clauses did not apply to

Australia, New Zealand or Newfoundland until 'adopted' by their own parliaments. Australia delayed until 1942; New Zealand until 1947; Newfoundland gave up Dominion status during the depression in 1933 and joined Canada in 1949. Today, the 1931 Act is given as the reason for a little oddity to be found in Secretariat lists of Commonwealth members, which have Australia, Britain, Canada, New Zealand and South Africa 'joining' the Commonwealth in 1931. A footnote explains that the Statute of Westminster is 'for convenience regarded as the beginning of the Commonwealth'.[4] As we have seen, this explanation is quite inaccurate. The beginnings of the idea of 'Commonwealth-as-family' go back at least to Victorian times, if not to the American Colonies. Even the formal usage pre-dates 1931.

For Dominion status, the Balfour definition and the Statute of Westminster spelt the beginning of the end. As Leo Amery explained quite emphatically in 1926, 'freely associated' also implied a 'right to dissociate'.[5] The Irish were the first to grasp this. In 1932 the government of the Free State, which had played a very constructive role in producing both the 1926 declaration and the 1931 Act, changed. Eamon de Valera, the new Taoiseach (prime minister), had opposed the 1921 treaty setting up the Free State and he had fought against the government in the Civil War. In 1921 he had produced his own alternative scheme for a settlement based on a republic in a united Ireland 'associated' with the Commonwealth. His prime aim was to exclude the British Crown from any role in Irish domestic affairs, but he would have been prepared to accept the King as 'head of the Association'.[6] After coming to power in 1932, he could not undo partition, but he could exclude the Crown. The British were asked to recall the Governor-General; his Irish replacement eventually ceased to function and the office lapsed. The oath of allegiance was ended, as were appeals to the Privy Council.

De Valera's masterpiece was the External Relations Act of 1936 defining Ireland's relations with the Commonwealth. As long as the Free State was associated with Britain and the other Dominions, with the King recognised by those nations as the 'symbol of their cooperation' and continuing to act on behalf of each (on the advice of their respective governments) for diplomatic purposes, he would do the same for the Free State. Next, after a referendum in 1937, a republican-type constitution was adopted whereby the Free State became a sovereign, independent, democratic state styled 'Éire or Ireland'.[7] The British and Dominion governments agreed to treat it as a Dominion in external association with the Commonwealth. Ireland's neutrality in the

Second World War was a clear demonstration that Dominion status had become fully independent status.

By the end of the Second World War, Ireland's position had shown that Dominion status was, in effect, redundant. Moreover, Canada, New Zealand and South Africa had each made separate decisions to enter the Second World War. Only in Australia did the Prime Minister take it that Britain's declaration applied to his country. All four old Dominions joined the UN as independent members.

Clement Attlee, who became Britain's prime minister in 1945, hoped that Éire would return to Commonwealth conclaves, and de Valera was interested, but only if partition could be discussed. Moreover, the subtle nuances of 'external association', so meaningful for him, were a bone of contention for the Inter-party Government which succeeded him in 1948. They determined to make the break. On 7 September 1948, during a press conference in Ottawa, after attending a meeting of the Canadian Bar Association, Prime Minister John A. Costello announced that the External Relations Act was to be repealed. Asked if this meant that Ireland would leave the Commonwealth, he spoke somewhat ambiguously, about continued 'association' with Britain and Commonwealth countries, but admitted that Ireland would quit.[8] At midnight on 17/18 April 1949 the Republic of Ireland left the Commonwealth and on Easter Monday the new republic was celebrated. Five days later Nehru announced that India would stay in as a republic. Fifty years on, as Irish leaders on both sides of the partition line seek a cooperative future for Ireland, hopes are expressed that Ireland will come back into the Commonwealth it once did so much to shape.[9]

Although the Statute of Westminster and the Irish anomaly made Dominion status redundant, and Canada and South Africa fretted about the ancient phrase 'Dominions beyond the Seas' in the royal title, Dominion status had a final unexpected fling of utility in 1947 as a device for arranging a speedy transfer of power in the Indian Empire.

Equal status, as described in the 1926 formula, was not a *new policy*, merely a succinct definition of a relationship, which had evolved over nearly a century since debates in British North America in the 1820s and 1830s about self-government. The system, first authorised in respect of Nova Scotia in 1846, and put into practice there, and in Canada in 1848, had evolved from controversies lasting two decades involving the transfer to the colonies of an up-to-date version of the contemporary British practice of parliamentary government.[10]

Students, when asked today to define 'responsible government' usually say 'good government' or 'government with a sense of responsibility'. But in Commonwealth history it has the much more specific meaning of **an executive responsible to the legislature.** A government must be answerable to a parliament and have majority support in that parliament to get its measures through. It means in practice, government by leaders of the parliamentary majority and the Crown acting on the advice of ministers. At first, when it began in the 1840s, this applied only to internal affairs, and certain general powers were reserved to the British Parliament. Over the next 80 years these imperial reservations were removed, one by one, in pragmatic decisions, with the whole matter tidied up by the Statute of Westminster in 1931. Dominion status, as it emerged after 1907, was the distinguishing label which marked the countries with responsible government from the directly ruled dependencies, the greatest of which was India.

In India representative legislatures were progressively developed, but there was great reluctance to go beyond and give in to Indian demands for responsible government. It was not conceded as an ultimate goal until 1917, and an experimental half-responsible system, known as dyarchy, tried in the 1920s, left Indian nationalists dissatisfied. Although the declaration of equality in 1926 briefly excited Indian leaders to demand Dominion status, by the time this was accepted by Britain as the goal in 1929, the Indian radicals were calling for complete independence. During the Second World War, Leo Amery, who had had a key part in the 1926 Declaration, tried to persuade Churchill to promise Dominion status after the war, but Churchill refused. By now, even the chances for a united India were slim. The big concessions the British made during the war were that Indians could write their own constitution after the war; could stay in or go out of the Commonwealth; and that some provinces might even constitute a separate state. But constitution writing was liable to be a contentious and lengthy process and there were fears of a complete breakdown of law and order after the war, as some elements looked to violent revolution.

As a short-cut to an orderly British withdrawal and a peaceful transfer of power to well-known and moderate leaders, the idea of independence through Dominion status was revived by some Indians in 1946. The Viceroy's Reforms Commissioner advised that a grant of Dominion status under the Statute of Westminster could provide the framework of an immediate transfer of power to an elected government even before the new constitution was completed. Therefore, in 1947, a simple piece of legislation, specifically titled the Indian

Independence Act, was passed by the British Parliament providing for the creation of two Dominions, India and Pakistan. Ceylon, the first Colonial Office dependency deemed ready for independence, demanded the same status and also joined the Commonwealth as a Dominion in 1948.

By this time, it was realised in London that the ambiguities which had persisted over the previous 20 years could not go on. It was agreed that 'Dominion' should be dropped in favour of 'Commonwealth country'; instead of 'Dominion status' the new formula would be 'fully independent member of the Commonwealth'. The Dominions Office became the Commonwealth Relations Office, into which the India Office was soon merged. 'British' was dropped in front of 'Commonwealth of Nations' in the overall title.[11]

Old habits die hard. In 1951 the Labour government, which had negotiated the momentous transfers of power in South Asia, went out of office. The Conservatives (under Winston Churchill), who came in, did not contemplate granting independence to some 40 dependencies, some with populations of less than one million. Self-government – yes; but Commonwealth membership – surely not! Some 'mezzanine status' with self-government, but not involving Commonwealth membership, was sought. The now 'vacant' label, 'Dominion status', was revisited, but turned down. As each dependency came up for independence in the era of accelerating decolonisation after 1960, most countries would accept nothing less than full Commonwealth membership. Dominion status surfaced only once more, in the case of Fiji in 1970. Rival political leaders in the islands could agree that their country should advance to Dominion status – meaning 'become a fully sovereign independent State' – and 'seek membership of the Commonwealth'. Here, then, was final confirmation of what had been implicit in 1926 and explicit since 1947.

The story of Dominion status should not be discounted. It is unique in the history of decolonisation and represents the Commonwealth's contribution to one of the great transitions of the twentieth century. Arnold Smith, the first Secretary-General of the Commonwealth, was fond of recounting how he once lectured a Soviet audience about the non-revolutionary way to freedom, which he dubbed the path of 'persuasion and dialogue'. He put it slightly differently to an audience of American editors when he said of Canada: 'instead of cutting the umbilical cord that bound us to the centre of the Empire, as the Americans had done, we pulled and stretched and twisted this cord out of all recognition and made it work both ways'.[12]

3
Republic Status and the 1949 Declaration

India, Pakistan and Ceylon became Dominions and members of the Commonwealth, but Burma, which became independent in 1948 a month before Ceylon, became a republic outside the Commonwealth. As it was well known, from the end of 1946, that India's new constitution would also be for a 'sovereign independent republic', did this mean that India, too, would leave the Commonwealth?

This question highlighted, in the most acute form, the problem of the Commonwealth's future. The Irish link was tenuous; even the more well-disposed Irish leaders complained about 'anomalies and anachronisms'. Before Indian independence, Attlee was warned by the British Cabinet Secretary, Sir Norman Brook, that a new basis for the Commonwealth had to be found. From an ex-Indian civil servant, P. J. H. Stent, came the idea of a two-tier Commonwealth of monarchical and non-monarchical or associated states, on the ground that Asian countries would never accept a white king.[1] Sir Walter Monckton, who had been constitutional adviser to the Nizam of Hyderabad, pointed out that the King could never be independent India's head of state, but he might be acceptable as 'Head of the association'[2] – a suggestion similar to that made by de Valera in 1921.

Attlee created a ministerial committee on Commonwealth Relations in 1947 to find a formula that would enable the greatest number of newly independent states to adhere to the Commonwealth without undue uniformity in their domestic constitutions. Another contributor to the discussion was Malcolm MacDonald, a pre-war Colonial Secretary, who as Governor-General of Malaya in 1947 was concerned about the impact that events in South Asia would have on Southeast Asia. He feared a domino effect if India and Burma were to leave the Commonwealth and wondered if the Irish model could provide a way.

(MacDonald remembered his negotiations with de Valera in the 1930s and he had supported Éire's external association.) MacDonald also wondered if the King might be recognised as 'Head of the Commonwealth'.[3] These ideas were discussed by a committee of senior Whitehall officials in 1948 which favoured the nomenclature changes such as dropping 'Dominion status'. It, too, saw merit in the concept of the King as 'Supreme Head of the Commonwealth', possibly with some diplomatic role on the Irish model.[4] Brook was sent by Attlee to sound out the leaders in Ottawa, Wellington and Canberra before the 1948 Prime Ministers' Meetings (PMM), the first to be attended by the prime ministers of the three new Asian Dominions. Before Brook got home, however, the Irish option was eliminated by Costello's announcement that Ireland would quit the Commonwealth. Informal discussions at the time of the 1948 PMM failed to reach any formula to cater for India's continued membership as a republic.

Could the Commonwealth accommodate a republic? No one, it seems, remembered that the South African Republic (the Transvaal) had existed under British suzerainty in Victorian times, though it was not a propitious precedent. Certain things were clear. India would certainly become a republic. However, it wished to remain in the Commonwealth. There was little inclination among the other members to exclude India. Attlee believed there had to be some link through the Crown; so did his ministers and the other Commonwealth leaders. But a major conceptual breakthrough was made by Patrick Gordon Walker, the former Oxford history tutor, now Parliamentary Under-Secretary in the Commonwealth Relations Office, to whom Attlee entrusted the donkey work. Gordon Walker suggested in a paper of 31 December 1948 that instead of regarding some link with the Crown as the founding principle, they should focus on the will and intent of the members:

> What I have in mind is not a weakening of the connection through the Crown to the lowest possible point but the deliberate and friendly snapping of the Crown-link by mutual consent and the simultaneous adoption of a completely non-monarchical Dominion into the Commonwealth, but a Dominion that genuinely and sincerely wishes to remain in the Commonwealth.

Let there be two declarations, he said: 'in one India would say it wished to stay in as a republic; in the other the rest would say they agreed.'[5]

This approach was accepted, after considerable grumbling, by the British Cabinet. Emissaries were sent around all member capitals to sound out the prime ministers in preparation for a conference in London. Nearly everyone wanted India to stay in. Only in New Zealand was there difficulty about severing the Crown link. Three options were presented by Lord Listowel, Attlee's emissary to Wellington: India as a member without allegiance to the Crown; as a foreign state in close treaty relations with the Commonwealth; or as a foreign state with no treaty relations. Peter Fraser, the Scots-born New Zealand prime minister (who had once worked as a carpenter in the Houses of Parliament in Westminster) did not want to 'cheapen the link or weaken the Crown'. He thought the price was too high. 'What do we get from all this sacrifice?' He feared it would be 'nebulous good-will and endless conferences'. He said an association could not be 'based on nebulae ... we would have a flabby Commonwealth'. He was 'terribly doubtful' about the whole idea and was determined to demand in London what India would give in return. Would they come to the defence of fellow members? His permanent head of the External Affairs Department, Alister McIntosh, was even blunter. He thought it inevitable that a two-tier system would emerge – he felt it best to let India go.[6]

The matter was settled remarkably smoothly at a special conference in London in 1949. As the premiers began to arrive, the Republic of Ireland left the Commonwealth on the 18 April. The very next day Lester Pearson, the Canadian Minister for External Affairs (standing in for his prime minister), called at Number 10 to talk with Sir Norman Brook, who was emphatic that India should be allowed to stay in. The coincidence of two republics moving in opposite directions at the same time is only one of the great ironies of the occasion. The other was the attitude of Buckingham Palace. The Prime Ministers' conference began with sherry at No 10 followed by lunch at the Palace with the royal family, where the ambience of gold plate and family feeling caused the genial Anglophile Canadian to hope that the Asian leaders were suitably impressed. He was, himself, delighted to discover from an old friend, the King's Private Secretary, that the Palace had been looking into precedents and was reassured to find that the Holy Roman Empire had included the Republics of Danzig and Lübeck![7]

When the leaders got down to business, the idea of two declarations did not meet favour, so a single document was tried. In the first draft the King was cited as 'Head of the Commonwealth and symbol of the free association of the independent members'. Prime Minister

Jawaharlal Nehru jibbed at the *former* formula, since his Cabinet had authorised him only to accept the *latter*. In private meetings, Sir Stafford Cripps explained that the King was Head because he was symbol – the 'symbolism created the Headship'. Nehru preferred the formula of Head '*as* symbol' rather than '*and* symbol'.[8] Daniel Malan, the South African prime minister, was very happy to accept the idea of a republic, since his own country was thinking along the same lines, but he feared the concept of Headship might suggest some sort of super-state. The Ceylon and Pakistan prime ministers both felt the Indian precedent would cause people in their countries to press for a republic. Malan was satisfied by a formula (first supplied by Pearson) that the King would be 'the symbol of the free association ... and *as such* Head of the Commonwealth'.[9]

The London Declaration (as it came to be called) was published. But two agreed minutes to satisfy South Africa that the Headship had no constitutional significance, and to satisfy Pakistan that further requests for republican status would be favourably considered, remained secret. It was also agreed that there could be local variations of the royal title. George VI would be cited, separately, as 'King of [Great Britain, Canada, Australia, New Zealand, South Africa, Pakistan, and Ceylon]' and 'of his other realms and territories, Head of the Commonwealth'.[10] 'Defender of the Faith' became optional. 'Dominions beyond the Seas' would go. At the end of the conference, the top Whitehall mandarins had some sport in brushing up their classics to produce a Latin version. The prime ministers all went to Buckingham Palace to tell the King about their labours, a task performed on their behalf by Attlee. The King thanked them, and said that he hoped there would not be too many republics. By the end of the twentieth century, 48 years into his daughter's reign, there would be 32! This meant that when Australians debated passionately in the 1990s whether to vote for a republic (and New Zealanders did the same with less enthusiasm) the issue of Commonwealth membership had no part of the debate.

4
The Secretariat and the 1971 Declaration

The most significant landmark in the organisation of the modern Commonwealth was the creation of the Secretariat in 1965. Strong support for the proposal from the new African members took the 'old' Commonwealth members by surprise.[1] Yet the idea was not a new one; there had been similar proposals from Australia in 1907, 1924, 1932 and 1944 and New Zealanders had suggested a central council in 1909 and 1956. The earlier proposals were largely aimed at gaining direct links with the British government untrammelled by Whitehall departments handling the routines of colonial administration.

As well as resisting all these moves, Whitehall never did erect a unified imperial secretariat.[2] Colonies came under the Colonial Office (CO), and after the Dominions asserted their distinctiveness in 1907 they did not get a separate department for several years. A Dominions division was created inside the CO. Not till 1926 was a separate Dominions Office (DO) created and it shared a minister with the CO until 1930 and the same building until 1946. The Indian Empire came under the India Office, but a separate Burma Office was created in 1937. The DO became the Commonwealth Relations Office (CRO) in 1947 and, after Indian and Pakistani independence a month later, it absorbed the former India Office. Of course, anomalies abounded. The Foreign Office (FO) had ruled, for a time, a number of African protectorates and held on to the largest territory, the Sudan (known as its 'hobby colony'), to the end. In 1966 the CO and CRO merged to form the Commonwealth Office and two years later it joined the FO to create a single department for external relations. Tradition, however, prevailed in the titling. Instead of becoming a Ministry of External Affairs, it was called rather cumbrously the Foreign & Commonwealth Office (FCO).

Servicing Commonwealth meetings was, for years, shared by the CRO with the Cabinet Office. Between the wars, the Committee of Imperial Defence (CID) and its hierarchy of sub-committees had a considerable secretariat, and its secretary, Sir Maurice Hankey (also Cabinet Secretary), has been referred to as a virtual Secretary-General of the Commonwealth.[3] After the Second World War the CID was not revived, but the Cabinet Office grew more powerful. Until 1966 the Cabinet Secretary was Secretary-General of the Prime Ministers' Meetings, while the preparatory work was done by the CRO. It was largely to get away from this CRO/Cabinet Office matrix that the new Secretariat was sought in 1964.

Whitehall did not resist, on this occasion, because by the mid-1960s rapid decolonisation had considerably disillusioned the British about the Commonwealth. Equality of status as agreed in 1926 had applied only to Britain and the six white Dominions, which retained their common allegiance to the Crown. Common allegiance became optional after 1949, but the eight-member Euro-Asian Commonwealth still had a semblance of unity based on the symbolic Headship of the Commonwealth. Would the 40 or more other dependencies, large and small, be able to join this Club?

Sudan, which became independent in 1956, emulated Burma and did not join. Various ideas for an intermediate or 'mezzanine status' falling short of full membership were mooted.[4] Ghana became the first African member in 1957. Malaya became an independent constitutional monarchy in the same year. By the 1960s, Britain's standing in the world had plummeted as a result of the disastrous Suez adventure of 1956. The European Economic Community (EEC) had come into being after the Treaty of Rome in 1957 but Britain did not join. The whole context of colonialism was changed irrevocably after 1960 by France's grant of independence to 13 African territories, Belgium's grant of independence to the Congo, and UN Resolution Number 1514 on ending colonialism. The CO, under Iain Macleod's leadership, found that timetables looking to gradual growth towards independence in East and Central Africa by about 1970, had to be dramatically accelerated. Therefore, in the post-Suez era, and particularly after 1960, the Commonwealth's cosy club, with its periodic Premiers' Meetings around the Cabinet table in 10 Downing Street, was drastically transformed.

The watershed year, 1960, was one of paradox for the Commonwealth. Nigeria, Africa's most populous state, joined the Commonwealth, and Harold Macmillan, the British prime minister, made his famous 'Wind of Change' speech to the South African Parliament. At the same time the prospect of Cyprus (with a population of only 500,000) joining the Commonwealth led to another effort to keep out small countries. Everyone realised that Cyprus could be the precedent for some 30 very small states. But no reasons could be found to keep Cyprus out. If new countries could join the United Nations but not the Commonwealth, the tradition of amicable transfers of power would be compromised and the association damaged. But it also meant that the membership would be altered out of all recognition.[5] In 1961 another significant conjuncture, akin to the Ireland/India decisions of 1949, occurred when the Republic of Cyprus joined the Prime Ministers' Meetings only two days before the Republic of South Africa quit. In 1962 the Cabinet Secretary anticipated another flood of new members leading to a possible total of 35 by 1970. The British smarted under Dean Acheson's aphorism that they 'had lost an Empire and not yet found a role'. In 1964 *The Times* published a feature article by 'A Conservative' (Enoch Powell) declaring that the Commonwealth had become 'a gigantic farce'.[6]

There were, however, those who took a less pessimistic view. In the aftermath of Suez, Macmillan instructed the Colonial Office to do a cost/benefit analysis of the remaining colonies to determine the future path of decolonisation and the impact on the Commonwealth. A Commonwealth Economic Conference was held in Montreal in 1958 where it was decided to bring together several trade monitoring agencies under the aegis of a Commonwealth Economic Advisory Council housed in a 'Commonwealth House' in London. For this purpose the Queen invited the British government to use Marlborough House, a royal palace on The Mall, designed by Sir Christopher Wren and formerly the home of George V's consort, Queen Mary. After minor modernisation it became the home of various economic and educational agencies. Between 1962 and 1966 it was also the venue of the Prime Ministers Meetings.

Within the CRO, a Planning Unit created in 1959 to consider the next ten years, included the idea of a Commonwealth Secretariat on its proposed agenda. A seminar organised jointly by the CRO and the Ditchley Foundation in 1963 concluded that the Commonwealth was worth saving and that practical measures for assisting development in the new and poorer members should be attempted. By 1964 the total membership had reached 18 and some of the new members were, in the view of Sir Alec Douglas-Home (now the prime minister), 'not the easiest of associates'.[7] He suggested to the 'old' members (Australia,

Canada and New Zealand) that a package of practical measures might convince the new members of the tangible advantages of membership. Five proposals in a package entitled *The Way Ahead* included technical assistance in development, a Commonwealth Foundation to foster professional links, capital assistance for higher education, training and research in public administration, and regional organisations for technical advice in planning.

In the run-up to the 1964 meetings, there were prophecies of doom, but also some calls for a revival of the Commonwealth. John W. Holmes, a former diplomat and President of the Canadian Institute of International affairs, argued in *The Times* on 7 January 1964 that the Commonwealth could not survive the present apathy or live in a 'state of anaemia'. It was needed 'to promote understanding rather than uniformity' and it ought to 'put some meaning into the phrases about consultation'. The Royal Commonwealth Society, the premier voluntary body for fostering interest in the Commonwealth, held a seminar in London for 39 non-governmental organisations interested in the Commonwealth and issued a manifesto appealing to the prime ministers to help bridge the gap between developed and developing countries.[8]

As the leaders gathered in Marlborough House in 1964, the press geared themselves to report fireworks over Britain's handling of the request for independence from the minority white government in Southern Rhodesia. Some commentators expected that the Commonwealth would dissolve. The British agenda arrangements were upset when, in the opening discussion on global trends, President Nkrumah of Ghana chided the 'old' members over their preoccupation with the Cold War. The real global problem, he declared, was the gap between the 'Haves' and the 'Have-Nots'. Here was the issue members should focus on, and he called for a 'central clearing house' in London to serve the Commonwealth as a whole. It could prepare plans for trade, aid and development, and circulate information about this for members. Nkrumah was supported by Milton Obote of Uganda, who used the word 'Secretariat', and Eric Williams of Trinidad who formally proposed that a Commonwealth Secretariat should be created. The Canadian and New Zealand prime ministers did not refer to the idea, but Menzies of Australia gave general support.[9] After the meeting, Nkrumah sent a memorandum to Douglas-Home explaining his ideas. Starting with a quotation from John Holmes's article in *The Times* about fostering understanding, he argued that the CRO's dual role of distributing information for all members and being the British FO-for-the-Commonwealth were incompatible.

The same view was taken by Sir Saville Garner of the CRO, who warned Douglas-Home that, in view of all the African enthusiasm, it might be damaging to reject the idea. He was not sure what a secretariat would do; indeed, he feared it might develop into an African pressure group. But when the Commonwealth senior officials had a first look at the proposals, Garner said Britain should welcome the proposal. He enunciated two principles that he would stick to tenaciously: the Secretariat should pool and disseminate information, but *not* be an executive or policy-making body. All the officials favoured the idea. When Sir Burke Trend, the British Cabinet Secretary, sent their report to Douglas-Home, he added his private view that although Britain could not oppose the idea, they should realise that it did represent a major landmark. It would be the first formal administrative step in detaching the Commonwealth's organisation from British control and that, he said, was 'quite a significant thing to do'.[10]

In this rather unexpected manner the British *Way Ahead* initiative, including the development projects and the foundation, were overtaken by the Secretariat idea. The 1964 Communiqué envisaged a body to disseminate factual material, to assist official and non-official agencies in the promotion of links, and to coordinate Commonwealth Meetings. It would be a 'visible symbol of the spirit of co-operation'.

The details were worked out by the senior officials during Marlborough House meetings in January 1965 and in July just before the next PMM. There was a debate between a restrictionist view of the secretariat, led by Australia, and an expansionist view, adopted by the Africans supported by the Canadians. An 'Agreed Memorandum', published after approval had been granted by the PMM, included four sentences which managed to reconcile the rival approaches and were cherished by Garner, their chief author, as 'splendidly antiphonal'. The Secretariat should not 'arrogate to itself executive functions', but it would 'have a constructive role to play'. It would 'operate on a modest scale' but its staff and functions could 'expand pragmatically in the light of experience'.[11]

The Commonwealth Secretariat began work in August 1965. The first Secretary-General, a Canadian diplomat, Arnold Smith, who was by previous experience a 'cold warrior', had first encountered the 'new' Commonwealth at the 1964 meetings. In his ten-year term he had four major achievements to his credit. He asserted the independence of the Secretary-General as the servant of the Heads of Government collectively. This meant rebuffing some petty protocol rearguards from the CRO. He asserted a political role for the Secretariat and sided with the

African members over Rhodesia. He even urged the British to send in paratroops to avoid a unilateral declaration of independence. He created a role for the Secretariat in arranging multilateral technical assistance for planning and development in poorer countries. After some resistance from the 'old' members, he got agreement for the Commonwealth Fund for Technical Co-operation (CFTC) in 1971. Above all, he stamped the Secretariat with a philosophy of consultation and a jargon with which to proclaim it. Consultation rather than confrontation was his constant plea. 'Consultation is the lifeblood of the Commonwealth' became his motto, and he said, 'We have to learn to share the planet.'

The first Secretary-General was not responsible for one of the many landmarks of his period, namely the Declaration of Commonwealth Principles which was also adopted in 1971. The meetings that year were held in Singapore, and were the first to sport the new title, 'Commonwealth Heads of Government Meetings' (Chogm). They were dominated by controversy over British arms sales to South Africa and Commonwealth bitterness over events in Southern Africa generally. In an endeavour to make a constructive approach and provide guidelines for the future, President Kaunda of Zambia proposed a set of principles that members held in common.

The 1971 declaration provided a new definition of the association, in place of those of 1926 and 1949: 'The Commonwealth of Nations is a voluntary association of independent sovereign states, each responsible for its own policies, consulting and co-operating on the common interests of their peoples and in the promotion of international understanding and world peace.' In addition six principles were declared. **Members pledged their *support for* peace, liberty and international cooperation; they *stood against* racial discrimination, colonial domination and wide disparities of wealth.**

Such bland assertions were unremarkable, but one striking sentence pulled a far greater punch than is usual in anodyne conference communiqués: 'We recognise racial prejudice as a dangerous sickness threatening the healthy development of the human race and racial discrimination as an unmitigated evil of society.' Members pledged themselves to 'combat this evil' in their own nations and they accepted that no country would afford to regimes that practised racial discrimination 'assistance which in its own judgement directly contributes to the pursuit or consolidation of this evil policy'.[12] Much of the history of

Commonwealth relations over the next two decades would focus on this issue.

*

In the broad historical perspective, the Commonwealth changed, during the middle third of the century, from being a small, white, imperial club to a large multicultural, multilateral, international association. The Balfour Declaration of 1926 proclaimed the doctrine of equality. The London Declaration of 1949 facilitated republican membership, confirmed multi-racialism, and created the symbolic Headship. The Singapore Declaration of 1971 made equality and multi-racialism dynamic principles to be pursued in international affairs. That this was not an easy task may be illustrated by a look at the two great crises of decolonisation in the 1960s and 1980s.

Part II
Shadows of Decolonisation

5
Rhodesia's UDI and the Crisis of the 1960s

The first three decades of the 'New Commonwealth' were overshadowed by Britain's disenchantment with the association. Although fears that the Secretariat would develop simply into an African pressure group were not realised, Commonwealth meetings were, indeed, dominated by African issues. One African historian, Eli Mazrui, called this the 'Third Commonwealth'.[1] The first had comprised Britain and the six Dominions; the second followed South Asian independence; the third began in 1960 when Nigeria's independence created a permanent non-white majority. The British now found themselves perpetually on the back foot, especially on matters relating to Southern Africa.

The low points were 1966 and 1986. In 1966, Kenneth Kaunda, of newly independent Zambia, talked of 'throwing Britain out of the Commonwealth' because of its handling of Rhodesia. So much pressure was put on Harold Wilson that he hit back with the cry that Britain, too, was independent: 'We are being treated as if we were a bloody colony.'[2] In 1986, the issue was apartheid in South Africa and Commonwealth demands for the application of sanctions. Margaret Thatcher breached consensus at a mini-summit in 1986 by refusing to go along with the proposed measures. During the Edinburgh Commonwealth Games of 1986 more countries boycotted the events than competed. Chogm communiqués in 1987 and 1989 signalled specific caveats by the words: 'with the exception of Britain'. Showing cheerful defiance, Mrs Thatcher once threw out: 'If it's one against 48, then I'm sorry for the 48.'[3] On Southern African issues, then, British leaders refused to be pushed around by the Commonwealth. This, in turn, accentuated a rapid de-Britannicisation process, which, on less contentious issues, was an entirely positive trend. On Africa, however, the British found themselves in a no-win predicament.

The crisis of the 1960s was about UDI, Rhodesia's unilateral declaration of independence in 1965. This became the most dramatic breach in the process of orderly, negotiated transfers of power to democratically elected governments. (The others were in Palestine, Cyprus and Aden.) Rhodesia defied the independence-by-persuasion-and-dialogue method so extolled by Arnold Smith. This can only be understood as the end-product of Rhodesia's unique and anomalous position in the former empire. UDI became a possibility in 1964 when the prime minister of Southern Rhodesia was not invited to Commonwealth meetings where his predecessors had been observers for over a quarter of a century.

The key point in understanding these issues is that Southern Rhodesia (later Zimbabwe) had, in fact, never been ruled from London like the other colonies.[4] First settled by a chartered company, the Rhodesian colonists conquered the rulers of the African-majority peoples – the Ndebele and Shona – in the 1890s, and enjoyed, from the start, a measure of self-government. When the company charter expired, many expected Rhodesia to join the Union of South Africa. In 1922, however, the tiny white electorate opted for responsible government as a separate colony. In status it became like the Dominions in the mid-nineteenth century. The premier was soon accorded the title prime minister and he (and later his federal successors) were invited, in a personal capacity, to attend Commonwealth conferences as observers from 1937 to 1962.

By the time of the Second World War Rhodesia was a quasi-Dominion and there was talk of merger with copper-rich Northern Rhodesia and even neighbouring Nyasaland – virtually a supply depot for recruiting well-educated African labour. These amalgamations were not allowed. But after 1948, when an Afrikaner-dominated government, pledged to a policy of apartheid and exclusion of British influence in the Union, came to power in South Africa, the idea of a Central African Federation was viewed more favourably. The Rhodesias and Nyasaland could pool resources for development and move on to eventual independence and Commonwealth membership. For Britain, the prospect of a 'loyal Dominion' as a counterpoise to South Africa now suddenly became attractive. The Conservative governments of the 1950s still regarded the Commonwealth as a small club for big members.

The Federation went ahead in 1953 against the wishes of its African majority peoples, who were not consulted. Thus African nationalist parties became vocal in all three territories, demanding the same rights as Ghanaians and Nigerians. The nationalists in the two northern protectorates abhorred, especially, control from Salisbury and demanded independence for themselves. Federation lasted only ten years. Malawi (former Nyasaland) and Zambia (former Northern Rhodesia) became independent in 1964. They then became entitled to Commonwealth membership leaving long-time self-governing Southern Rhodesia high and dry with neither independence nor Commonwealth membership.

Rhodesian-born Ian Smith, who became prime minister in 1964, claimed that he had the right to attend Commonwealth meetings like his Southern Rhodesian and Federal predecessors. Sir Alec Douglas-Home and his 'old-member' colleagues feared Smith's presence would be disruptive. After determining that the majority of the members were against sending an invitation, Douglas-Home left Smith off the list for the 1964 meetings. Yet Rhodesia's demand for independence was well known and there were fears that Smith would act unilaterally. The British hoped that this issue would not dominate the agenda in 1964 and they produced the *Way Ahead* programme partly to direct discussion into constructive channels. But the Rhodesian issue – more bluntly, a white minority demanding sovereign independence – would not go away.

Although in legal terms Rhodesia was still a British dependency, its white population of about 250,000 and their predecessors had enjoyed self-government from the early days of settlement, and near-Dominion status since 1923. They boasted a colour-blind franchise based on educational and property qualifications, but in fact only a tiny handful from the four million African population had the vote. A new constitution in 1961 provided for 50 constituencies and 15 electoral districts to elect a-65 member Assembly by a system of dual electoral rolls. Whites predominated on the higher income/education roll and Africans on the lower roll. If African parties were willing to cooperate (which they were not) they might expect 15 seats initially, with a gradual increase as more qualified for the higher roll. It would be a very gradual process. Smith told people that white supremacy would be maintained in his lifetime. In the context of the 1960s and decolonisation elsewhere, any British government that granted Rhodesia independence on this basis could expect to be denounced in the United Nations.

In the Commonwealth, the new African member countries were reinforced by their Asian and Caribbean colleagues, and also the Canadians, in efforts to pin Britain down to a policy of majority rule in Rhodesia. Their aims came to be known as 'Nibmar' – No Independence Before Majority Rule. They argued that as a colonial

power Britain had often resorted to force; it should do so now to forestall UDI and impose Nibmar. At the 1964 Prime Ministers' Meetings,
the Rhodesian question appeared on the agenda under an item about
'Progress of British Territories towards Independence and
Commonwealth Membership', but the British were given an unexpected jolt. After Duncan Sandys, the Secretary of State for
Commonwealth Relations, led off with a panegyric on Britain's proud
record of bringing countries to their freedom, he was rebuked in a
jovial intervention by the conference new boy, Dr Hastings Banda of
Malawi, whose country had attained independence just three days
before: 'Now come, Mr Chairman, let's be frank with each other,' said
Banda. 'It has not been all voluntary.' He recalled that he had himself
been in jail for only a few months, but he went round the room totting
up the considerable prison sentences of some of his distinguished
fellow leaders, referring especially to those of recently deceased Pandit
Nehru. Somewhat stiff laughter was defused into more relaxed amuse-
ment when Canadian Prime Minister Lester Pearson, sensing an exclu-
sive circle emerging, asked if he would qualify for membership on the
strength of being detained by British military police during the First
World War.[5] More serious evidence of Canadian identification with the
Afro-Asian members was the first substantive paragraph of the
Conference communiqué – a declaration (drafted by the Canadians) on
racial equality and non-discrimination. On Rhodesia, the meeting welcomed the British warning that UDI would not be recognised and
looked forward to independence based on majority rule.

As a basis for discussions on constitutional change in Rhodesia the
British government laid down five principles: there should be unim-
peded progress towards majority rule; guarantees against subsequent
retrogressive amendments; an immediate improvement of the political
status of Africans; a progressive removal of discrimination laws; and
the British government must be satisfied that any settlement was
acceptable to the Rhodesian people as a whole. In other words, if Smith
had been willing to give a few more Africans the vote and provide
them with more seats in the assembly, Britain would have probably
granted independence *before majority rule*. Smith and his supporters,
however, refused to budge and detained many of the African nationalist leaders.

After the British general election of October 1964, the Labour government of Harold Wilson took office with some grandiose professions
of enthusiasm for the Commonwealth. On Rhodesia they maintained
the five principles as their basis of policy and tried negotiating with the

Smith regime. They added a sixth principle that there should be no repression of the minority by the majority, or vice versa. At the 1965 PMMs the British confirmed that they regarded 'one man, one vote' as the basis of democracy and that this should be applied to Rhodesia. In their 1965 Communiqué, the Heads of Government warned against a UDI and urged Britain to call a conference representative of all Rhodesian groups and to grant independence only on the basis of majority rule. They appealed to the Smith regime to release political detainees. If the Rhodesian government failed to attend such a conference and release the detainees, Britain was enjoined to suspend the 1961 constitution, appoint an interim government and repeal discriminatory legislation. Smith remained unmoved. On 11 November 1965 he declared independence unilaterally, in what was now dubbed 'IDI' – the illegal declaration of independence.

The problem was primarily one for Britain as the sovereign power, but it had potential for destroying the Commonwealth. Asian and African leaders – some of them posturing at their first PMMs – wanted Britain to impose majority rule by force. Wilson argued that this was impracticable as Britain lacked the means, since there was no British official in the colony except the Governor, and he was chosen by the Rhodesians. Arnold Smith, the Secretary-General, and several African leaders talked blithely of 'sending in the paras', but Wilson ruled out the use of force. The policy adopted was one of refusal to recognise the rebel regime and the application of trade and financial sanctions to bring it down.

A special heads of government meeting, held in Lagos in January 1966 (which was boycotted by Menzies, Nyerere and Kaunda), heard Wilson plead for time. His officials had advised him that sanctions would bring down the rebel regime in 'weeks rather than months'. Wilson promised that if sanctions did not succeed in this way by mid-year, he would call another Commonwealth meeting and go to the UN Security Council to seek mandatory sanctions against trading with Rhodesia.[6] When the deadline passed, Wilson tried to get the Canadians to host the conference in Ottawa, but, in the event it took place in London in September 1966. Here, after three days of inconclusive debate, 14 Asian-African-Caribbean members met in caucus to seek a formula to pin Britain to Nibmar. Wilson refused to give such a pledge and pleaded for Smith to be given a 'last chance'. Wilson outlined in some detail what the 'offer' to Smith would be. There must be a return to legal rule – IDI must be rescinded and the Governor form a broad-based government representative of all races. The police and armed forces would be responsible to the Governor. Once a legal government was in place, Britain would negotiate a constitutional settlement that would be submitted for approval to the Rhodesian people as a whole. Independence would be granted only when the British Parliament was satisfied that the constitution was acceptable. It would have to be based on the Six Principles, and Britain would also seek Commonwealth and UN endorsement.

After bitter words and frayed tempers a communiqué (drafted by the Canadian prime minister, Lester Pearson) gave Wilson his breathing space, but it put on record that 'most' of the heads of government did not agree with the British approach. The use of force and Nibmar were the chief points of disagreement. But Wilson conceded that if Smith rejected his 'last chance', the British government would withdraw the offer, go to Parliament for Nibmar and go to the UN for mandatory sanctions.[7]

There were talks with the Rhodesians aboard a British warship off Gibraltar in 1966, when Wilson tried to persuade Smith to improve African political rights enough so as to give a plausible promise of majority rule. Had Smith accepted, Wilson was still prepared to give independence before majority rule. Smith refused, so Wilson closed the door and adopted Nibmar. In the end, the notorious 'weeks rather than months' stretched to 15 years.

It took a civil war to bring an end to the rebel white regime. With the main African leaders in detention, African nationalists began guerrilla activities from neighbouring Zambia, Tanzania and Mozambique. A compromise formula for meeting the Six Principles, agreed with Smith in 1971, was rejected by the Rhodesian majority after a visiting Royal Commission sounded local opinion. After 1972 the African 'liberation struggle' developed into a regular war. At first, the Rhodesian Security Forces held the initiative, but, after the Portuguese revolution of 1974 produced a government which gave independence to Mozambique in 1975, a huge flank was opened in the Rhodesian defences. By the late 1970s both sides were suffering and the Americans tried to organise a settlement to check the spread of the Cold War in Africa. To forestall these moves, Smith made his own 'internal settlement' in 1978. With a change of name to Zimbabwe-Rhodesia, an African-majority parliament and an African prime minister, Bishop Abel Muzorewa, Smith hoped that international recognition would follow, even though the police and armed forces remained under white control. As this settlement coincided with the election of Mrs Thatcher's Conservative government to power in

Britain, the world waited to see if Britain would finally shake off the Rhodesian incubus and recognise Zimbabwe-Rhodesia.

The Commonwealth, which had survived the bitterness of 1966, helped to deflect Mrs Thatcher from recognition. It assisted in the search for a settlement in four ways. First, at the Chogm in Lusaka in 1979 influential leaders such as the host, Kenneth Kaunda, the Australian prime minister, Malcolm Fraser, and Jamaica's Michael Manley, combined to persuade Mrs Thatcher to withhold recognition and to make a final act of leadership by calling a conference of all the parties in London. Second, during the arduous Lancaster House Conference, from October to December 1979, influence was exerted behind the scenes by the Commonwealth Secretary-General, Sonny Ramphal, and the presidents of neighbouring Zambia and Tanzania in persuading the rival African leaders, Joshua Nkomo, Robert Mugabe and Prime Minister Muzorewa, to accept the plan which the British proposed. This involved sending a British Governor to rule by ordinance and to call general elections. In fulfilling these arrangements the Commonwealth's third contribution was a joint military force to monitor a cease-fire in the war between the Rhodesian Security Forces and the rival guerrilla armies. Assembly points were established for the guerrillas to come out of the bush. The Commonwealth force also monitored the Security Forces' adherence to the cease-fire. Fourth, a Commonwealth Observer Group went to report to the Heads of Government collectively as to whether the elections were fair. These activities represented, for some commentators, the Commonwealth's 'finest hour'.[8]

After winning an overwhelming number of seats in the new Assembly, Robert Mugabe took office as prime minister. Zimbabwe became independent in 1980 and became the last of the populous African states to join the Commonwealth. To help the Zimbabwe economy recover its feet and to meld the old security forces and the guerrilla armies into a national force, Mrs Thatcher agreed that a British Military Advisory and Training Team be sent to Zimbabwe. At a camp near the Mozambique border, British and Zimbabwean officers and NCOs trained units of the Mozambique army to protect the rail routes to the Indian Ocean ports through which Zimbabwe traded.

The Zimbabwe settlement removed a 20-year burden from the backs of British policy-makers, but they still faced an even bigger hurdle to the south. South Africa, once one of the four great Dominions, became the source of renewed controversy in the Commonwealth in the 1980s.

6
Apartheid and the Crisis of the 1980s

The end of UDI and the admission of Zimbabwe into the Commonwealth in 1980 removed the most bitter bone of contention of the previous 15 years. But it brought little respite for Britain. In his report for the 1981 Chogm, Secretary-General Ramphal said that the resolution of the Rhodesia issue had not taken Southern Africa off the agenda. If the Commonwealth were to be true to its principles, it had to bring apartheid in South Africa to an end. Therefore the 1980s were years of further crises for the association. If disintegration never seemed likely (as it had in the 1960s), consensus was now breached – and by none other than Britain.

Denis Austin once quipped that South Africa 'helped rescue the Commonwealth from boredom but at the cost of rather too much excitement'.[1] It is ironical that a state which had quit the Commonwealth in 1961 was the continuing focus of attention and source of friction. However, Oliver Tambo, president-in-exile of the African National Congress, told a London audience in 1986 that 'we never left the Commonwealth' – that had been done by the Afrikaner regime. He looked to the day when South Africa would return.[2]

That apartheid gave the Commonwealth such a stormy passage through the 1980s was largely due to Britain's attitude. We have seen how at Mrs Thatcher's first Chogm in Lusaka, shortly after she came to power in 1979, she had been prevailed upon by influential voices to withhold recognition of the new Zimbabwe-Rhodesia regime and to go for a settlement involving free and supervised elections. The headline 'The Day Mrs Thatcher Wept' may or may not have been accurate reporting, but it probably registered the impact that the Lusaka Chogm made. The next time such pressures were put on Britain, she was more entrenched in power, more ready to ward off her antagonists. At

Lyford Cay in the Bahamas in 1985, she weakened briefly on sanctions against apartheid because of the blandishments of 'two good-looking men' – Rajiv Gandhi and Brian Mulroney[3] – but in the following year she dug in her heels. Consensus could not hold. There was talk of a 'binary Commonwealth', but not, significantly, of break-up. The association learnt to take action by general agreement – 'with the exception of Britain'.[4]

Mrs Thatcher maintained her independent status with, perhaps, too much relish. This meant that Britain's viewpoint on South Africa was rarely accorded serious assessment. Successive British governments had always deplored apartheid, but were not prepared to jeopardise commercial relations with, and investments in, South Africa. Mrs Thatcher's government genuinely differed from most of its Commonwealth partners on the tactics for dealing with apartheid. As with its response to decolonisation, Britain's response to apartheid was coloured by the past – by chagrin and discomfiture at its position of a declining colonial power. South Africa, especially the Cape of Good Hope, had formerly been one of the keystones of Empire. Cape Colony and Natal had been British white settlement colonies not unlike the old Dominions. Over a third of the population of South Africa was English-speaking. Britain was South Africa's fourth largest market, South Africa Britain's second largest place for overseas investment. Long-standing economic ties were not to be jettisoned lightly for the likely benefit of Germans, Japanese and others.

South Africa had also had a prominent role in the evolution of the Commonwealth The denizens of the Round Table had first come together in South Africa in the aftermath of the war of 1899–1902 and had played a part in the forging of the Union. The 1926 declaration of equality of status had been largely in response to South African promptings. Field Marshal Jan Smuts became one of the most respected Commonwealth leaders during the Second World War. There was disappointment when he lost power in 1948 to the Afrikaner Nationalists pledged to the policy of apartheid. Although racial segregation in various guises had long been a feature of social life in many British colonies, South Africa's systematic legislative programme and physical relocations of people from the 1950s shocked the world. The disenfranchisement of non-whites, enforcement of residential, educational and employment segregation, the banning of marriage and sexual relations across colour lines, the classification into racial groups of all citizens, were compounded by a territorial division which kept the bulk of the land for the white minority. On the 14 per cent reserved for the

African majority, a series of tribal homelands, Bantustans, were made, in the 1970s, into parodies of sovereign states.[5]

The campaign against such racial injustice had a long history. Mahatma Gandhi had begun his agitational career and evolved his philosophy of non-violent resistance in South Africa. The Government of India had spoken out in favour of Indian rights in the Union at the Imperial Conferences between the wars. After independence, India carried the attack on apartheid to the United Nations. By 1960, as the tidal wave of decolonisation was gathering momentum, Macmillan made his 'Wind of Change' speech in the Cape Town Parliament Buildings during the fiftieth anniversary of the Union. He also made it clear that Britain would not support apartheid. A little over a month later, on 21 March 1960, the shooting of 67 and wounding of 87 Africans at Sharpeville led to the growing isolation of South Africa.

Withdrawal from the Commonwealth in 1961 did not remove South Africa as a target of censure. The Rivonia trials of 1963 kept the spotlight on the Republic. On 12 June 1964 the sentencing of Nelson Mandela and seven others to life imprisonment for sabotage reminded the world of the reality of apartheid. In his four-hour speech from the dock, Mandela told how in 1961 a conscious decision had been made to prepare for a violent liberation struggle because the door to constitutional action was closed when African political parties were banned. He said he was prepared to die for the idea of ending white domination.[6]

Sporting boycotts became the most visible means for expressing disapproval of the apartheid regime. South Africa was excluded from the Olympic Games in 1964 and expelled from the Olympic movement in 1970. The Gleneagles Agreement of 1977 and the Commonwealth Games Code of Conduct of 1982 were designed to seal off South Africans from Commonwealth sports. South Africa was further isolated by the independence of Angola and Mozambique following the Portuguese coup of 1974. The ex-Portuguese territories joined Commonwealth members, Botswana, Swaziland, Tanzania, Zambia and Zimbabwe, as the 'Front Line States' in the battle against apartheid. South Africa was also condemned by the international community for the continued occupation of South-West Africa [Namibia] in defiance of the United Nations' revocation of the mandate for the territory.

From the mid-1980s, the campaign against apartheid had become a virtual crusade for Sonny Ramphal, as he moved to a third term as Commonwealth Secretary-General. If the Commonwealth was to be true to itself, he declared, 'it has no option but to be in the vanguard of the final push against apartheid'.[7] At the Nassau Chogm in 1985 the

Heads of Government adopted a four-pronged strategy. First, they condemned the South African government for the three-fold sins of apartheid, occupation of Namibia and destabilising military attacks on the Front Line States. Second, they demanded a programme for scrapping discrimination laws, release of detainees, unbanning of African political parties and dialogue directed towards electing a non-racial representative government. Third, an Eminent Persons Group (EPG) was appointed to visit South Africa and a seven-member group of Heads of Government from Australia, Bahamas, Britain, Canada, India, Zambia and Zimbabwe, was appointed to work with the Secretary-General on 'modalities of this effort'. Fourth, a list of 'economic measures' was endorsed. They were called 'measures' rather than 'sanctions' to overcome Mrs Thatcher's reluctance and enable consensus to hold.[8]

The EPG, headed by Malcolm Fraser, former Australian prime minister, and General Obasanjo, former Nigerian head of state, visited South Africa early in 1986 and found the reality of apartheid 'awesome in its cruelty'. Its report outlined a 'possible negotiating concept'.[9] This would involve the government removing troops from African townships, allowing freedom of assembly, releasing Mandela and other political prisoners, and unbanning African political parties. It also required the African National Congress to eschew violence to achieve its ends. To the Heads of Government, the EPG suggested that the negotiating concept offered a last chance to avoid the type of bloodshed not seen since the Second World War.

When the seven Heads of Government met to consider the EPG report, in the so-called Mini-Summit of June 1986, a new list of sanctions was drawn up. But Mrs Thatcher now refused to go along with them. Britain, she said, abhorred apartheid, but was not prepared to apply any measures not agreed by the European Community. She favoured humanitarian and educational aid to Africans from the Republic and aid to the Front Line States. No doubt she remembered Wilson's humiliation over the 'weeks rather than months' remark and the failure of sanctions over Rhodesia. She also insisted that sanctions would hit those it was intended to help by creating African unemployment. From the mid-1980s, as the Commonwealth debated sanctions, Britain stood aloof.

At the 1987 and 1989 Chogms the communiqués carried repetitions of the phrase 'with the exception of Britain'. The high point of Mrs Thatcher's defiance came at Kuala Lumpur in 1989, when, after approving a declaration on South Africa which included specific reservations of the British position, she permitted her delegation to release only an hour later a paper explaining the British position. For several days she was vilified with varying degrees of abuse, from Robert Mugabe's 'despicable, unacceptable', to Lynden Pindling's 'it's not cricket'. In reply, Mrs Thatcher declared herself 'astounded' that democratic leaders would deny her free speech.[10]

Already, however, the thaw had begun in South Africa. The new State President, F. W. de Klerk began to lift restrictions, release prisoners and modify apartheid. In 1990 Mandela was released after 27 years in jail. At the 1991 Chogm in Harare, his appearance as a guest of the host Robert Mugabe gave him the appearance of a president-in-waiting. John Major, Mrs Thatcher's successor as British prime minister, worked carefully to mend fences. His genial, conciliatory manner impressed the conference. He maintained some British reservations, but said they related to tactics, not general aims. He conferred with Mandela. He went in to bat in a charity cricket match. In the following year, white South Africans voted in a referendum in favour of an equal rights constitution. Quickly following the remarkable all races election of April 1994, South Africa returned to the Commonwealth after a 33-year absence. And, at the Auckland Chogm in 1995, tall, colourfully dressed and deliberately spoken President Mandela was hailed as the man of the moment. He was one of the keynote speakers at the opening ceremony, and he was lionised by a 200,000 crowd at an open air concert.

The Commonwealth's role in the ending of apartheid needs to be seen in perspective. For Chief Anyaoku (who had been involved since his pre-Secretariat days as a junior Nigerian diplomat at the UN),[11] it was the association's greatest achievement. But in the end the new South Africa was forged by South Africans. It arose from the long-term persistence of the African National Congress and from the remarkably sudden turn about by the Nationalist leadership in 1989–90 under F. W. de Klerk, probably induced by the financiers and industrialists who saw the incompatibility of apartheid and development. External pressures undoubtedly played their part, but they were not solely the work of the Commonwealth. The United Nations had imposed the arms embargo; the Olympic movement banned South Africa from its sports; in the economic boycotts Britain broke Commonwealth solidarity; and the withdrawal of major American corporations also had its role. Yet the Commonwealth embraced the most persistent opponents of apartheid. India's opposition to South Africa's racial laws had been taken to the United Nations as early as the 1940s. Canada took up the cause in the 1950s. From the 1960s, the new states of Africa and the Caribbean were in the forefront of the campaign against apartheid. Tanzania's Julius Nyerere and the governments of Nigeria, Africa's most populous state, stood out. Of all the boycotts, the severing of rugby ties went to the heart of the Afrikaner self-image. Even though a New Zealand government defied the world in 1981 by permitting a Springbok rugby tour, protesters invaded the field causing the first test match to be called off, which gave Nelson Mandela, in prison on Robben Island, new hope. He later recalled that 'it felt like the sun coming out'.[12] The new South Africa arose from negotiations between the parties in the early 1990s, and it is now known that Chief Anyaoku played an important role behind the scenes in preparing the way.[13]

*

For Britain, 1994 marked the end of 30 years of Southern African embarrassments. Decolonisation had brought its agonies and disappointments and the emergence of a Commonwealth very different from the cosy Statute-of-Westminster Club. But virtue was made of necessity. The New Commonwealth was accepted, reluctantly by many, with enthusiasm for its potentialities by a few. The creation of the Secretariat in 1965 took most of the chores, and some of the heat, off Whitehall.

Rhodesia and South Africa presented crises for Britain in its relations with the Commonwealth, basically because its governments felt helpless. UDI and apartheid were policies that had been adopted by self-governing countries, albeit countries dominated by white minorities. Both countries lived in a time warp and were isolated from the postcolonial world which had evolved so rapidly in the 1960s. Commonwealth leaders, including the Secretaries-General, wanted to respond to UDI and apartheid in various ways. But Britain, too, was trapped by its own past. Its policies were quite explicable in those terms, but they invited considerable condemnation, which blighted Britain's whole attitude to the Commonwealth. By the mid-1990s with the incubus of UDI and apartheid resolved, Britain was free to rediscover the Commonwealth without the burden of an imperial hangover.

Part III
Symbolic Commonwealth

7
The Head of the Commonwealth

During the Edinburgh Chogm in 1997 the British hosts perpetrated a minor coup by getting agreement in principle that the Prince of Wales would succeed to the Headship of the Commonwealth. This was done in an oblique fashion without, it seems, discussion by the Heads of Government. It is probable that a good number of them did not understand some of the implications of what they were doing. The Communiqué simply recorded that Heads of Government endorsed the report of an Inter-governmental Group on Criteria for Membership and that one of these criteria was acceptance of 'Commonwealth norms and conventions'. One has to read the group's report to discover that these norms included acceptance of the 'British monarch' as Head of the Commonwealth. When asked at the final press conference what the use of the term 'British monarch' did to the status of the Canadian monarch, Prime Minister Tony Blair (who clearly did not understand the question) shrugged it aside with a laugh. One observer commented that it was 'the silliest question of the conference'. However, a senior public servant suggested that the decision about the Headship was the most significant outcome of the Edinburgh meetings.

He was right, because symbols are important even if, as in Edinburgh, they are rarely analysed or discussed. Elizabeth II, in her role as Head of the Commonwealth, provides the association's best-known and most visible symbol. The symbol may lack the fervour and mass excitement of the Commonwealth Games, but it is an on-going symbol, which is seen at many levels and in many countries. It has dignity, colour and glamour which people enjoy and identify with, and for many years it provided the Commonwealth's most popular element after the Commonwealth Games.[1] It is ironical, therefore, that the Queen's visibility and continuity are most often associated with her quite different role as Head of State of Britain and 15 other countries.

We have seen how the symbolic headship arose from quite specific political circumstances. Although foreshadowed by the Irish republican de Valera in 1921, it was mooted from several different sources at the time of South Asian decolonisation and, specifically, in response to India's desire to stay in the Commonwealth as a republic. Since the landmark definitions of 1926 and 1931, 'Common allegiance to the Crown' had become the residual linkage of the Commonwealth. But the Canadian citizenship law of 1946 and subsequent agreement about separate nationalities in 1947, as well as the possibility of republican membership, rendered 'common allegiance' obsolete. Indeed, the legal authority Sir William Dale has argued that 'the Crown' was really a metaphor and hardly accurate as the unifying element since there were 'separate Crowns' in each member country; hence the deliberate decision to snap the Crown link in favour of the symbolic headship.[2] As Sir Stafford Cripps pleaded with Nehru in 1949, the symbol created the headship. Thus the London Declaration of 1949 laid out the new arrangement in four succinct sentences.

First, the governments of the eight countries, which were at that time united as members of the British Commonwealth of Nations and owed a common allegiance to the Crown, which was the 'symbol of their free association', announced that they had considered India's impending change. Second, the Declaration went on to say that the Government of India had informed the other members that it would soon become a 'sovereign, independent, Republic', but wished to stay in the Commonwealth. It would accept the King 'as the symbol of the free association of the independent member nations and as such Head of the Commonwealth'. Third, the governments of the other countries, 'the basis of whose membership was not changed', accepted and recognised India as a member. Finally, the eight countries declared that they remained 'united as free and equal members ... co-operating in the pursuit of peace, liberty and progress'.[3] In place of the Crown as the symbol, the unifying link became a personal one – the King as symbolic Head. Dale called it 'an imaginative act, a brave return almost to medieval conceptions'.[4] There were, however, no precedents, no rules of succession, no specified functions, other than simply being the 'symbol of the free association' of the members.

George VI died in 1952 before he had had much opportunity to develop the Headship. Elizabeth was thrust, unexpectedly, at a young age into the role. But in his letter of condolence for her father's sudden passing Nehru, prime minister of the only republican member, welcomed the Queen as the 'new Head of the Commonwealth' and this was agreeable to the rest.[5] Since then, over a period spanning virtually the second half of the twentieth century, the Queen enhanced the Headship in many interesting directions. At Edinburgh in 1997, where she attended and spoke at a Chogm session for the first time, her address was preceded by a video tribute to her activities in many member countries. After viewing it, she began her speech laconically with 'Haven't I been busy'. She also spoke during the Durban opening in 1999 and marked the fiftieth anniversary of the Headship by quoting the 1949 pledge to cooperation in 'pursuit of peace, liberty and progress'.

Commentary on the Queen's role must make, at the start, the vital distinction between the two symbols, Crown and Headship. In the member countries where the Queen is Head of State (16 of them), the Crown is the metaphor for sovereignty, authority, in effect, executive government. By the 150-year-old conventions of **responsible government, the Crown acts on the advice of ministers**. Thus in Britain, the Queen herself, and in the countries retaining allegiance, the governors-general (her vice-regal representatives) are the symbols of the sovereignty of their respective nations. The summoning of prime ministers, the opening of parliament, the speech from the throne, the assent to bills – all are symbolic functions of constitutional monarchy.

Considerable efforts have been made to make governors-general symbols of national identities. Instead of British aristocrats (including members of the royal family) or famous British military leaders, governors-general are now local citizens. The first Australian, Sir Isaac Isaacs, took office in 1931 and in the following year de Valera ensured an Irish governor-general, who lived in a suburban house and did not function in the office other than to sign bills. In New Zealand, General Freyberg (who, though British-born, had been brought up in New Zealand and commanded its soldiers in the Second World War) became Governor-General in 1946. The first New Zealand-born Governor-General was Sir Arthur Porritt in 1967, but his career had been in Britain. Since then, all have been New Zealanders, including an ex-prime minister, Sir Keith Holyoake (1977–80), a part-Maori ex-archbishop, Sir Paul Reeves (1985–90), and one woman, an ex-mayor of the country's largest city, Dame Cath Tizard (1990–6). In Canada the last British Governor-General was Lord Alexander of Tunis (1946–52). An odd idea from the Secretary of State for External Affairs, Lester Pearson, that after Alexander the Governor-Generalship should be put 'in commission' with a member of the royal family residing for a few months each year at Rideau Hall, Ottawa, was quickly dropped.[6] (A similar idea was explored a year later in Neville Shute's Australian novel *In the Wet*, which envisaged the monarch flying by delta-winged jet between residences in Ottawa, Wellington, Canberra and Pretoria.) The first Canadian was Vincent Massey, in 1952, former High Commissioner in London and Ambassador in Washington. Pearson expected that under Massey everything would be done in 'a proper and protocolaire way'; he thought people would be reassured 'by the royal atmosphere which will soon prevail at Rideau Hall'.[7] There was talk of Massey being succeeded by the Queen Mother, but this idea was also scotched and Canada's vice-regal representatives have alternated between Anglophone and Francophone Canadians including two woman, Jeanne Sauvé (1984–9) and Adrienne Clarkson (1999–), who is Hong Kong-born. Alone among the old Dominions the Governor-General's residence in Ottawa is guarded by sentries in scarlet and bearskins (who include women), members of the Governor-General's Foot Guards of Ottawa and the Grenadier Guards of Montreal. In Australia, the last British Governor-General was Lord de l'Isle (1960–5). Since then there have been three former ministers of foreign affairs, Lord Casey (1965–9), Sir Paul Hasluck (1969–74) and Bill Hayden (1989–96), three judges, Sir John Kerr (1974–7), Sir Vivian Stephen (1982–9) and Sir William Deane (1996–2000), and a law professor/vice chancellor, Sir Zelman Cowan (1977–82).

The role of Head of State in 16 countries amounts to a considerable part of the Queen's visibility around the Commonwealth, but this is the constitutional monarchical function and something quite different from the Headship of the Commonwealth. For this, nothing was laid down in 1949. It was left for conventions to evolve. For example, new applications for republican membership were submitted formally to the Queen. Beginning with Pakistan in 1955, Sir Winston Churchill sent the application to the Queen, as Head of the Commonwealth, indicating the British government's endorsement. It was then initialled 'Approved E. R.'.[8] Ghana's application in 1960 was sent by Harold Macmillan on behalf of the other prime ministers who met in that year. Various ideas mooted by Nkrumah to give new content to the role and to give the Queen some special relationship with Ghanaians under the republic, such as 'First Citizen of Ghana', were not adopted. During these discussions in 1959 her private secretary, Sir Michael Adeane, wrote: 'There are in fact no functions of the Queen as Head of the Commonwealth that I am aware of, therefore, it is impossible to say that such functions are to be given a new content.' He went on: 'the idea of the "Head of the Commonwealth" is quite a fragile flower of which life can be endangered just as easily by too much watering as too little.'[9]

The most common activities were those which flowed over from the monarchical role. There were state visits, which eventually took the Queen to every member country except the two most recent – Cameroon and Mozambique.[10] Entertaining at the time of the old Prime Ministers' Meetings involved a banquet at Buckingham Palace for the Heads of Delegations, receptions for ministers and senior officials, another for selected media representatives, and private audiences for all heads of delegations. Both the visits and entertainment were fused with the advent of rotating Chogms outside Britain, with only two breaks. These were in 1966 at the time of the Lagos special meeting on Rhodesia and in 1971 at Singapore, when British Prime Minister Edward Heath, advised the Queen to stay away because the British were in such bad odour over arms sales to South Africa. Thereafter, the Secretary-General ensured that there were always invitations from the hosts for regional or member country visits to coincide with Chogms. Thus the banquets, receptions and audiences continued around the world, often held on board the royal yacht *Britannia*, which became increasingly a mobile base rather than a means of transport until its decommissioning in 1998. The private audiences for heads of delegation continued until the membership grew so large in the 1990s that they were confined to new Heads of Government or those who especially wished to confer. Starting in 1964, on Jomo Kenyatta's suggestion, the meetings began with a formal exchange of greetings with the Head of the Commonwealth. Since 1966, the first conference organised by the Secretary-General, he has sent a bound copy of the proceedings to the Head of the Commonwealth.

After nearly half a century, visits to nearly every member country and meetings with a galaxy of distinguished Commonwealth leaders (several generations of them), the Queen has built up a store of Commonwealth experience unsurpassed by any other person. She also sponsored other tangible symbols. As Patron of the Commonwealth Games, she inaugurated the 'Queen's baton' relay starting before the Cardiff Games of 1958. The baton conveys a message from the Queen to the Games. It is conveyed around the Commonwealth by relays, according to a protocol involving medal winners of the previous Games and representatives of the previous and present host venues. In the final stage of the relay the baton is conveyed into the stadium, after the opening parade, by medallists from earlier Games (whose identities are not revealed until their entry). The baton is presented to the Queen (or her representative) who reads the message and formally opens the Games. Another such symbol is the Commonwealth mace. This was presented to the Queen by schoolchildren of the Commonwealth in 1992 to mark the fortieth anniversary of her reign. The golden mace, adorned with the flags of the member countries, was laid before the podium at the opening of the Limassol Chogm in 1993. Thereafter, it has lain in the well of the conference table during Chogm plenary sessions.

The symbolic Headship has, therefore, provided a very tangible symbol in a way that is visible and personal. The Duke of Edinburgh has also been associated in various informal ways. A scheme of Winston Churchill's during his last PMM in 1955 to have the title 'Prince of the Commonwealth'[11] conferred on Prince Philip was not pursued, but from 1955 to 1990 he was President of the Commonwealth Games Federation and opened most of them on behalf of the Queen. In 1956 he inaugurated the Duke of Edinburgh's Commonwealth Study Conferences and from the mid-1960s to mid-1980s was patron of the Comex expeditions of young people, which adopted as symbol a Green Pennant incorporating Prince Philip's cipher. The Headship of the Commonwealth provides continuity in the association and gives symbolism a face. The editor of the magazine *Commonwealth* commented in 1986 at the time of her sixtieth birthday: 'In terms of diplomatic skill and sheer physical endurance Queen Elizabeth has given, and continues to give, an astonishing performance.'[12]

It was, however, a performance which was not without critics, especially in Britain. The most persistent was Enoch Powell, the only member of the House of Commons to vote against the Royal Titles Bill. His 'gigantic farce' article in *The Times* in 1964 declared that:

> It is dangerous to prostitute to the service of a transparent fiction the subtle emotions of loyalty and affection on which that heritage depends. A great and growing number of people of these islands do not like to see the Sovereign whom they regard as their own by every claim of history and sentiment play an alien part as one of the characters in the Commonwealth charade.[13]

Similar adverse views were expressed in the British media as the Queen, in her Queen-of-New Zealand role, became embroiled (as some might say) in controversies over indigenous rights. On visits to New Zealand in 1980s she was pelted with eggs and by a dirty T-shirt. By the 1990s, she was making formal apologies to Maori tribes for acts of state done or omitted in Queen Victoria's reign. But this was the **Crown of New Zealand acting on the advice of New Zealand ministers** – the Queen was not acting as Head of the Commonwealth.

Perhaps the most serious media debate about the Headship took place during the 1980s at a time when Mrs Thatcher's disenchantment with the Commonwealth contrasted with the Queen's evident interest in, and enthusiasm for, the association. In 1983 the Queen's televised Christmas Day broadcast followed shortly upon a visit to India, and she recalled this in the broadcast against a background of video shots of her conversing with Prime Minister Indira Gandhi. The Queen then uttered some sentences which provided the spark for a quite unexpected and remarkable debate:

> But in spite of all the progress that has been made the greatest problem in the world today remains the gap between rich and poor countries and we shall not begin to close the gap until we hear less about nationalism and more about interdependence. One of the main aims of the Commonwealth is to make an effective contribution towards redressing the economic balance between nations ... Perhaps even more serious is the risk that ... mastery of technology may blind us to the more fundamental needs of people. Electronics can't create comradeship; computers can't generate compassion; satellites can't transmit tolerance.[14]

To anyone familiar with the recent debates about underdevelopment and a 'new international economic order', these words would have been very old hat, almost cliché, but they raised a fascinating debate about the Head of the Commonwealth.

The *Daily Express* wanted to know who was telling the Queen that 'her role as Head of the Commonwealth is so valuable that it is worth putting in jeopardy her role as Queen of the United Kingdom and Head of our State'.[15] Enoch Powell returned to the fray in a speech early in 1984, accusing ministers of putting into the Queen's mouth words suggesting she had the interests of other countries more at heart than those of her own people. The Prime Minister's Office immediately pointed out that the Queen's Christmas broadcast was a personal one, not subject to ministerial advice. *The Times* went further and reminded readers that the Head of the Commonwealth had 'no constitutional character'. There were no 'formal responsibilities' and no 'repository of ministerial advice'.[16] Powell found this 'peculiar and alarming' and felt quite secure that his criticisms could not be taken as disloyalty or impugning the Queen's judgement because 'ministerial advice that ministerial advice is not requisite is also ministerial advice, for which ministers must take the responsibility'. He went on to claim that as Head of the Commonwealth she could never be advised by ministers because 'the Commonwealth as such' had no ministers. It was 'not a political entity, or indeed an entity at all except in make-believe'. 'Head of the Commonwealth' was only a 'title', therefore he regarded the Christmas broadcast as 'a hiatus in the normal chain of advice and responsibility'.[17]

Powell did not err in his constitutional logic, but Lord Blake, an Oxford historian, explained that twice a year – on Christmas Day and Commonwealth Day – the Queen sent personal messages to the Commonwealth. They were the only times she spoke without advice. Normally, when she spoke in Britain, it was on the advice of British ministers; when she spoke in another of her realms it was on the advice of its ministers; when she spoke as a visitor in a republic or indigenous monarchy, she spoke on the advice of British ministers. But Powell would not let go his 'hiatus' in advice for the two annual messages: 'When was this convention declared?' he demanded. 'And what ministers were responsible for it, remembering that advice that advice is not requisite is also advice.' This was trumped by Lord Blake's splendid reply: 'If ministerial advice is not needed, ministerial advice that it is not needed is also not needed.'[18]

Powell again took up his cudgels two years later at the time of the disastrous Commonwealth Games boycotts when there were rumours that Buckingham Palace and Downing Street were at odds over the Commonwealth. *The Times* speculated on 16 July 1986, that the Queen might have to intervene to save the Commonwealth. Powell insisted that ministers should not attribute personal opinions to the Queen or suggest she might not accept advice constitutionally offered. Her role as Head of the Commonwealth could not affect the issue because there is 'no function corresponding to that title' which the monarch could perform for the simple reason that there was 'no constitutional source of advice to the sovereign as "Head of the Commonwealth" because as such she has no responsible ministers on whose advice to act'.[19]

It was left to H. V. Hodson, a veteran of Commonwealth affairs for over 50 years, to point out that Powell was strong on logic and weak on historical perspective. The British constitution, said Hodson, was 'almost entirely conventional rather than legally structural'. Ministerial advice was a conventional not a statutory right, and it was in keeping with this tradition that the Headship of the Commonwealth role evolved by convention. 'Whatever the Queen does as head of the Commonwealth, not being contrary to existing convention, is inherently precedent, which grows into convention, in turn being part of the unwritten constitution.' The Queen was, he said, at liberty to 'consult whatever persons she pleases on whatever matter'.[20]

By the mid-1990s, as the Commonwealth experienced a renaissance and membership went past the 50 mark, both the Crown and the Headship came in for new sorts of criticism. H. V. Hodson, wrote again on the 'Crown and Commonwealth' in *The Round Table* in 1995. With vocal republican movements in Australia and New Zealand (but not Canada), criticism of the expenses of the monarchy in Britain, and media obsession with the private lives and marital misfortunes of the Queen's children, some novel notions were being aired. Some suggested that Charles, Prince of Wales, should not succeed to the throne. Tony Benn, a socialist republican relic from the hey-day of the welfare state, called for a quadrennial rotation of the Headship. Hodson reminded us of the distinction between Crown and Headship. The wearer of the Crown and performer of its functions was a matter of hereditary succession, he said. 'British monarchs are not chosen by opinion poll. Popularity should be neither their boast or their purpose. Their conduct as Head of State is what matters.' Of the Headship of the Commonwealth he went on: 'this is not an hereditary office. When Queen Elizabeth II dies ... or if she abdicates, the Headship of the Commonwealth will be vacant. Neither the accession nor the Coronation will make the new monarch Head of the Commonwealth.'

Here, indeed, said Hodson was the real hiatus. In 1952 there had been unanimous agreement by the eight members. 'There are no other precedents and times are changed.' If the Headship rotated, as Tony Benn proposed, where would the incumbent live, how would he or she be paid and transported? Was the Headship even necessary? asked Hodson. Were not Secretariat, Secretary-General and Chogms 'institutions enough to embody the Commonwealth's over-all purpose'? Should the Headship lapse at the end of Elizabeth's reign? Hodson's answer was that an institution without a head was an institution without a heart and that there were bonds of feeling as well as interest. If Elizabeth II lived as long as her mother or reigned as long as Queen Victoria, he said, the decision could be put off until the 2010s.[21]

However, in the same year as Hodson wrote, the advent of new members, Cameroon and Mozambique, and the applications in the pipeline from several other countries, made it imperative to review the criteria for membership. The task was given to an Inter-governmental Group made up of London High Commissioners from the countries, which had hosted Chogms. At the same time, domestic reviews were put into motion in Britain on the monarchy's role and finances. There was also a realisation that if the Queen's reign were to end abruptly, an unseemly debate about the Commonwealth Headship could ensue among the more than 50 members. It would be better for the succession to be determined in tranquil times to avoid a potentially messy emergency debate. The Secretariat and the Palace gave thought to this matter. The Inter-governmental Group on Criteria presented a useful opportunity. A preview of its conclusions was published in *The Round Table* in 1996 in an article by the New Zealand High Commissioner, the group's convenor.[22]

That something was in the wind and going rather further than mere criteria was evident at the Secretary-General's opening press conference in Edinburgh in 1997. In answer to a question about the Headship, the Secretary-General remarked that 'at the moment' it was the Queen. This prompted some immediate wildly speculative questions. Was she about to abdicate in favour of Prince Charles? Would the Headship of the Commonwealth become elective? Was Nelson Mandela a candidate? The answer was, in due course, found in the Inter-governmental Group's report defining the 'conventions and norms' for membership, which included the recognition of the 'British Monarch' as the Head of the Commonwealth.[23] This formula did not have the benefit of discussion by the Heads of Government. Its implications were certainly not understood by one prime minister, who was surprised to be told, but brushed it off saying he was a republican anyway. The questioner at the closing press conference, who asked what the new formula did to the status of the Canadian monarch, was raising a point which arose from the comments of Sir William Dale and H. V. Hodson.

The London Declaration referred to 'The King'. The current Head of the Commonwealth is Queen Elizabeth. There has been a strong line of interpretation that the Headship was always a personal role. And, as Dale reminded us, there were several Crowns. Thus by citing only the 'British Monarch', the formula used in the criteria report appeared to demean the status of the Queen of Canada, the Queen of Barbados, the Queen of New Zealand, the Queen of Papua New Guinea, and so forth. A contrary view might follow the line of the Canadian Prime

Minister, St Laurent, at the time of the Coronation in 1953, who said the Queen was Queen of Canada because she was Queen of the United Kingdom: 'It is not a separate office.'[24] But the symbolic Headship *is separate* precisely because there are member-countries who do not subscribe to a 'common allegiance', but give allegiance to their republic or their own monarch. Moreover, for those who might hope for Ireland's return to the Commonwealth, the specification of 'British Monarch' would surely cause some disquiet. A more felicitous wording might have referred to 'the Queen's successors', which would have confirmed the equal status of the 16 monarchies. If the intention was, indeed, to ensure the succession of Prince Charles, the effect would have been the same. There was no sign that anyone wanted to change the symbolic Headship of the Commonwealth, but it was unfortunate that in Edinburgh the 'habit of consultation' was circumscribed and a major innovation with less than felicitous wording went through on the nod.[25]

8

The Logo, the Venue and the Argot

The Queen as the Head of the Commonwealth is a symbol well known throughout the world. The Commonwealth logo, by contrast, is one of the most obscure. Unlike the five rings of the Olympic Games which people instantly recognise, those who are shown the Commonwealth logo invariably fail to identify it.

The symbol first appeared in 1973, on the initiative of the first Secretary-General, Arnold Smith, who was soon sending his friends ties sporting the motif. He recorded in his memoirs that soon after his election he had lunch with several Heads of Government when Milton Obote of Uganda suggested that in due course the Secretariat would need a flag and a symbol. 'When you do, don't ask heads of government to approve a design. We have enough to divide us... . Decide what you can do for yourself, and do it.'[1] Once the Secretariat's information service got underway in the early 1970s, Smith consulted Derek Ingram, founder of Gemini News, the only news agency that concentrates on the Commonwealth and which made a speciality of clear graphic design.[2] A member of the agency, Cliff Hopkinson, produced a design consisting of a stylised globe encircled by a capital 'C', formed of hatched lines radiating from the globe. This appeared modestly on the Secretary-General's fourth report, more prominently on the 1973 edition of the booklet *The Commonwealth Today*, and on a blue flag which adorned the Secretary-General's car for the Ottawa Chogm. The Canadian government also incorporated it in the Chogm decor and thereafter it has adorned Secretariat letterheads and publications.

In recent years, the straight 'hog's back' hatchings, forming the capital 'C', have often been rendered in 'tapered spear' form. This has a more eye-catching effect when rendered in colour (normally gold on blue); in black and white it 'thickens' the hatchings to become much more recognisable as a 'C'. Yet it still eludes the uninitiated. Generations of students, confronted with the symbol and asked about what it conveys, could only lamely offer 'the globe' or 'the rising sun'. What a contrast to the impact of the Olympic rings, one of the world's most popular and instantly recognised symbols!

In Edinburgh, the British government used a much more colourful design as the decorative motif for the 1997 Chogm. This was blatantly borrowed from the Royal Commonwealth Society (RCS), the oldest private organisation for fostering interest in the Commonwealth. The role of the RCS and a recent crisis in its affairs will be recounted in Chapter 21. But in 1997 it marked the start of a new era in its life with a colourful new logo designed by Linda Morey Smith, consisting of green, blue, red and orange strands entwined right across the society's letter head and bulletins. The bright colours signified vibrancy, and the strands symbolised the Commonwealth interwoven in friendship and cooperation around the world.[3] Edinburgh streets were adorned with banners carrying this motif, and the official Chogm symbol rendered the same colourful entwined strands in a circle, as if wrapped around a globe, which made an unmistakable and attractive visual impact. Whether the symbolism was appreciated by onlookers is doubtful. Interestingly, the Francophone community also adopted a roundel made of segments in yellow, green, mauve, red and blue. For the Durban Chogm the colours in the South African flag – yellow, black, green, red, and blue – were rendered as concentric crescents to make a circular logo.

A few other visual symbols have been attempted from time to time. The Royal Commonwealth Society's Ottawa Branch simplified the globe encircled by 'C' by rendering the 'C' as a normal, single-curve capital letter. The Commonwealth Air Transport Council superimposed a head-on silhouette of an aircraft on the logo, producing a very handsome symbol. The Commonwealth Human Ecology Council uses the 'C' encompassing the globe as the start of its logo CHEC, and in place of the lined hatchings, it puts the names of the member countries. The Commonwealth Foundation has skewed the logo sideways to give a pleasant 'planetary' symbol. The Commonwealth Partnership for Technology Management makes a colourful 'C' in the form of lines of members' flags. For more than a decade before the appearance of the Secretariat logo, the Commonwealth Games based their symbols on the Commonwealth Games Federation's circular badge with a crown and initials encircled by a chain. In Cardiff (1958) this was surmounted by a red dragon; in Perth (1962) by a kangaroo; in Kingston, Jamaica

(1966) by a local coat of arms; and in Edinburgh (1970) it was incorporated in a thistle. A break was made for the Xth Games in
Christchurch, New Zealand (1974), which adopted the most striking of
all Games logos – a red, white and blue Roman numeral X made up
from the initials NZ, which also echoed the Union Jack. Since then,
red, white and blue have featured in all the Games' logos, but each
host venue produced its own design.

*

If the Commonwealth lacks a visual symbol as popular as the symbolic
Headship, does it have a suitable venue with which people can identify? It certainly has a venue of immense grandeur in Marlborough
House, a royal palace on Pall Mall and overlooking The Mall in central
London. Now the home of the Secretariat and the Foundation, its use
for Commonwealth purposes preceded the creation of the Secretariat
by six years.

The idea of some focal point for the Commonwealth away from
Whitehall arose at the time of the Trade and Economic Conference held
in Montreal in 1958. As they prepared for this meeting, British officials
considered the idea of bringing a number of Commonwealth inter-governmental organisations concerned with economic and trade matters
under an identifiable umbrella title. Lord Home, the Secretary of State
for Commonwealth Relations, also threw in the idea of a
'Commonwealth House' in London to bring these bodies under one
roof. During the Montreal conference, it was agreed that
'Commonwealth Economic Advisory Council' would be the umbrella
title and there was considerable enthusiasm for the idea of a
'Commonwealth House'. The search was soon on for a site in London.
Several were considered. The Commonwealth Institute (formerly
Imperial Institute) was shifting from Victorian Renaissance buildings in
South Kensington to a striking contemporary structure in Holland Park,
and the idea was floated that this site might be shared. Somewhere
closer to Whitehall was preferred, and among sites mentioned was the
Banqueting Hall where a lease was coming due. If a purpose-built place
was preferred, there was talk of a site next to the National Gallery in
Trafalgar Square or the former Westminster Hospital site close to the
Abbey and Parliament, formerly earmarked for the Colonial Office. A
working party set up by the prime minister to find a Commonwealth
House felt it must be 'a worthy symbol of Commonwealth co-operation
… which would attract the imagination of the public'.[4]

Derick Heathcoat Amory, the Chancellor of the Exchequer, bumped
into the Duke of Edinburgh at a German Embassy function, where they

talked about the Montreal Conference and the search for a centre. The idea of using Marlborough House came up. It had been the home of Queen Mary until her death in 1953 and the Duke suggested to Amory that the Queen might agree to its use for the Commonwealth. Sir Norman Brook, the Cabinet Secretary, gave Prime Minister Harold Macmillan the considered view of senior officials on 27 October 1958. They felt that the Commonwealth Centre had to be presented as an imaginative project. Most importantly, it should have a theme. In this respect, merely providing a home for the Commonwealth Economic Committee staff would 'not quite do'. A permanent home for Commonwealth meetings would be more appropriate. Although there was 'great psychological value' in using the Cabinet Room at 10 Downing Street, the PMMs were getting too large. It would be better to have a permanent meeting-place which had 'a Commonwealth character'. Marlborough House would fit the bill and 'it would certainly strike the public imagination if the Queen, as Head of the Commonwealth, were to make it available as a Commonwealth centre'. Failing Marlborough House, Brook suggested they build on the Westminster Hospital site, close to the Houses of Parliament.

Macmillan and Home were both enthusiastic about Marlborough House, though money would have to be spent on installing central heating and modern lavatories. On 22 December 1958 Macmillan approached the Queen, who signified her approval on 15 January 1959. As Sir Michael Adeane, the Private Secretary, put it, she was not offering the house to the Commonwealth as such, but making it available to the British government to use for Commonwealth purposes, provided this was agreeable to Commonwealth governments. The Heads of Government were all happy, except Dr Verwoerd, who did not like the idea of a 'Commonwealth Centre' as a joint venture, since it might 'lead to interpretations' which conflicted with clearly stated South African views. Macmillan replied that it would not be called 'Commonwealth Centre' but keep the name Marlborough House. The project was announced in the House of Commons on 17 February 1959 and the first PMM to use the new facilities gathered in 1962.

Initially, the house was used for the staff of the Commonwealth Economic Committee, the Commonwealth Educational Liaison Unit and the Association of Commonwealth Universities, which administered the Scholarship and Fellowship Plan started in 1959. The 1964 and 1965 PMMs, which made the decisions about creating the Secretariat and the Foundation, met there. Later, in 1965, the Secretariat began to move in and was joined by the Foundation a year later. Eventually the Secretariat absorbed the economic and educational tenants, and the ACU moved out. As a venue for PMMs, Marlborough House had a very short life. There was a gap between meetings from 1966 and 1969 when Lancaster House nearby was used. From 1971 onwards, the new-style Chogms started in Singapore and then rotated around the Commonwealth. The only returns to Britain since that date were in Lancaster House in 1977 and the Edinburgh International Conference Centre in 1997.

As symbol for the Commonwealth, Marlborough House has its ironies, ambiguities and its critics. Macmillan believed that members would prefer Marlborough House to a modern building. He surmised, somewhat incongruously, that its association with the Royal Family and the first Duke of Marlborough would be 'acceptable even to the newer and more republican-minded members'. Sir Norman Brook, who was very keen on the idea, balked at the prospect of embarrassing offers of help with the furnishings: 'We certainly do not want to see the house cluttered up with statuary from India or Ghana, or even modern furniture from Canada or Australia.'[5] Tactful forestalling was in order by emphasising the architectural and artistic significance of Christopher Wren's last great building. The Ministry of Works obliged with a blurb describing it as the work of Britain's greatest architect done for Britain's greatest general.

After a few years it was evident that Marlborough House was not big enough to house either all the Secretariat or the PMMs. As for the symbolism, one must wonder about the impact on Commonwealth visitors. How does an official from, say, Tuvalu respond as he or she climbs the grand stairways, surrounded by vast murals depicting Marlborough's European victories? And does the Secretary-General, as he works in a vast and elegant office, once Queen Mary's bedroom, feel that he inhabits a very special brand of ivory tower remote from the experience of the Commonwealth's hundreds of millions of citizens? Perhaps a purpose-built Secretariat could have been made into a more appropriate symbol for the modern Commonwealth.

*

Another aspect of the symbolic Commonwealth, only recognised by a few enthusiasts, is Commonwealth Day. In Britain there was an Empire Day, 24 May (Queen Victoria's birthday), which was renamed **Commonwealth Day** in 1958. In Canada they still have it as Victoria Day. In 1966 a Commonwealth Day multi-faith service was held at the Church of St Martin-in-the-Fields in Trafalgar Square, building on an experiment begun during the pioneer Commonwealth Arts Festival of the previous year. The service was attended by the Queen and the Duke of Edinburgh and conducted by the Bishop of Kensington, but aroused the ire of some Anglicans because of the 'heathen' elements in the service. Therefore, from 1968 to 1972 the Guildhall became the venue for these services, until the Queen suggested the use of Westminster Abbey, a 'royal peculiar' not under the jurisdiction of a diocese. These celebrations, however, were confined to Britain.

In 1975 Pierre Trudeau of Canada, in a new-found mood of enthusiasm for the Commonwealth, suggested that there should be a simultaneous Commonwealth Day celebrated in all member countries. Senior officials, meeting in Canberra the following year, found that the second Monday of March was a rare occasion which would find all schoolchildren around the Commonwealth at their desks. The first of the new Commonwealth Days was 14 March 1977. It is not a public holiday, therefore hardly noticed by anyone. Generations of students, asked to say what *they* did at school on Commonwealth Day, usually look blank. In a few cases, where they had teachers with knowledge or interest, advantage was perhaps taken of a hand-book produced by the Secretariat suggesting possible activities, such as debates, quizzes, country projects, ethnic food experiences, talks by visitors on their homelands, films, junior-Chogms and other activities. The Queen's message can be distributed in leaflet form.

Commonwealth Day is marked by a few, but has not become a popular symbol. In London and a few Commonwealth cities it is preceded on the Sunday before by religious services, where the flags of the member countries (and, if known about, the blue and gold flag sporting the Commonwealth logo) are paraded down the aisle by young people and the Queen's message read out. In Westminster Abbey it remains a multi-faith observance and children bring in fresh flowers from around the world and some also meet the Queen. For the few who experience it, the symbolism can be memorable. But in a Commonwealth Day broadcast in 1978, the Secretary-General admitted, 'I don't think people know enough of what's going on in the Commonwealth.'[6]

A further way in which the symbolic Commonwealth fails to match the appeal and popularity of the Headship and the Games is the language of Commonwealth discourse. It may amount to a somewhat ambiguous achievement, but the Commonwealth now embraces an argot of its own. Bureaucracies love to spawn jargons suffused by acronymese. Denis Austin once poked gentle fun at the Commonwealth's links with other international organisations, which, he said, bordered on fantasy: 'agreements with "Imco, Unesco, Unido, Unep, and Habitat" like some strange language of the unknown'.[7] Barely a few years after its formation, Secretariat statements became recognisable by the broadening inflexions of a ComSec-Speak comprehensible only to the *cognoscenti*. By the 1990s, as the Secretariat joined the global cyber-community, we learnt of Combinet (Commonwealth Business Network), Comnet-IT (Commonwealth Network of Information Technology For Development) and CENSE (the Commonwealth Electronic Networks for Schools and Education). The COL (Commonwealth of Learning) extols the rising role of ICT (Information and Communications Technology) and GKP (the Global Knowledge Partnership). When it opened its website in 1997, the Secretariat issued a glossary of abbreviations, indicating those acronyms pronounced as words (such as Nato and Chogm) that are written as such in lower case; otherwise they stay as initials.

The globe is encompassed by a galaxy of regional organisations such as Anzus, Apec, Asas, Asean, Caricom, Canidad, EcoWas, Esecap, Nafta, Saarc, Sadcc and Sacu. In conversation we refer to ComSec and the SG, Chogms and the CoW (Committee of the Whole). The CFTC (Commonwealth Fund for Technical Co-operation) works alongside Cida (Canadian International Development Agency) and tries to foster TCDC (technical cooperation between developing countries). A voluntary body is a non-governmental organisation or NGO – an inelegant acronym in itself, but one that lends itself to extensive, almost poetic, ramifications. Thus, the Pacific Islands Association of NGOs is Piango; the Association of NGOs in Aotearoa (New Zealand) is Angoa, and the South African National NGO Coalition is Sangoco. For a time, national NGOs were coordinated by a Commonwealth Liaison Unit or Clu. The pioneer report titled *Non-Governmental Organisations: Guidelines for Good Policy and Practice,* produced a taxonomy of such bodies that reads like a comedy: Quangos – quasi-autonomous NGOs; Pongos – politically organised NGOs; Fongos – funder-organised NGOs; even Bongos – business-organised NGOs; and Gongos – government-organised NGOs. And none of these a 'true' NGO![8] In 1999, the organisers of the unoffical forum in Durban improved the argot with its use of NPOs – not-for-profit organisations.

New words appear almost annually, like Capam (Commonwealth Association for Public Administration and Management), Congosam (Commonwealth Office for NGOs in South Africa and Mozambique), Dawn (Developing Alternatives for Women of the New Era) and Instraw (International Research and Training Institute for the

Advancement of Women). The COL contributes to a global distance education network (DistEdNet) and to FOCODLA (the Federation of Commonwealth Distance Learning Associations). In one case the new argot was mobilised to disguise past associations. The former Commonwealth Agriculture Bureaux, the major umbrella organisation embracing the pioneer inter-governmental organisations in the agricultural sciences, was initially CAB. Then it became, from 1986, an international organisation in its own right, including non-Commonwealth members, called CAB-International. Finally, as it became self-financing in the 1990s and intent on de-emphasising its Commonwealth origins, it became simply CABI – spoken as 'Cabi'.

My own offering to the new lexicon is a slogan designed to emphasise the *positive side* of the voluntary Commonwealth. Designations like 'unofficial' and 'NGO' and 'NPO' define such bodies by what they are *not*. Americans prefer 'private voluntary organisations' (PVOs) or 'voluntary agencies' (VolAgs). One positive suggestion, 'public interest groups' (Pigs), makes a nice counterpoint to heads of government (Hogs). Others use 'informal sector' or 'organic' Commonwealth. D. A. Low threw the net wider to embrace 'personal, professional and philanthropic' linkages.[9] But this neglected the most popular element of all – sports, the Games, the CGF and, more recently, the Chogm Committee on Co-operation Through Sport (CCCS). A better, all-embracing formula is **'voluntary, independent, professional, philanthropic and sporting organisations'** – **VIPPSOs** (pronounced Vippsos). Here is a designation indicating both their nature (voluntary and independent) and their main functions (professional, philanthropic, and sporting). Or perhaps, Professor Austin had a point!

Part IV
Political Commonwealth

9
Membership

At the time of writing there were 54 members of the Commonwealth. Of this total, over half had populations of less than one million at independence when they joined. Between the era of the five-nation 'British Commonwealth of Nations' – an unwritten alliance in the Second World War when it was still a Great Power – to the time of Namibia's accession as the fiftieth member in 1990, the association was totally transformed. The engine of change was the dissolution of the British Empire. This, in turn, was only part of the mighty tide of decolonisation – one of the grand themes of the twentieth century. The evolution of the 'New Commonwealth' was the peculiar contribution made by the British fellow-nations to this momentous process. Deryck Schreuder once wrote of imperial expansion in the nineteenth century: 'The Empire … died as it grew.'[1] Cynics contemplating decolonisation during the suspense-ridden 1960s liked to hint that 'The Commonwealth grew as it died.' But the putative morticians were to be confounded. The return of post-apartheid South Africa to the Commonwealth in 1994, after an absence of 33 years, made the total membership equal to the original United Nations in 1945. A year later this was followed by the admission of Cameroon, a largely Francophone country, whose accession surprised everyone. This perhaps tempered the surprise which also greeted the approval, in the same meetings, for the admission of Mozambique, a wholly Lusophone country, no part of which had ever been ruled by Britain. In 1997, there was considerable delight at the return of Fiji, after a 'lapse' in membership of ten years. Such was the apparent attraction of membership that a minor build-up of new applicants led to the appointment of the working group on criteria in 1995. There was talk of 70 by the end of the first decade of the new century.

The atmosphere had not always been so buoyant. Those who had cherished the old Commonwealth of Nations – Australians, Britons, Canadians, New Zealanders and English-speaking white South Africans – found the transformation traumatic. Virtue may have been made of necessity, but the strains of decolonisation were often hard to bear. At each stage of the decolonisation process there were regrets about the impending changes and numerous attempts to apply the brakes. The original five-member club, dating from Imperial Conference days and the close comradeship of two world wars, was reluctant to open its doors to new members. Some felt almost overwhelmed by the pace of change and depressed by the periodic spurts of dramatic acceleration.

From the 1940s to the 1960s, there were numerous ministerial committees, official study groups and inter-departmental enquiries in London to review the nature of the Commonwealth. Officials were forever compiling lists of dependencies, classifying their progress, assigning them to categories and drawing up tentative timetables. At the end of the Second World War, the colonial empire comprised some 50 dependencies. Every few years, officials would tot up their populations, progress, resources and likely futures. Dependencies were allocated places in a hierarchy of constitutional categories. For a long time, it was assumed that most of them were **unqualified to become independent nations**. Yet Britain's colonial policy had been trumpeted during the war as one of encouraging colonies to become self-governing nations within the Commonwealth. What had not been decided – let alone announced – was how far self-government and independence also meant membership of the Commonwealth 'as now understood'. For many years there was talk of a 'two-tier' system. This was always firmly rejected, yet in practice, there were always preliminary in-group consultations between London, Ottawa, Canberra and Wellington.

*

The first phase of decolonisation passed off without too much strain and led to considerable self-congratulation.[2] Attlee's postwar Labour government granted independence to India, Pakistan, Burma and Ceylon in the years 1947–8; they gave up the Palestine Mandate and prepared to end Indirect Rule in Africa. The device for achieving a quick transfer of power in India and Pakistan, to avoid a major bloodbath (which, in the event, was not avoided especially at the border), was the grant of Dominion status. Burma also wanted Dominion status and to become a republic. The former was refused; the latter meant that Burma never joined the Commonwealth which probably contributed to its subsequent tragic and isolated history. Ceylon was not, at first, lined up for Dominion status because, as we have seen, the concept was already out of date and about to be dropped. But Ceylon insisted, and became the third Asian Dominion. All three Asian Dominions attended the 1948 PMMs for the first time, when informal discussions took place about the question of whether India could stay on as a republic. Burma had not been allowed to; Ireland was about to cut its last ties; but India wanted to stay. As we have seen, the matter was resolved with considerable skill and goodwill in 1949. The old Club became an 'Eight', with members still eager to row in the same boat. But as it settled its multiracial rules, the Eight were not yet contemplating further boats on the river.

What, then, would become of the junior cousins? The same ministerial committee that considered the future of India, the largest country, also heard demands from one of the smallest dependencies, Gibraltar. Attlee was dismayed to discover that there was no body of principle covering the problem; so he set up a special enquiry into the future of the smaller territories, made up of officials, MPs and academics. Their task was to consider the future of 21 of the smallest colonies. Their secret report in 1951 concluded that independence was not always the appropriate goal – some 'satellite' status was needed and the committee's idea was for 'City or Island States'. Nine of the 21 might achieve self-government. For the rest, some permanent form of dependency was envisaged. This report was never published. A month after its completion Labour lost in a general election. The 'Island or City State' concept was deemed 'attractive intellectually but academic and un-English'.[3] The new Conservative government of Winston Churchill was diverted by more dramatic developments.

The second phase of postwar decolonisation began in 1951 when the first elections under universal suffrage took place in the Gold Coast. The Convention People's Party, whose leader, Kwame Nkrumah, was in jail, won them. The Governor, in a move dubbed by Roland Oliver as the 'Gamble for Africa', summoned Nkrumah from jail to Government House and called him to be 'Leader of Government Business' in the new Assembly. Nkrumah immediately demanded Dominion status for the Gold Coast, which horrified CRO officials, who envisaged 'acute and far-reaching problems' since 'numerous possible candidates' might try to emulate the Gold Coast. In South Africa there was particular alarm at the prospect of a black Dominion. The Conservatives faced a real dilemma: did the official policy – self-government leading to independence – really mean what Dominion status had come to mean – full membership of the Commonwealth, a ticket to enter the Club? In the short run, the Colonial Secretary bought time by fobbing off Nkrumah with the title 'prime minister' and telling him that, while Britain could negotiate terms for independence, Commonwealth membership needed approval by the Club committee – the existing members. Meanwhile, some 'mezzanine status' was sought, or independence without full membership.

Officials dusted off the 1951 Smaller Territories report and considered an 'intermediate' status, akin to Southern Rhodesia's after 1923. Future federations, in the West Indies, East Africa and Central Africa, might qualify for membership, along with the Gold Coast, Malaya and Nigeria. The whole shape and nature of the Commonwealth was also re-examined. There were indications that Sudan desired membership. Yet another option – integration with the United Kingdom on Ulster or Channel Islands lines – was contemplated briefly for Malta. Indeed, the Malta Committee came up with a possible solution to the general problem. This was the concept of 'statehood' – full internal self-government with defence and external affairs handled by Britain. But Nkrumah would not settle for anything short of full membership of the Club. The Governor warned that if he were blackballed, the rest of Africa would be lost. A good three years before independence was finally achieved by the Gold Coast the decision was made to sponsor it for Commonwealth membership.

Although in 1956 Sudan was the first (and geographically largest) African dependency to be granted independence, it followed Burma into the wilderness. And like Burma, Sudan's isolation could well have contributed to its subsequent unhappy history. Ghana and Malaya, independent in 1957, became members. Singapore, which also demanded Dominion status in 1956, was denied it, and became the only self-governing 'state' in 1959. Nigeria's independence in 1960 converted the club of 'Eight' into an 'Eleven' – a team, which found the field of play of the mid-1960s so rugged that it began to drop the whole 'club' image in favour of the newly fashionable garb of a 'multilateral international association'.

The turning point was passed during the third phase of decolonisation known as the 'Wind of Change' from 1959 to 1963. In the aftermath of the 1956 Suez crisis, Macmillan sought to resume friendly play with the existing Eleven and became the first British prime minister to tour the Commonwealth. He went to India, the Far East, Australia and New Zealand, and later Canada and Africa. Meanwhile, he set the officials to look again at their lists and timetables. They were given three specific tasks – to report on the future pattern of decolonisation, to compile a 'profit and loss account' of the cost and value of colonies to Britain, and they were to search, yet again, for some arrangement short of selection for the Eleven to cater for the smaller territories. The really urgent and critical case here was Cyprus, which had a population of only 500,000.

The now-famous 'profit and loss' report of 1957 concluded that new members expecting to join the team over the next ten years included Malaya and Nigeria (already in train), the West Indian and Central African Federations, and the larger West and East African states. Of the smaller territories, **some could never expect independence**, and the others, though of little value, **could not be abandoned**, as that would be 'discreditable and dangerous'. In the economic and financial account, the picture was 'evenly matched'; Britain's investment should not be the determining factor.[4]

Cyprus was regarded as a special case. Since Suez it had become the main British Middle East base. Its Greek majority population had to live with a 20 per cent Turkish minority. Since 1955 a campaign of sabotage and killings was being waged by the puritanical EOKA movement favouring *Enosis*, or union with Greece. This in turn alarmed the Turks. Military action failed to suppress EOKA; the governor's wife once found a bomb in her bed in Government House. By the end of the 1950s Macmillan sought a negotiated settlement. The exiled Greek nationalist leader, Archbishop Makarios, was prepared to trade *Enosis* for an independent republic guaranteed by Greece, Turkey and Britain, the latter retaining two small sovereign base areas.[5] Cyprus became independent in 1960 but was not, at first, selected for the Commonwealth Eleven. That would create a precedent for numberless small territories. Everyone realised it. The search for some alternative status resumed. Could not a line be drawn? New Zealand, then at two million, was taken as a sort of demographic bottom line. The 'Island or City State' and 'Statehood' concepts were re-examined; the old lists were re-assembled and the categories re-ordered. The CRO now offered the concept of a 'Commonwealth State' – independence in association with Britain.

The Cypriot leaders made it clear that they did not want 'a place in the second XI'. Yet to admit Cyprus would end chances of persuading the rest of the smaller territories to enter some lower league. In a private discussion at Number 10 in 1960 someone (probably Lord Home, the Secretary of State for Commonwealth Relations) said, 'If Cyprus was admitted as a fully independent member all the other tiddlers would demand this treatment.' Macmillan still cherished the

Club but asked, 'was it to be the RAC or Boodles?'[6] In 1960, the matter was put to the Commonwealth prime ministers who set up a Study Group of senior officials. During a week at Chequers they pored over the lists again. Cyprus was their big headache, but the New Zealanders provided a new source of irritation by announcing that they would soon be giving independence to 100,000 Western Samoans. For one British official this was too much – a *'reductio ad absurdum'* – but the New Zealanders expected that the Samoans would not want to join the Commonwealth, at least for a while. After pondering the lists and redesigning the categories, the senior officials concluded that by 1970 the total membership would reach between 17 and 24. They also said that it would be a negation of much of what the Commonwealth stood for if, on gaining independence, a country could join the United Nations but be debarred entry to the old Club. Full membership was the principle most consistent with the aspirations of new nations and the ethos of the Commonwealth. So Cyprus joined in 1961, two days before South Africa took its leave.[7]

As the 'Wind of Change' gusted to gale force during Iain Macleod's colonial secretaryship, between 1959 and 1962, the timetables and lists were constantly revised. Tanganyika became the first East Africa territory to become independent in 1961, followed by Uganda in 1962 when Sierra Leone (in West Africa) also joined. With the break-up of the short-lived West Indies Federation in 1962, Trinidad and Jamaica immediately became members. The Cabinet Secretary warned Macmillan in 1962 of another rush of candidates for full membership. Instead of 17–24 members by 1970 it was now more likely to be between 21 and 35. As the expanding PMMs shifted to Marlborough House in 1962, some procedural streamlining was tried. Macmillan admitted to Menzies during an elegiac exchange of letters in the same year: 'I am bound to confess that I now shrink from any Commonwealth meeting because I know how troublesome it will be.'[8] Out of this atmosphere came Nkrumah's Secretariat proposal in 1964. Twenty-one members made the decision to go ahead, and selected the first Secretary-General in 1965.

By this time, Labour had returned to power in Britain under Harold Wilson, and the penultimate phase of colonisation, symbolised by his 'Withdrawal from East of Suez', began as financial crises induced military retrenchments and closure of overseas bases. By now, too, alarm about what had happened to the old Club was not confined to British Conservatives. When the Canadian government was consulted over the admission of Malta in 1964, Lester Pearson, the Canadian prime minister, who was a veteran of the cosy days in Number 10, during the 1940s, had minuted: 'This really is becoming ridiculous.' In the following year he tackled Wilson about the findings of the 1960 Chequers group, which amounted to what Pearson called 'the principle of universality'. Realising that the new timetables were already obsolete, he wondered if 'some criteria for membership' were not desirable.[9] Wilson found himself in the same predicament as his Conservative predecessors. On what grounds, he asked, could the existing Club members deny full membership to countries that were able to join the United Nations? But he admitted that the Colonial Secretary was reviewing 31 remaining dependent territories. The results of this review were available in May 1965.

The Colonial Secretary told Wilson they were almost at the 'last stage' of decolonisation. The policy was to give independence to every territory that wanted it and was capable of sustaining it. He saw five possible options for the list of 31: independence as a separate sovereign state or united/federated with another state; independence with a treaty arrangement for Britain to handle external affairs; free association with an independent state; integration with an independent state, or continuing dependency. From the list only about a dozen were candidates for independence.[10] For the rest, New Zealand was providing a possible model. Its dependency in the Cook Islands (pop. 20,000) was granted responsible government in 1965 in 'free association' with New Zealand. The UN Committee on Colonialism was invited to observe elections in which the Cook Islanders signified their consent. Although the British did not approve of inviting a UN presence in case a precedent was created, they saw possibilities in the Cook Islands model. In 1967 they created a group of Caribbean 'associated states' with internal self-government. In 1970 Commonwealth membership had not, in fact, quite reached the most pessimistic 1962 projection. It stood at 31 rather than 35.

After 1970, the final phase of decolonisation involved a gradual hauling down of the flag on distant enclaves, and a closing of the last files on empire. Reluctant Pacific Island countries began to accept independence. At the Singapore Chogm in 1971 Fiji and Tonga were welcomed, along with Western Samoa, independent since 1962. Papua New Guinea followed in 1975, the Solomon Islands in 1978, and the Gilbert and Ellice Islands separated as Tuvalu and Kiribati in 1978/79. The New Hebrides rounded out the new political geography of the Pacific, under the name Vanuatu, in 1980. In the same year, Rhodesia's UDI was terminated (with considerable Commonwealth help as we have seen) and Zimbabwe joined the Commonwealth. The experiment of associated states in the Caribbean was short-lived. One by one the 'little eight' in the Leeward and Windward Islands became members of the Commonwealth, so boosting its small-state majority. By 1990, when Namibia (former South-West Africa) joined, the total hit the half-century: 50 dependencies into 50 Commonwealth members had taken less than 50 years.

The new problem of the 1990s was the appearance at the portals of the old Club (now converted into a large international association) of applicants whose claims for consideration were by no means straightforward. Cameroon had been a German colony before the First World War. Under the League of Nations Mandate system, the greater part of the territory was administered by France, but two north-western slices, known as Northern and Southern Cameroons, went to Britain. The large French territory gained independence in 1960. By plebiscites in the British enclaves in 1961, Southern Cameroons opted to join the former French territory and Northern Cameroons joined Nigeria. Thus, even though only an eighth of Cameroon had ever been under British rule, its application to join the Commonwealth was approved in 1995. Mozambique, a former Portuguese colony, was neither English-speaking nor a former mandate. But as a major transport outlet for the inland Commonwealth states, as a vital haven on Zimbabwe's path to independence and as a Southern African state having borders with six Commonwealth members, it was admitted as a 'special case' on Mandela's recommendation in 1995.[11]

At this point it became essential to do what Pearson had recommended 20 years earlier – establish criteria by which other new applicants could be judged. In 1997 the Palestinian Authority, Rwanda and Yemen were in the running. Other possible candidates are Bermuda, Somalia, even Israel, Sudan, Myanmar (Burma) and Ireland.

The Inter-Governmental Group which advised the Heads of Government on criteria consisted of representatives of countries which had hosted Chogms – Australia, Bahamas, Britain, Canada, Cyprus, India, Jamaica, Malaysia, New Zealand, Singapore, Zambia and Zimbabwe – chaired by John Collinge from the previous host country, New Zealand. They took as their starting point the general criteria embodied in the 1991 Harare Declaration (which we will be examined in Chapter 11). In brief, this meant historic links and shared traditions (through earlier British rule or an administrative link with another member) and adherence to Commonwealth values (summarised as democracy, human rights, good governance and the rule of law). The

Inter-Governmental Group decided that these principles had to be complied with prior to admission to membership. There were also certain 'non-controversial' prerequisites for membership which it termed **Commonwealth 'norms and conventions'**. These were – that the applicant had **broad-based domestic consent for joining**; that the applicant **accepted the English-language as the *lingua franca* of the Commonwealth**; and that the applicant **accepted the British monarch as the Head of the Commonwealth.**[12]

In the Edinburgh Communiqué the Heads of Government endorsed the Group's report in one general sentence. They agreed that in order to become a member of the Commonwealth, an applicant country should, as a rule, have had a constitutional association with an existing Commonwealth member, that it should comply with Commonwealth values, principles and values as set out in the Harare Declaration; and that it should accept Commonwealth 'norms and conventions'.

In the light of these criteria the three Edinburgh applicants were not admitted. But they were not rejected. Palestine's historical link was acknowledged and a decision was postponed until a decision had been made on Palestinian state sovereignty. Rwanda's and Yemen's applications would be kept under review. At Durban in 1999 there were no new applicants. Nauru attended as a full member for the first time, but Tuvalu's request for the same status was deferred, but was accepred in September 2000. The old Club had become a rules-based international association.

10
At the Summit – Chogms

The Heads of Government Meetings are the only aspect of the Commonwealth to make headlines, apart from the Queen and the Games. To use the argot, they represent the 'Commonwealth at the Summit' and are known by the flat neologism 'Chogm'. Generally forgotten is the fact that they are the world's oldest and largest gatherings of Heads of Government. They are, indeed, the contemporary successors of the Colonial Conferences, which began with Queen Victoria's golden jubilee in 1887, continued as Imperial Conferences between 1911 and 1937, and the Prime Ministers' Meetings which ran from 1944 and 1969.

When 45 heads of delegation, each with two officials, met around the table in Vancouver in 1987, only the editor of the quarterly journal *The Round Table* thought to recall that it was the centenary of the first Colonial Conference. In 1887 there had been a slightly smaller gathering, of 123 representatives from Britain and the Empire. When the experiment was repeated for Victoria's diamond jubilee in 1897, attendance was smaller, being confined to the Premiers of the self-governing colonies. For the next meeting, at the time of Edward VII's coronation, it was smaller still; there was now only one prime minister from newly federated Australia. By the time of the first Imperial Conference in 1911, the four South African colonies had become a single Union, so making the conference even smaller.[1] The unique Imperial War Cabinets of the 1914–18 war consisted of Australia, Britain, Canada, Newfoundland, New Zealand and South Africa. The Irish Free State added a sixth Dominion in 1922. We have seen how Newfoundland gave up Dominion status in 1933 and Éire adopted a republican constitution in 1937; both were absent from the conferences after 1930.

For the new series of Prime Ministers' Meetings, which started in 1944, the much used and cherished designation of a 'club' was entirely appropriate for the group of five. A usage which lingered long in the minds of many participants, it can still be encountered today. But, with the addition of the three Asian Dominions in 1948, the 'Eight' became less intimate – strategic secrets were not for sharing. With the arrival of the first Africans, the 'Eleven' of 1960 generated such tension that South Africa quit in the following year. Thereafter, as we have seen, rapid decolonisation totally transformed the Club into a multilateral international association, almost a mini-United Nations. Twenty-one members decided on the Secretariat in 1965. The first Chogm, in Singapore, comprised 31. A decade later, 42 gathered in Melbourne and at Edinburgh in 1997 there were over 51 – the same as at the UN meeting in London in 1946. In 1999 all 52 eligible members sent delegations to Durban. Only Tuvalu (a special member) and Pakistan (suspended from meetings) were absent.

As the meetings grew in size, they outgrew both Number 10 Downing Street and Marlborough House. They now required very large convention centres. In the 1990s they used the Harare International Conference Centre (1991); the Meridian Hotel near Limassol (1993), with the opening ceremony 100 km away in Nicosia; the Aotea Centre, Auckland (1995); the Edinburgh International Conference Centre (1997); and the Durban International Convention Centre (1999). Once inside these anonymous places, delegates must feel they could be anywhere in the world.

Chogms have become part of the tightly packed international meeting circuit. But the use of English and regular attempts to retain informality, as well as some developing friendships among leaders of long-standing, does permit more intimacy than many such gatherings. Those who have attended testify that 'people really talk to each other'. The most serious device in the direction of informality is the weekend Retreat, which seeks to emulate the earlier weekends at the British prime minister's country house Chequers in Buckinghamshire. However, even before the meetings began to rotate around the world, they outgrew Chequers, and the nearby ministerial residence, 'Dorneywood', had to be used as back up. Pierre Trudeau revived the weekend and called it a Retreat in 1973, when the Heads of Government and their spouses, without officials, went off to a resort hotel at Mont Tremblant, Quebec, some 120 km north of Ottawa.

As the size of the meetings grew, their length became circumscribed and the Retreat seemed under threat. From the 1940s to 1960s the

PMMs lasted for a week to ten days, sometimes including two weekends. The Chogms began in the 1970s with nine days in Singapore, but were down to a week by the 1980s to only five days in 1987. Kuala Lumpur (1989) and Harare (1991) were the last week-long conferences; Limassol (1993) was back to five days, and, since then, it has been three-and-a-half days. In New Zealand they were evenly split between conference and Retreat. In Edinburgh, the Retreat was reduced to a Sunday Away-a-Day on a vintage Pullman train across the Forth Bridge to a golf course at St Andrews. Tony Blair apologised and admitted it was too short.

*

For all the variety of place and personality, the contemporary Chogms have evolved a well-established pattern, which includes five main features: ceremonial and ritual; political responses to world events; the on-going work of the Commonwealth; getting together at various levels; and the communiqués.

The ceremonial and ritual aspects are widely reported and always make a considerable impact on the host city, if only for the traffic hold-ups, tight security arrangements and some accompanying demonstrations. There is the visit by the Head of the Commonwealth, which usually involves meeting local dignitaries, visiting institutions, as well as touring the conference facilities, audiences with Heads of Delegation, the banquet and formal group photograph with Heads of Government, a reception for Ministers and Senior Officials, and one for selected media representatives.

The **opening ceremony** today is usually a grand, publicised and, often, televised event in contrast to the brief opening meetings of the earlier PMMs, when, after a few words of welcome, they simply ran through the agenda and arrangements. Modern opening ceremonies involve large-scale performances of political theatre in impressive auditoria, before more than 1,000 invited guests, including all the delegations and most media people, as well as host country politicians and NGO leaders. Cultural warm-up sessions precede the opening proper. In Harare there were African water dancers and the massed choirs of local high schools clad in striped blazers. At Limassol young people in white danced with banners and flowers in the aisles and sang 'Give Peace a Chance'. In Auckland the New Zealand Symphony Orchestra offered music by Commonwealth composers and a Maori group performed a traditional (menacing) welcome. For Edinburgh, the new Labour government banned bagpipes and bearskins and the warm-up had actor John Thaw sitting on a stool telling 'Commonwealth stories', giving some graphic and personal illustrations of the work of the specialist Commonwealth agencies. There was a brief routine by non-white dancers flourishing coloured streamers matching the Chogm motif and a youth choir who sang a new Commonwealth song. Durban provided a mix of song and dance from South Africa's European and African heritages. Such performances are all together too time-consuming in comparison with the time now allotted for genuine consultation.

Heads of Government are preceded into the auditorium by their spouses, after which the heads of delegation take their places in the podium. A convention had developed that the opening speakers would represent the five main regions. Following the welcome speech by the host Head of Government and one by the Secretary-General, there would be five others including the previous host. In Edinburgh, the British waived this tradition. A smaller auditorium meant that only selected delegation staffs and even fewer media people attended. On the occasion of her golden wedding, the Head of the Commonwealth attended for the first time, and sat at the centre of the podium with the Duke of Edinburgh and the Prince of Wales. The Queen addressed the meeting and the only other speeches were by the host Tony Blair, the Secretary-General, and the Prime Minister of India, in recognition of the fiftieth anniversary of the ending of the Raj. The same pattern was followed in Durban to mark the fiftieth anniversary of the creation of the Headship. Had a new tradition been formed?

The second and most significant aspect of the Chogm **is political consultation by the leaders** and their responses to global and Commonwealth trends. These sessions represent the prime *raison d'être* of the gathering, the fulfilment of the adage that 'consultation is the life-blood'. With over 150 people in the room, real informality can hardly be possible. Vast circular or rectangular tables have to be constructed which often test the capacity of the room. Voice enhancement gear is provided. Large floral displays adorn the well between tables. In place of a preliminary global trends or keynote issue discussions, which in the past could take up the best part of a week (as in the case of the Rhodesia debate in September 1966), very little can be covered in one-and-a-half days of executive sessions. Much of the business is pre-processed by ministerial committees or inter-governmental working groups. Detailed drafting is left to the senior officials. Only a few Heads of Government get a chance to speak and heads of delegation of lesser rank traditionally hold their peace.

Each Chogm tends to focus on a few contentious issues which reflect urgent contemporary concerns, and these discussions (and the intense media speculation they engender) stamp each Chogm with its special character. In Harare in 1991, they looked to assisting an impending, and long-awaited, post-apartheid South Africa. The big personality of the Chogm was, in fact, a non-delegate, Nelson Mandela. Recently released after 27 years of jail, and invited to be present as the guest of the Zimbabwean President, Mandela had meetings with several Heads of Government, attended the Secretary-General's reception and gave a well-organised press conference. Harare also focused on the principles and values of the association as it contemplated its role in the post-Cold War environment. (The Harare Declaration expounding these values is discussed in the next chapter.) In Limassol in 1993 there was a proposal put forward by Anyaoku for giving a lead to the world for a Global Humanitarian Order, in face of the descent into barbarism in former Yugoslavia, Somalia, Rwanda and Sudan. Muslim leaders spoke forcefully about the fate of their fellow religionists in Bosnia. There were also continuing concerns about the reduction of international trade barriers, especially as they effected primary producers.

Auckland in 1995 had the themes of 'Nukes and Nigeria'. South Pacific countries were incensed about French nuclear tests at Mururoa Atoll and Britain's refusal to denounce them. The military government of Nigeria's execution, on the very day the Conference opened, of nine Ogoni activists (the son of one of them was present at Auckland) and the continued incarceration of some 40 political leaders, including the winner of the recent presidential election, prompted emotional responses and the first suspension of a member state. In Edinburgh in 1997, Nigeria's suspension was renewed. The main theme in Edinburgh was improving trade and investment and the elimination of poverty. The meetings were preceded by the first Commonwealth Business Forum and produced an economic declaration, intended to match the political Harare declaration. In Durban in 1999, Pakistan's suspension from Commonwealth councils following a recent military coup was confirmed. The Chogm tried to grapple with the problem of globalisation and the growing role of the private sector in Commonwealth endeavours.

The third, and much less reported, aspect of the Chogm is **the on-going work of the association**. The Secretary-General presents his biennial report on the work of the Secretariat. The Committee of the Whole (CoW) of senior officials chaired by a deputy secretary-general, works through Commonwealth functional cooperation. The 1990s were a time for thorough reviews of the Commonwealth's role in the postcolonial, post-Cold War world. The final session of the Chogm is normally devoted to Heads of Government perusal of this on-going

functional work. Convenors and directors of the main inter-governmental agencies have their opportunity to report. The Commonwealth
Fund for Technical Co-operation, the Commonwealth Foundation, the
Commonwealth of Learning, the Commonwealth Institute and the
Committee on Co-operation through Sport each have their moment in
the sun. For the practical work of the Commonwealth these are vital
matters and a Chogm is rather like a board of governors' meeting.

A fourth and much cherished part of the Chogm is the chance for
'getting together' at many levels. As well as the Chogm itself, the
occasion is utilised by Heads of Government for many bilateral,
regional or special interest meetings. The Retreat, at least in intention,
is designed to enable the Heads and their spouses to relax informally,
play golf or tennis, go for walks, shop in the nearby village, go to
church and even mingle with the locals. But they now also include
vital business talks, and some of the critical decisions (like Nigeria's
suspension) were taken during the Retreat.

The meetings of the CoW facilitate similar interaction among
officials, who often face similar administrative problems in their own
states. Until 1993 there were separate political and economic CoWs
and at Limassol, when they were first combined, the pressure was so
intense that there were all-night sessions and grumbles about the
'Committee of the Black Hole'. In subsequent meetings the officials
started two days earlier than the Heads of Government. There is also
much getting together among the media people, many of them veter-
ans of similar jamborees around the world.

In recent years, **media centres** have been fully equipped with on-line
facilities, booths for broadcasting, briefing rooms for press conferences
conducted by Secretariat officers or political leaders, and also refresh-
ment and lounge arrangements. The exception was Harare, where the
media facilities were abysmal, probably symbolic of the way the media
were regarded in Mugabe's Zimbabwe. The hubbub of the media centre
stems from the work of up to 1,000 representatives, accredited by the
Secretariat, to photograph, film and report the Chogm for broadcasting
networks, newspapers, magazines and even academic journals. Among
the horde will be well-known TV presenters, distinguished commentators and editors, a galaxy of journalists from around the world, even a
handful of professors masquerading as reporters. The latter dubbed
themselves the SCEPTICS, or Special Committee of Eminent Persons to
Investigate the Commonwealth Spirit.

Until the 1990s, representatives of NGOs, who wished to lobby delegates or report the Chogm for their bulletins and journals, required

media accreditation along with the rest. In 1993 a new era dawned for the 'People's Commonwealth' with the long-sought-after appointment of an NGO Liaison Officer in the Secretariat. For Limassol he arranged a special NGO accreditation and separate lounge and document facilities for representatives of 12 pan-Commonwealth organisations. In Auckland this had risen to 18; for Edinburgh and Durban it was over 60, amounting to some 300 people. Also in the wings of the Edinburgh Chogm was the first unofficial 'Commonwealth Forum', partly financed by the FCO, where 80 voluntary organisations (not necessarily specialising in the Commonwealth) mounted exhibits, ran mini-conferences and gave press briefings. The experiment was repeated in Durban with a large 'Commonwealth People's Centre' next door to the Chogm venue. The Edinburgh and Durham Chogms were also preceded by the first and second 'Commonwealth Youth Forums'. Thus the opportunities to get together for media and other interested groups are extensive. The moment when Heads of Government and the media and the unofficial groups mingle is the Secretary-General's reception, which usually precedes the opening. Here, media people mix informally with Heads of Delegation in an off-the-record atmosphere which makes the event one of the highlights of this aspect of the Chogm. In Cyprus, President Clerides had a wind-up party, virtually for all comers.

Finally, there is the public record of the Chogm, **the Communiqué**. This results from the continuous drafting endeavours of the CoW. It becomes the historic record and is enshrined now in the two-volume, *The Commonwealth at the Summit* – a vital reference source. It is not the only source of information, and a study of press reporting of Chogms would reveal that there are few secrets. If you look at the verbatim archival record of a meeting now open under the 30-year rule (say 1964 when the Secretariat was mooted) and compare it with a systematic file of press clippings, you find that the reporters usually did an excellent job. Maybe the credit should go to the PR briefing teams!

Before the Chogm opens, the Director of Information of the Secretariat briefs the media about arrangements and the Secretary-General runs through the agenda. After each executive session a Secretariat official summarises the discussions on a non-attributable basis. At the end, the Secretary-General and the host prime minister present the Communiqué. On each occasion there are questions embodying every possible nuance of provocation. Sometimes (as with Nigeria's suspension) the host Head of Government will present the paper part way through the conference. Many Heads of Government brief their own media on a daily basis; others give general press conferences to get their views across and answer questions. Thus around the 'secret' executive sessions, waves of speculation and news leakages build up to a pretty accurate public picture. For a few days, at least, the Commonwealth makes headlines. It then tends to fade away until the next meeting or the next Games.

Table 10.1 Expansion of PMMs and Chogms

Year	Venue	No. of Days	Total Members Attending
1944	London	16	5
1945	London	10	5
1946	London	33*	5
1948	London	12	8
1949	London	6	8
1951	London	10	8
1953	London	7	8
1955	London	14	8
1956	London	10	8
1957	London	10	9
1960	London	11	10
1961	London	10	13
1962	London	10	16
1964	London	8	18
1965	London	9	21
1966	Lagos (Jan.)	3	19
1966	London (Sep.)	10	22
1969	London	9	28
1971	Singapore	9	31
1973	Ottawa	9	32
1975	Kingston	8	33
1977	London	8	34
1979	Lusaka	7	39
1981	Melbourne	8	42
1983	New Delhi	7	42
1985	Nassau	7	46
1987	Vancouver	5	45
1989	Kuala Lumpur	7	46
1991	Harare	7	47
1993	Limassol	5	47
1995	Auckland	$3^1/_2$	48
1997	Edinburgh	$3^1/_2$	51
1999	Durban	$3^1/_2$	52

* Included adjournments to attend the UN General Assembly in Paris.

11
Ethos, Values and the 1991 Declaration

In the argot of the contemporary Commonwealth, groups of buzz-words have been assembled to highlight the values that member countries strive to uphold. Democracy, human rights, good governance and the rule of law are seen as the concomitants of sustainable development, free trade, the role of the market economy, equal opportunities and consensus building. Each of these phrases has the superficial quality of a slogan, but, on definition and analysis, they sum up the endeavours and aspirations of a quarter-of-a-century and they were restated at the start of the 1990s to signify a minor revolution.

Previous enunciations of Commonwealth principles and values were never designed as charters or constitutions; nor were they intended as theoretical exercises in politics and ethics. They each arose from specific circumstances. Just as the declaration of equal status in 1926 arose from specific South African, Canadian and Irish concerns, and the creation of the symbolic Headship in 1949 arose from India's republican constitution, so the 1971 Declaration of Principles arose from anger over British policies in Southern Africa and the 1991 Harare Declaration was a response to the end of the Cold War. Similarly, in 1995 an action plan for fulfilling the Harare values was drawn up because of the persistence of 'errant states' under military rule, notably Nigeria.

The 1971 Declaration was a statement of guiding norms, not of mandatory rules. They provided generalised political commitments and were reinforced in the 1970s and 1980s by a series of declaratory elaborations. We have seen how the members pledged themselves *to support* peace, liberty and cooperation.[1] This was reinforced by the 1983 Goa Declaration on International Security and the 1985 Nassau Declaration on World Order. The members also *denounced* racial discrimination, colonial domination and gross disparities in wealth. The first of these was reinforced by the 1977 Gleneagles Agreement on Racism in Sport, which became a key Commonwealth commitment because of the sheer visibility of infractions arising from the great popularity of sport.[2] There were also declarations relating to Southern Africa in 1985, 1987 and 1989.

The legal authority, Sir William Dale, has suggested that the 1971 Declaration incorporates statements 'of a constituent nature', and that the body of elaborations are 'agreed commitments as well as aims'. The Gleneagles Agreement especially, he said, contained obligations that were 'binding morally and politically'.[3] Stephen Chan, a political scientist and former Secretariat officer, went much further and saw 'a gradually-evolving political and moral point of view', which began to look like a charter. The declarations formed 'a dynamic constitutional structure that derives from international conditions and the Commonwealth's response to them'.[4] When Chan wrote in the late 1980s his interpretation seemed far-fetched. Ten years later, in the late 1990s, as Nigeria faced the possibility of expulsion, Chan's approach had more point. The 1971 Declaration of Principles consisted of guidelines for conduct. They outlined a Commonwealth value system, which could not be enforced, but could, hopefully, be upheld through consensus.

By 1989, as the Commonwealth began to display a new sense of confidence, the apartheid regime in South Africa began to thaw, and the Soviet domination of Eastern Europe to falter. The decade of the 1990s, with a new generation of leaders, promised different challenges. Thus the Kuala Lumpur Chogm in 1989 – the 45th anniversary of the first PMM – appointed a High Level Appraisal Group (HLAG – pronounced in the argot as H-Lag) to report on the role of the Commonwealth in the 1990s and beyond. To arrive at the membership of the group, invidious personal choices or intricate regional juggling were avoided, by adopting the simple device of taking those countries which had hosted Chogms – namely, Australia, Bahamas, Britain, Canada, India, Jamaica, Malaysia, Nigeria, Singapore and Zambia. The convenor was the recent host Prime Minister, Mahathir Mohammed of Malaysia.

The full H-Lag met only once, on the eve of the Harare Chogm, in 1991. Earlier meetings were postponed first because of the outbreak of the Gulf War and then by Rajiv Gandhi's assassination. The work of the group was done by senior officials of Cabinet Secretary rank (or equivalent) chaired by the Secretary-General of Malaysia's External

Affairs Department. As well as input from the member countries, the group had the benefit of the Secretary-General's ideas, and submissions from invited individuals, at least two of whom subsequently published them.[5]

As its starting point the group assumed a distinctive and enlarging role for the Commonwealth. The new global environment was marked by the end of the Cold War; the rising economic influence of Germany and Japan; the resurgence of ethnic, religious and cultural conflicts; the globalisation of finance, manufacturing, and information technology, and the consequent fear that the developing nations were being marginalised. The latter now constituted the overwhelming majority of the Commonwealth, which was somewhat crudely divided into 46 developing countries and only four developed ones were cited, namely Australia, Britain, Canada and New Zealand. To meet the challenge of the 1990s, it was accepted that good government and sound administration were essential, and that private capital investment and business competitiveness would have a major role. Newer problems crying out for urgent attention were environmental threats, drug trafficking, HIV/AIDS and the continued subordination of women.

The Commonwealth had comparative advantages for meeting these challenges in the habits of consultation, the use of English as a common language, and the breadth and depth provided by its official and unofficial agencies. The great needs were seen as education and training, capital and technical assistance, and help in strengthening democratic institutions and human rights. The Secretary-General had practical ideas for implementing this outline. The developed members needed to be encouraged to increase their aid contributions to Commonwealth programmes. Member states, it was suggested, should double their contributions to the CFTC by the end of the century. Educational exchanges should be increased and Commonwealth ministerial groups should be created to provide a continuous basis for consideration of international economic cooperation and the problems of small states. The Secretariat would have to make resources available to give advice in economic restructuring, the role of women in development and strengthening democratic processes.

The sweep of the H-Lag's work proved to be comprehensive. It reaffirmed the Commonwealth's usefulness and set out many appropriate directions for its future work. However, in the view of the British representative, Lord Armstrong (the former Cabinet Secretary under Mrs Thatcher, 1979–87), its draft report was overlong and unfocused.

The new British prime minister, John Major, asked him to produce a more succinct draft embodying the same basic ideas. When the H-Lag Heads of Government finally met in Harare, on the eve of the 1991 Chogm, they found themselves diverted by discussions about the future of South Africa and gave no attention to the details of the report. Only as they broke for lunch did John Major draw their attention to this and the shorter British draft, which was duly accepted, subject to a few changes by senior officials. Thus, the report, based on the British draft, became a series of headings, each of which signalled very large areas of concern. Possibly the Secretary-General was not pleased that his proposed practical remedies had been severely watered down.

After the Retreat at Victoria Falls, the H-Lag's work was published as the *Harare Commonwealth Declaration.*[7] After reaffirming the principles of the 1971 Declaration, the Harare Declaration addressed first the 'protection and promotion of the fundamental political values of the Commonwealth' summarised as:

- democracy, democratic processes and institutions which reflect national circumstances, the rule of law and the independence of the judiciary, just and honest government;
- fundamental human rights, including equal rights and opportunities for all citizens regardless of race, colour, creed or political belief.

Continuing action to end apartheid and establish a free democratic, non-racial and prosperous South Africa were also advocated. Second, the economic goal stated as 'the promotion of sustainable development and the alleviation of poverty' through:

- a stable international economic framework within which growth can be achieved;
- sound economic management recognising the central role of market economy;
- effective population policies and procedures
- sound management of technological change;
- the freest possible flow of multilateral trade on terms fair and equitable to all, taking account of the special requirements of developing countries;
- an adequate flow of resources from the developed to developing countries, and action to alleviate the debt burden of developing countries most in need;

- the development of human resources, in particular through education, training, health, culture, sport, and programmes for strengthening family and community support, paying special attention to the needs of women, youth, and children.

Third, because of some strong special pleading, additional social and environmental concerns were singled out for mention: equality for women; universal access to education; respect for human rights; protection of the environment; combating drug trafficking, drug abuses and communicable diseases; and assistance to small states.

To face up to this formidable agenda, the report called on all intergovernmental and non-governmental organisations to play a full part. Presenting the declaration on the evening of Sunday, 20 October 1991, the Secretary-General, who probably would have preferred some more specifics, dubbed it the Commonwealth mission statement – it would be 'our guide and beacon for the new century'. John Major said it was 'not a string of words to forget, but a road map for our future progress'.[8]

One commentator, Stephen Chan, suggested that the Harare Declaration proclaimed the political and socio-economic values of the victors of the Cold War.[9] It certainly had the virtue of highlighting three major Commonwealth problems. First, there were member countries under military or one-party rule that did not match up to the criteria. Harare was, in this respect, an exercise in finger pointing. Second, with a majority small-state, developing nation membership, the Commonwealth had colossal investment, technology and human resource needs. These, however, were under the risk of being marginalised because of the massive problems of rehabilitating post-Cold War Eastern Europe and the former Soviet Union. Could the Commonwealth small states' needs be met in the new environment? Third, the Commonwealth had some new applicants, whose character and ethos might not fit the historic pattern. To meet these problems, the Commonwealth needed more specific guides and tools, as the Secretary-General knew too well. These were forthcoming in Auckland in 1995.

Against a background of euphoria about South Africa's return to the Commonwealth after the epoch-making 1994 elections; anger at continuing human rights abuses in Nigeria; growing prosperity in the Asian Commonwealth, notably Singapore, Malaysia and Brunei, but continuing financial and environmental vulnerability in the small island states, the Heads of Government sought to give teeth to the Secretary-General for meeting the Harare goals. From the retreat at a resort, among snow-capped peaks and green fairways near Queenstown, in New Zealand's South Island, came the Millbrook Commonwealth Action Programme (MCAP or M-Cap), succinctly summarised as a three-head mandate for advancing **fundamental political values**, promoting **sustainable development**, and facilitating **consensus building**.[10]

To advance the fundamental political values, a three-fold strategy was outlined. First, positive measures for supporting processes and institutions included Secretariat assistance in constitutional and legal drafting, in democratisation programmes, in the conduct of elections, in strengthening the independence of the judiciary, in public service reform and activities to strengthen 'the democratic culture'. Second, to tackle the negative side, responses to violations of the Harare principles would include expressions of collective disapproval; use of the good offices of the Secretary-General to facilitate a return to democracy; the sending of eminent persons or groups as investigators; the setting of deadlines for the holding of elections; the exclusion of errant regimes from Commonwealth meetings and assistance programmes; and the application of a range of sanctions. Third, the mechanism to deal with 'serious or persistent violations' of the Harare principles was a Commonwealth Ministerial Action Group (CMAG) of eight foreign ministers. The first members of C-Mag (to use the argot) came from Britain, Canada, Ghana, Jamaica, Malaysia, New Zealand, South Africa and Zimbabwe.

For the promotion of sustainable development it was agreed that the CFTC, the Commonwealth Foundation and the Commonwealth of Learning needed enhanced resources. Greater investment should be encouraged through a new Commonwealth Private Investment Initiative. The poorer countries were to be assisted by 'innovative mechanisms for relief on multilateral debt'. Voluntary organisations were called on to create self-help schemes to help alleviate poverty. The special problems of HIV/AIDS were to be tackled by strengthening the Southern Africa Network of AIDS Organisations. Finally, the Commonwealth's unique experience in consensus building through its many organisations should assist the international community in building bridges across traditional divides.

By creating the C-Mag, and by giving the Secretary-General this range of instruments, the Millbrook action plan proclaimed an association with standards it was determined to maintain. Nigeria's suspension during the same meeting indicated that Heads of Government were prepared to move beyond argot to action. Indeed, when the government of Pakistan was overthrown in a bloodless military coup in 1999, the C-Mag moved fast to recommend the suspension of Pakistan from Commonwealth councils. This was endorsed by the Durban Chogm in the following month. Similarly, when the Fijian Prime Minister and 30 supporters were taken hostage in May 2000, the C-Mag recommended another suspension from Commonwealth councils – Fiji's second lapse only five years after its return. The as yet unanswered question is – how far C-Mag suspensions really have any impact? Nigeria's turn around could partly be attributed to the fortuitous deaths of the two main antagonists. Can the Commonwealth ever really stop tough guys grabbing or abusing power within member states?

12
Below the Summit

As the Chogms became shorter, meetings below the summit – those of ministerial groups and senior officials – took on a greater significance. The three-and-a-half-day pattern established by the Heads of Government in the mid-1990s left no opportunity for the leisurely reviews of global trends that had prevailed in the past. On the positive side, this also eliminated the posturing that had once been endured from set-piece orations or the weeklong donnybrooks like that which occurred over Rhodesia.

The most significant Commonwealth statements and actions of the 1990s emerged from below-the-summit endeavours stretching over many months. The Harare Declaration came from the H-Lag. The criteria recommendations, including confirming the hereditary Headship, came from the Inter-governmental Group of High Commissioners. The recommendation for the extension of Nigeria's suspension in 1997, and setting a deadline for the restoration of democracy, came from the C-Mag. This group also moved quickly in 1999 to recommend Pakistan's suspension from the association's councils and Fiji's in the following year.[1] At the turn of the century, C-Mag had emerged as one of the most significant of the Commonwealth's new organs.

The value of ministerial, official and expert groups has long been appreciated. They are utilised both for the light they can shed on particular issues and the sense of continuity they provide. The Colombo Plan, one of the pioneer programmes of technical assistance in Asia, is so-named after the unique Commonwealth Foreign Ministers' Meetings held at Ceylon's capital in 1950. Although foreign ministers, as a group, did not meet again, a variety of ministerial meetings began to occur in-the-wings of major international agencies. Commonwealth Finance Ministers meet before the annual councils of the International

Monetary Fund/World Bank; Health Ministers meet in association with the World Health Organisation Assembly; Labour Ministers at the time of the International Labour Organisation Conference, and Agriculture Ministers at the time of the Food and Agriculture Organisation meetings. There are also periodic meetings of Law, Health and Education Ministers. The last of these now provide the main 'pledging' times for government contributions to the Commonwealth of Learning, the association's agency for cooperation in distance education (the subject of Chapter 17).

The Ministerial gatherings never tried to muster a comprehensive attendance from all member countries. They were, however, used by relevant ministers to float ideas, seek expert studies, monitor trends and solve problems. Such meetings were expanded to include Women's Affairs (from 1985), the Environment (from 1989) and Youth Affairs (from 1992). In 1998 it was suggested that Ministers for Science and Technology should meet triennially. The more important recommendations from these meetings go forward for endorsement by Chogms. Among the most important have been schemes produced at Finance Ministers' Meetings for easing the debt burden of poorer members.

Reviews of the implementation of Chogm decisions, and planning for the next meeting, are tasks for the senior officials who meet at a point roughly halfway between the Chogms. In the days of the Downing Street and Marlborough House PMMs, the senior official's usually only gathered just before the meetings to finalise the agenda. When the Secretariat and Foundation proposals came up in 1964, the senior officials met in January 1965 to draw up the schemes, which were endorsed by Heads of Government in June 1965. The first of the modern Chogms in Singapore in 1971 was blighted by bitter conflict over South Africa; by the presence in the room of four officials per delegation; and by some excessively long-winded set speeches. Therefore, the youthful Pierre Trudeau of Canada undertook to sharpen Chogm arrangements, a matter tackled first by senior officials in 1972. Thereafter, the pattern of regular between-Chogm Senior Officials Meetings (SOM) was established. From 1993 a Steering Committee of Senior Officials (Scoso) met to approve triennial funding allocations in the Secretariat.

Representing a wider range of expertise, there are triennial Commonwealth Health, Education and Law conferences. In contrast to the ministerial meetings in these fields, the conferences are mainly for professionals. The first Law Conference in 1955 became the pioneer of such gatherings that now attract several thousand participants and are among the largest Commonwealth events outside the Games. From these conferences came proposals to create a Law Division in the Secretariat and to found new specialist legal associations. The first Education Conference in Oxford in 1959 produced the Commonwealth Scholarship and Fellowship Plan (CSFP).

Consideration of certain international conflicts affecting particular member states have been entrusted to special groups. Turkey's invasion and continued occupation of northern Cyprus led to the creation of the Commonwealth Action Group on Cyprus. Guatemala's boundary dispute and land claims on Belize was watched by the Commonwealth Committee on Belize. Intra-Commonwealth disputes, however, notably those between India and Pakistan over Kashmir, were always carefully left as a UN matter. In civil wars, as in Nigeria over Biafra and Sri Lanka over Tamil separatism, and recently in the cases of violent outbreaks in Sierra Leone, the Solomon Islands, Zimbabwe and Fiji, the Commonwealth as such has treated these matters as part of domestic jurisdiction. But for humanitarian reasons the Secretary-General attempted to use his good offices, and in some cases Commonwealth neighbours were involved in attempts at settlement – Ghana in the case of Nigeria, India in the case of Sri Lanka, Ghana and Nigeria in Sierra Leone, and Fiji in the Solomon Islands.

In the 1970s and 1980s the Heads of Government began to authorise the Secretary-General to commission expert groups to study particular problems in the general area of development. Because of the vocal clamour from the Third World, organised in the Non-aligned Movement, the Group of 77 developing nations in the United Nations, and the Africa-Caribbean-Pacific group under the Lomé Conventions (ACP), a majority of the Commonwealth member countries (who were variously involved in these groupings) were demanding urgent attention to the problem of inequality. Therefore, starting with Ramphal's first group of 'Ten Wise Men' to investigate a 'New International Economic Order', there followed over a 15-year period a series of expert groups on commodity trade, financial flows, protectionism, indebtedness, industrialism, women's rights, youth employment and climate change. These reports became the main Commonwealth contribution to what was dubbed the North/South Dialogue. There was a great deal of study, some excellent analysis and a dozen informative reports, but the end product was more understanding than action.[2]

By the 1990s the goals had become more modest, the rhetoric less apocalyptic, the view of possibilities more realistic, but the effects were probably more positive. Three examples may be singled out for comment.

First, the Commonwealth contributions to the ending of apartheid and the return to membership of democratic South Africa, are regarded by many as its greatest collective achievement. The 1986 Eminent Persons Group (EPG) and the Committee of Foreign Ministers on Southern Africa (CFMSA) set up in 1987, enabled the Commonwealth to maintain pressure on the South African regime in spite of the different tactics adopted by Britain. At the Harare Chogm of 1991, when Mandela was welcomed as a guest, the Secretary-General was given the task of coordinating constructive assistance to facilitate a peaceful transition in South Africa. For the next few years Anyaoku was a vital go-between among South African leaders.

Second, there is the important, widely impacting work in fostering sport. After some disastrous sports boycotts, notably at the Montreal Olympics in 1976 and the Edinburgh Commonwealth Games in 1986, and with rising financial burdens for hosting the Games – the Commonwealth's most popular events – the subject of sport was placed on the Chogm agenda by Canada in 1987. A working group, chaired by a Canadian judge, was appointed to consult with governments, sports bodies and the Games Federation. After reporting to the 1991 Chogm, the group was kept in being as the Chogm Committee on Co-operation Through Sport (CCCS), and went on to produce some eloquent reports on the role of sport in national and personal development and, above all, on the role of sport as the only point of mass identification with the Commonwealth. (A fuller treatment of these developments appears in Chapter 22.)

Finally, the Ministerial Action Group, the C-Mag, created in 1995, became the mechanism for the implementation of the Millbrook programme. Its task was to 'deal with serious or persistent violations' of the Harare principles by assessing the nature of the infringements and recommending collective action. In effect, the C-Mag had the job of determining the Commonwealth's response to the activities of what were called 'errant states' still under military rule. In 1995 these were Gambia, Sierra Leone and Nigeria. Between the 1995 and 1997 Chogms, C-Mag met roughly every two or three months, mainly in Marlborough House, but once in New York. It sent ministerial missions to Gambia and Nigeria.

It reported in 1997 that Gambia, which had been under military rule since 1994, had made a 'creditable transition' to democracy, but the C-Mag criticised the non-inclusive nature of the country's political system. In the case of Nigeria, it found the 'most blatant violations of Harare principles'.[3] The winner of the aborted 1993 presidential election and 43 other persons (including ex-Head of State Obasanjo, a co-chairman of the EPG), were incarcerated. The C-Mag recommended continuing Nigeria's suspension and, if satisfactory progress towards the restoration of democracy was not made by 1 October 1998, the Heads of Government should consider Nigeria's expulsion.

Over Sierra Leone, the C-Mag encouraged an interesting precedent. Civil rule had been restored after four years of military government. A general election in 1996, observed by four Secretariat officials, saw Ahmed Tejan Kabbah, a former UN official, elected President. But on 25 May 1997 a coup by junior army officers overthrew the new government, an event described by the C-Mag as a 'tragically retrograde step'.[4] It, therefore, recommended that the military junta should be debarred from Commonwealth councils and technical assistance programmes. Recognition was withheld from this illegal regime. President Kabbah was invited to the Edinburgh Chogm as guest of the host Prime Minister. The Heads of Government confirmed the junta's suspension from Commonwealth meetings. They suspended communications between the Secretariat and the military regime. But it was decided that 'emblematic representation' of Sierra Leone at Commonwealth meetings would continue; seats would be left vacant unless filled by representatives of Kabbah's government. Edinburgh thus set a precedent for continued involvement in the Commonwealth of a government-in-exile.[5]

Perhaps the biggest irony of the Edinburgh Chogm was that the same meetings which renewed the suspension of Nigeria, witnessed ousted Sierra Leonean President Kabbah praising the efforts of the military dictator of Nigeria (from his position in the chair of the West African Community) in endeavouring to restore democratic rule in Sierra Leone! It was a vivid reminder that regional ties could take priority over Commonwealth concerns.

*

As the twentieth century drew to a close, the C-Mag established itself as the Commonwealth's potentially most powerful instrument. Set up originally in 1995 for monitoring adherence to Harare principles, the original members of the group were the foreign ministers of Britain, Canada, Ghana, Jamaica, Malaysia, New Zealand, South Africa and Zimbabwe. The usual regional balance was biased in favour of Africa because all three 'errant states' under review were in Africa. This, no doubt, also influenced the choice for the chair of C-Mag, since instead of going to the 1995 host, New Zealand, it went to Zimbabwe. As well as reporting on the 'errant states' at Edinburgh in 1997 the C-Mag expressed a strong view that its own continued operation was vital for the protection and promotion of the Commonwealth's fundamental political values. It recommended that the mandate should be renewed biennially and that as many member countries as possible should serve in the Group on rotation. It also agreed that its focus should not be confined to military regimes or the unconstitutional overthrow of governments, but should be directed at all serious and persistent violations of the Harare Declaration. This was accepted by the Edinburgh Chogm, which now hailed the C-Mag as a 'standing ministerial mechanism'. A revised line-up included some old and some new members: Barbados, Botswana, Britain, Canada, Ghana, Malaysia, New Zealand and Zimbabwe. In its attention to the West African errant states it soon encountered ups and downs.

In Nigeria the sudden and unexpected death of General Abacha on 8 June 1998, followed by the release of prisoners and the broadcast of a timetable for the restoration of democracy on 20 July, prompted the C-Mag to make an interim report recommending that Nigeria's suspension should be lifted when an elected president took office. This was done on 29 May 1999 on the inauguration of recently elected President Obasanjo, the former head of state long incarcerated by the military regime.

The C-Mag had less happy experiences with Sierra Leone, On two occasions the legitimate government was again ousted from Freetown, the capital, and the UN Commissioner of Human Rights, who visited Sierra Leone early in 1999, reported violations of human rights on a worse scale than those in Kosovo. Yet Commonwealth involvement in assisting Sierra Leone was largely through the efforts of Nigeria and Ghana working through the West African Community. (This regional emphasis is a subject of Chapter 14.) The Commonwealth's most useful assistance was in reconstructing the Sierra Leonean police force and British and Indian participation in UN missions.

The future of the C-Mag, was discussed by a meeting of senior officials in Marlborough House in August 1999. They viewed the C-Mag as an 'important Commonwealth asset', which enhanced the association's credibility and international profile. The Group was seen as 'the most tangible expression of the Commonwealth's resolve to implement seriously its fundamental political values'. To diminish this would be a 'retrograde development'.[6] As well as assessing the unconstitutional overthrow of elected governments, the C-Mag should report on other threats to democracy. Guidelines were needed, and the C-Mag mentioned such things as postponement of elections beyond the constitutional life of a government; systematic bans or impediments to legitimate political activity by opposition parties; and widespread violations of human rights through the abrogation of the rule of law.

Shortly before the Durban Chogm events in Pakistan prompted the C-Mag into action. The elected government of Nawaz Sharif was toppled in a military coup on 12 October 1999. The C-Mag acted fast in condemning the overthrow of a democratically elected government. A C-Mag mission, led by the Canadian External Affairs Minister, visited Pakistan 11 days later. They found the constitution in abeyance, the legislature suspended, but the courts continued to operate. Martial law had not been declared. The mission warned that there were three options the Commonwealth might adopt – suspend Pakistan from Commonwealth councils, suspend its membership, or expel it from the association. The C-Mag recommended the first option and proposed that Pakistan be given two years to demonstrate progress towards the restoration of democracy. Thus Pakistan was not invited to the Durban Chogm in November 1999, which endorsed the suspension from Commonwealth councils.

The Heads of Government meeting in Durban commended the C-Mag for its functioning as 'custodian of the Harare Principles'.[7] It extended the mandate for two more years, revised the membership and laid down that henceforth no country would serve for more than two years. The C-Mag went into the twenty-first century made up of Australia, Bangladesh, Barbados, Botswana, Britain, Canada, Malaysia and Nigeria.

However, the future direction of this potentially powerful new instrument was to be a subject of study by a new High Level Review Group. The C-Mag was a demonstration that the Commonwealth aspires to having some teeth. In the clear cases of the erection or dismantling of military rule it had acted clearly and expeditiously. In this respect the C-Mag was a significant advance. But in seeking solutions to numerous local issues it was more or less impotent. The new century opened with serious human rights violations in Fiji, Nigeria, Pakistan, Sierra Leone, Sri Lanka and Zimbabwe, cases where C-Mag was not able to offer solutions other than to call for a return to democratic rule. The charge was made that C-Mag did not so much effect the protection of human rights as maintain the image of the Commonwealth. A more positive view would be that proclaiming principles without attempting mechanisms of monitoring and censure would be hypocritical. In organising for cases of humanitarian disaster and civil conflict, however, C-Mag's limitations were all too evident. It could only supplement the work of the global or regional organisations which were increasingly the major feature in international relations.

13
Rediscovery and the Generation Gap

The creation of the C-Mag to give the Commonwealth some teeth, the suspension of Nigeria and the partial suspension of Sierra Leone, Pakistan and Fiji came after a period of appraisal and reawakening. This suggests that the 1990s was a period of renaissance for the Commonwealth. This prompted interest in some quite surprising quarters. The rediscovery was spearheaded in Britain by the House of Commons Select Committee on Foreign Affairs. After 18 months' study, its report on *The Future of the Commonwealth* (FAC Report) was published in March 1996.[1] Elsewhere there were further reports and seminars which made similar examinations into the relevance of the Commonwealth and came up with very similar conclusions about its strengths and weaknesses. If the early 1990s were the years of the H-lag and Secretariat restructuring, the later 1990s became a time for critical outside scrutiny of the Commonwealth's overall utility and image.

The FAC Report was discussed by a somewhat critical seminar at the University of London's Institute of Commonwealth Studies (ICS) on 4–5 June 1997 and by a debate in the House of Commons on 27 June. A report of the ICS seminar, *Reassessing the Commonwealth*, was published by the Royal Institute of International Affairs (Chatham House) in 1997.[2] Meanwhile, two further enquiries were set in motion by the Secretary-General and gave rise to much quoted reports. In June 1995, Professor Tom Symons, former President of Trent University, Ontario, Canada, was commissioned to consider Commonwealth Studies at the tertiary level. The Symons Report, *Learning From Each Other* appeared in 1997.[3] The other enquiry was into the Secretariat's information services with a view to sharpening the image of the Commonwealth. This had been called for initially by the Scosc in 1995 and was conducted by

Derek Ingram, the doyen of Commonwealth commentators. The Ingram Report, *Review of the Commonwealth Secretariat's Information Programme*, appeared in April 1997.[4] Both the Symons and Ingram Reports were considered at the Edinburgh Chogm.

The wealth of information made available in all these reports, along with the range of viewpoints assembled, prompted similar investigations in Canberra and Ottawa. The Australian Federal Parliament's Joint Standing Committee on Foreign Affairs, Defence and Trade held a seminar in Canberra on 20 August 1997, in which former Prime Minister Malcolm Fraser was the opening speaker. A transcript of the proceedings and summary of recommendations, *From Empire to Partnership*, was published in October 1997.[5] In Ottawa, the Royal Commonwealth Society's Canadian National Council and the Ottawa Branch held a colloquium on 20–22 February 1998 and published a 'millennial challenge communiqué', *The Commonwealth in the 3rd Millennium*.[6] Both the Canberra and the Ottawa meetings made frequent references to the FAC, Symons and Ingram Reports. Thus, the years 1995 to 1998 witnessed unprecedented study and debate about the relevance of the Commonwealth in the contemporary world. In 1999 the British Foreign Policy Centre produced a radical pamphlet on *Reinventing the Commonwealth*.[7]

The general context of all these reviews was succinctly summarised at the start of the FAC Report. The committee had decided to make the inquiry at the end of 1994 because of the four-fold transition in the international scene marked by the ending of UDI and apartheid; the ending of the Cold War; recent economic growth of the Asia-Pacific region; and the transformation of the Commonwealth into a 'matrix of cross-linkages'. These discoveries indicated a rather tardy awakening of the British MPs.

In general, the overall spirit of all the enquiries was positive. The FAC admitted: 'Our enquiries and evidence have surprised us.' The committee members were particularly impressed by the economic opportunities offered to Britain by the (then prevailing) growth rates achieved around the Pacific-Rim and by the 'real Commonwealth vibrancy' encountered in the voluntary organisations. The Committee's conclusion struck a note of apology:

> Perhaps it was understandable for a few decades after the end of Empire that the Commonwealth was seen in the United Kingdom as a relic of an imperial past – a political albatross around the country's neck. Trauma and uncomfortable adjustment were inevitable ...

But that era is over, and so is its successor phase of 'decolonisation'. A new global pattern opens out in which the competition to maintain, let alone advance, living standards will be more intense than ever. In this new situation the United Kingdom has both friends and opportunities. They should be recognised and seized.

The first recommendation was that 'old Commonwealth ties could become, for the United Kingdom, the new Commonwealth opportunities'.[8] If the committee had met a year or so later, after the 1997 Asian financial 'meltdown', its findings may have been less fulsome.

By far the most eloquent and forthright spokesman for the Commonwealth was Derek Ingram. His submission to the FAC, dated 3 March 1995, was imbued with the authority of one intimately acquainted with Commonwealth affairs for over 30 years. A former deputy-editor of the *Daily Mail*, he had approached Arnold Smith with a proposal for a news agency specialising in the Commonwealth. On a shoestring, he started Gemini News Agency in 1967 and he personally reported every Chogm from 1969. He was also a prominent member of such key voluntary organisations as the Commonwealth Journalists Association, the Royal Commonwealth Society and the Commonwealth Human Rights Initiative. His overriding theme was disappointment about long-standing British official indifference to the Commonwealth. As he told the FAC:

Historically, the Commonwealth is Britain's greatest contribution to the international community, yet successive governments have shown few signs of understanding that or of exercising the political will to take advantage of the fortunate situation in which the country has found itself ...

It has often been said that if the Commonwealth did not exist no one would set about inventing it. That is true. But as a happy accident of history it is there, an organic development with strong and deep roots. The reality is that it is not going to dissolve. Britain should take a more positive and imaginative view of it than in the past and set about making much more use of this remarkable facility.[9]

Later the Ingram Report on sharpening the Commonwealth's information services took as its starting point, that the Commonwealth was well and truly established – a novel and exciting international concept without historical precedent that has widespread support – but one that suffered from a series of misconceptions due to chroni.c lack of information.

Opening the Canberra seminar in 1997, Malcolm Fraser former Australian Prime Minister (and a candidate for the Secretary-Generalship in 1989) also struck a highly positive note. He found the Commonwealth 'an enormously pragmatic organisation', which adjusted well to changed circumstances. He believed that the transition from an empire to an association of equals was 'really an extraordinary one'. The particular value he saw in Chogms was that leaders 'spent some time getting to know each other'.[10] He therefore regretted the recent curtailing of their duration. He also regretted the passing of the Heads of Government Regional Meetings (Chogrms), which he had inaugurated, especially because of their importance for small states in the Pacific.

Two other general comments from the Canberra seminar deserve attention. After interventions by two retired generals, Professor Allan Patience, from the Victoria University of Technology, drew a distinction between a Commonwealth of nostalgia – 'a very dangerous Commonwealth' – and a Commonwealth of multilateralism for which he saw 'a very splendid defence ... in terms of confronting the theory of the clash of civilisations'. The second comment was made by Ruth Inall, Secretary-General of the Commonwealth Association of Professional Centres, founded in Canberra only a year earlier. Her words vividly encapsulated the new spirit at work in the People's Commonwealth: 'I was struck by the fact that there was an entirely new spirit, if you like. The difference was that there was nobody on the giving end, and there was nobody on the taking end, but it was a meeting of partners who were exploring in what way we could help each other.'[11] Here was a vivid example of Ramphal's concept of an association with 'no centre and no periphery'. The Ottawa colloquium covered similar ground to that covered in Canberra, but the communiqué attached prime importance to the political Commonwealth: 'We believe that the Commonwealth's greatest tool is its political, as opposed to its technical influence. We urge it to continue its work helping member countries strengthen core institutions and their functions, because improvements in governance are critical to development.'[12]

Sweetness and light did not entirely pervade these inquiries. The *aficionados* were given their head, but the most consistent theme was disappointment over lost opportunities. There were also a few very negative comments about the Commonwealth itself. In a submission to the FAC dated 23 February 1995, Peter Unwin, former deputy

Secretary-General (1989–93), praised the voluntary organisations as being of 'unquestionable value', but was 'uncertain about the continuing utility of the official Commonwealth'. He suggested that it fell 'well short of playing any very significant operational role in major matters of multilateral political, economic or diplomatic concern'. Over a period of 30 years it had 'very largely been emptied of substantial content'. He concluded that: 'The Commonwealth Secretariat was not in my time a body of which I could be proud and efforts at reform have in my judgement been half-hearted.'[13]

There were also academic critics, as might be expected. Dr Thomas Young of the London School of Oriental and African Studies told the FAC at a hearing on 13 December 1995 that he was one of those who regarded the Commonwealth as 'a rather aimless, purposeless organisation whose functions are not very clear other than, as it were, a kind of balm for the loss of empire and that is an emotional need that is now clearly fading'. He also regretted the 'erosion of the language of sovereignty' and saw a danger that 'we are going to be saddled with various sorts of agendas of meddling in other people's affairs ...' He professed himself 'a strong sceptic about the Commonwealth from that point of view'.[14] A similar view was taken by Dr Rob Holland of the ICS, who dissented from the view of his colleague Dr Peter Lyon who favoured the post-Millbrook, rules-based Commonwealth. Holland was sceptical about making judgements on another country's affairs – 'People could be going through this revolving door, in and out, in and out, in and out, and no organisation, no club ... can survive for long when people are being admitted one minute and kicked out the next minute.'[15] The ICS seminar elicited a number of comments critical of the FAC Review. The author of the Chatham House summary of the conference, Rob Jenkins, suggested that portents for the Commonwealth had 'never been more ambiguous'. He felt that a grouping based merely on shared history and an institutional legacy was 'a bit out of place in the current context'. On the People's Commonwealth praised so lavishly in all the reports, he detected 'a sort of forced earnestness', and was sceptical of 'ritual intonations' about the value of the unofficial as opposed to the official Commonwealth. Neither, he suggested, would be so effective without the other.

It would be impossible to do justice in a small compass to the variety of evidence and opinion debated in the reviews of the later 1990s. One of the most valuable contributions lies in the reports themselves. The FAC Report was the most substantial. Its 333-page volume of *Minutes of Evidence and Appendices* was the fullest collection of up-to-date material on the Commonwealth to appear in recent years. Ten institutional memoranda were reproduced coming from such sources as the FCO, the Secretariat, the Foundation, the Commonwealth Parliamentary Association, the Royal Commonwealth Society (then part of the Commonwealth Trust), the Commonwealth Human Rights Initiative and two universities. Representatives of all these bodies appeared before the FAC at Westminster between June and December 1995. Memoranda were received, and published, from 70 individuals and organisations and a further 18 submissions were made available in the House of Lords Record Office. The Committee members visited Canada, Jamaica, Barbados and St Lucia in June 1995, and South Africa, Kenya, Uganda, Pakistan, India, Bangladesh, Malaysia, Australia and New Zealand in October. They talked with 160 people from presidents and prime ministers to politicians and professors.

For his tertiary study enquiry, Professor Symons consulted a panel of 55 people in 20 countries, as well as over 40 voluntary organisations. He had meetings in Oxford and Cambridge, at Cumberland Lodge in Windsor Great Park (which is discussed in Chapter 21) and with the Association of Commonwealth Universities Council in Malta. Derek Ingram talked with nearly 400 people in 13 countries as well as members of UN missions in New York. His report as published included responses and reports on actions by the Secretariat, the Foundation, and the COL.

*

Apart from the general points alluded to above, three themes from these reviews deserve special comment. First, the Commonwealth was seen to offer significant economic opportunities. This was the prime lesson for Britain drawn by the FAC. Second, the Commonwealth's public profile was depicted as a media disaster. The association failed to project itself positively and was therefore misunderstood or neglected. This crisis was the *raison d'être* of the Ingram Report. Third, a glaring 'generation gap' was revealed in sheer lack of elementary knowledge about the Commonwealth, mainly because it had disappeared from the educational curricula at all levels. Here was the problem for the Symons Report.

These media and educational crises were also discussed by the FAC and the Canberra and Ottawa seminars. The economic aspects of the FAC Report were, perhaps, the most surprising. The Committee was particularly impressed by the findings of the Australian, Katherine West, whose 1995 Chatham House discussion paper, *Economic Opportunities for Britain and the Commonwealth,* was one of the submitted papers. Dr West's theme was that growth in the Asia-Pacific region appeared, at the time, to be creating a new global economic centre of gravity. Growth rates in excess of 8 per cent per year were experienced in the late 1980s/early 1990s. 'Whatever the rhetoric, Britain's trade and investment overseas are in fact growing fastest not with Europe, but with the successful economies of Southeast Asia and the Pacific-Rim.' She also depicted the bonus of a 'Commonwealth business culture' provided by the English language, and various legal, commercial, accounting and financial procedures.[16]

Exporters who went for new markets could find within the Commonwealth, countries where the business and cultural environment gave easier access than many parts of the world. At the Canberra Seminar in 1997, Dr West developed this theme by emphasising that, in an increasingly competitive and globalising economy, regional and trans-regional ties were crucial and that this gave the Commonwealth 'a new kind of economic relevance' as a 'low cost, ready-made, trans-regional network – or series of networks'. She suggested that the biggest economic prizes would be won by countries and enterprises that 'can use a strong regional base to expand their economic activities in other regions as well'. She advocated a 'three-pronged ideal' (something she also termed the 'economic power of three') meaning mutually re-enforcing, bilateral, regional and trans-regional networks. In all this the Commonwealth was a major asset. She also called for 'smart partnerships' across the networks, taking advantage of the Commonwealth network as re-enforced by its 'ethnic diaspora networks'. 'Within the uniting framework of the Commonwealth business culture, we have a multi-diaspora Commonwealth – a multicultural Commonwealth within a uniting, English-speaking Commonwealth business culture.'[17]

An important aspect of the FAC Report was the figures it produced indicating the value of Commonwealth trade and financial links for Britain. Although the total size of the trade with the European Union, North America and the rest of the world was larger, it involved balance of payments deficits, while the balance of the smaller Commonwealth trade was in Britain's favour. Non-EU trade was seen as having an important role in moving Britain out of recession.[18] At the ICS Seminar David Howell (later Lord Howell), the Chairman of the FAC, stressed that 'capital and investment drove trade and that the former went where there was a common culture and good governance'. He said the central conclusion of the FAC Report was that the Commonwealth had new relevance in this regard. This was 'the leap in perception', he declared, 'that the most rapidly developing world was elsewhere and that some of it was in the Commonwealth'.[19]

The strongest words in all the recent reviews were expressed on the subject of poor public relations. The Ingram Report admitted that the Commonwealth had never been easy to project to the general public because it lacked a 'single focus'. For most people it was 'a blur'; it was taken for granted 'like a comfortable old shoe'.[20] But Ingram had told the FAC that the FCO and Downing Street often briefed journalists about the Commonwealth unenthusiastically, sometimes with hostility. The tabloid view depicted the Commonwealth as a 'collection of tinpot dictatorships and one-party states always holding out the begging bowl ...'[21] The FAC were themselves disappointed by the 'downbeat' report provided by the FCO and found the British government's attitude to the BBC World Service and British Council 'frankly incredible'. They managed to goad Baroness Chalker into saying that the 'C' in FCO did not stand for 'Cinderella'.[22]

In the Canberra seminar, Hugh Craft, President of the Royal Commonwealth Society branch, and a member of the Prime Minister's Department, admitted that knowledge about the Commonwealth was 'appalling' and that there was a 'dearth of relevant, up-to-date information about the Commonwealth in Australia, and one result is misinformation'.[23] Barry Jones, one of the members of the federal Parliament Joint Committee admitted he had never heard of *Commonwealth Currents*, the Secretariat's magazine. The Canberra seminar called for the creation of a Commonwealth Resource Centre and an Eminent Persons Group to publicise the Commonwealth.

The Ingram Report gave no fewer than 76 practical recommendations for sharpening the image. The most fruitful action to stir interest and knowledge, he suggested, would be to convene a conference of Commonwealth desk officers from all member foreign ministries to exchange ideas and to follow up such a one-off meeting with periodic meetings at the regional level. He also advocated giving the Secretariat buildings a higher profile in Pall Mall, with a larger notice at Marlborough House and a display window in Quadrant House across the road. He criticised 'a culture of quite unnecessary secrecy and confidentiality' which had grown up around the Secretariat. He also advocated upgrading the style and content of publications, training Secretariat staff in working with the media, and exploiting the 'good story' potential of many Commonwealth activities at the local level. Ingram also had strong things to say about the 'huge and deeply worrying generation gap' in knowledge about the Commonwealth.[24] This 'gap' emerged as the most significant theme of all the 1990s reviews.

The FAC Report called it 'the generation gap that exists in the under-standing of what the Commonwealth means'. One of its strongest rec-ommendations was that more needed to be done to 'enthuse young people' about the Commonwealth.[25] In the submission from the Royal Commonwealth Society, Prunella Scarlett told about a recent confer-ence at Cumberland Lodge where the young participants 'were so appalled by their lack of knowledge that they asked for a push to be made to get the Commonwealth into the National Curriculum'. Sir David Thorne, director-general of the Commonwealth Trust, said bluntly that if information is not got across, young people would not be interested, 'but, boy, we have found that time and again the moment we have a discussion about it with them their interest is very strong'.[26]

Addressing this 'gap' at the tertiary level was the task of the Symons Report. It found that too little was being done and insufficient atten-tion was being given to contemporary experience. There was a Centre for Commonwealth Studies at Stirling University and a Centre for Commonwealth and American Arts at Exeter University. Wollongong University had a Centre for the New Literatures. At Cambridge, a Malaysian-endowed Centre for Commonwealth Policy Studies had been created. The Symons Report suggested the creation of an Association for Commonwealth Studies and the publication of an up-to-date Survey of Commonwealth Affairs to follow the earlier Chatham House surveys which ended in 1969. It suggested that ComSec publica-tions should be deposited in university libraries and that its archives should be made available to scholars. It was also suggested that the Commonwealth Scholarship and Fellowship Plan might target some scholarships specifically for Commonwealth Studies.

Perhaps the most significant recommendation in the Symons Report was for a commission to investigate the problem at the school level. The Canberra seminar was told emphatically that 'students cannot know what they have not been taught'. The Ingram Report also addressed the problem of how to enthuse youthful imagination. He wanted to use the 'newspeg' of the Commonwealth Games to draw attention to other aspects of the Commonwealth. He endorsed the point made by the Symons Report that learning about the Commonwealth had to start at the school level. He included a curricu-lum outline from the Solomon Islands as a possible model. He deplored the absence of a simply written textbook on the subject and the fact that publishers were unconvinced that such books were worth producing.

A number of the themes which emerged in the reviews of the 1990s were taken up, in rather more strident language, by the 'Foreign Policy Centre' set up by the Blair government in London. Intended by Foreign and Commonwealth Secretary Robin Cook as a younger and more radical Chatham House, the Centre was described as an 'independent think tank committed to developing innovative thinking and effective solutions for an increasingly interdependent world'. Two young analysts from the Centre, without previous Commonwealth background, were given six months to take a fresh look at the association in the run-up to Durban. Their interim report, 'Making the Commonwealth Matter', sparked a debate that caused the authors to believe that 'there is clearly something very special about an idea that inspires so many good people for so long'. Their pamphlet *Reinventing the Commonwealth* was launched in Durban at a meeting sponsored by the Royal Commonwealth Society.

The pamphlet was offered as a call for radical change. It set out a 'reform agenda' to make the Commonwealth 'an internationally-recognised standard of good governance and growth'. Yet, in spite of the tough language, the pamphlet simply echoed recent trends. It looked towards 'the genuinely developmental state', which could combine growth and social development: 'it is only by combining democracy and markets that they can achieve sustainable growth which benefits their people.' The mechanism they proposed for this was the establishment of a 'Commonwealth Kite-mark' as a quality assurance of good governance to attract investors. To police the Kite-mark a permanent Good Governance Commission was envisaged. Criteria to be monitored would include holding free and fair elections; maintaining the rule of law and independence of the judiciary; tackling corruption and promoting honest government; promoting civil society and a framework for government/NGO relations; and respecting fundamental human rights, freedom of expression and the press. The Commission would maintain an 'at risk' register and issue warnings of defalcation. Kenya, Pakistan, Sri Lanka and Zimbabwe were in the doubtful category by 1999. Any future new member would have to undergo a 'full democratic health check'.[27] The Vippso world – the NGOs, civil society – was depicted as the 'supporters club' of the Commonwealth. A new compact was envisaged as a Harare-type Declaration of Civil Society. For all its robust language, the *Reinventing* report was a reiteration of the principles of the 1990s. In many respects the C-Mag was already performing the role of a Good Governance Commission. Perhaps the big change was that representatives of a younger generation, coming fresh to the Commonwealth, found themselves pointing stern fingers at the errant states.

From all this intense activity from 1995 to 2000, it became very clear that the Commonwealth was, after 30 years in the doldrums, being viewed more positively, especially in Britain. But the educational 'gap', which left young people almost totally ignorant of the subject, had yet to be addressed.

14
Globalisation, Small States and Regionalism

Although the Commonwealth encompasses a quarter of the world's peoples, it is not a large player as an international entity. This was vividly illustrated by three meetings which preceded the final Chogm of the twentieth century in 1999. They each highlighted the limitations to the association's role in world affairs.

First, the second Commonwealth Business Forum met in Johannesburg from 9 to 11 November 1999, to discuss the theme 'Making Globalisation Work'. The Forum's report to Heads of Government outlined conditions necessary for the private sector to help achieve what it called 'globalisation with equity'. Second, the Ministerial Group on Small States held its fourth meeting in Durban on 11 November 1999 on the eve of the Chogm. Like the Business Forum, it too tackled the question of globalisation. It pointed, in particular, to the 'transitional costs of integrating small states into a more globalised economy'. Third, on the same day, came the C-Mag meeting. As well as dealing with the straightforward cases of Nigeria's return and Pakistan's partial suspension, it reported on the tragic situation in Sierra Leone, where the restoration of civilian rule in 1996 had been twice subverted by dissident military groups. Here, Commonwealth endeavours had largely failed. Peace initiatives in the civil war had been the work of neighbouring countries through a regional agency, ECOMOG (the Economic Community of West African States' Monitoring Group), largely comprising Nigerian army units. These three themes – globalisation, the vulnerability of small states and the importance of regional organisations – mark the main features of the international environment in which the Commonwealth has to find its niche.

'Globalisation' is a word as yet absent from many dictionaries. Chambers gets as far as 'globalism' – the position which puts worldwide, international concerns above national or local. The OED calls this internationalism. To 'globalise' is to make global or worldwide. New Fowler notes that Marshall McLuhan's 'global village' concept of 1960 was a recognition that new information and communications technologies (ICT) were 'shrinking' the world into a single community. This highlighted the chief mechanism making globalisation possible. With this goes the concept of 'interdependence' and the reality that the process involves winners and losers.

Commonwealth leaders had long been aware of both the tendency and the dangers. Of the original 51 members of the United Nations the Commonwealth component – Australia, Britain, Canada, India, New Zealand and South Africa – made up only 12 per cent of the membership, even if they were disproportionately influential in the making of the organisation (see Table 14.1). Yet some contrary views were expressed by well-known Dominion leaders. Jan Smuts of South Africa viewed Great Power domination of the Security Council with equanimity and compared it with the Commonwealth model. In *status* all might be equal, but in *function* they were clearly not. On the other hand, Dr Herbert Evatt (Australia) and Peter Fraser (New Zealand) fought against the Great Power veto. Fraser told the UN organisation conference at San Francisco about another aspect of the Commonwealth model: the members 'as well as being independent ... are interdependent ... the future of the world depends upon our recognition of the interdependence of all nations'.[1]

Similar views were expressed by the Secretaries-General after the creation of the Secretariat. On the day of his election, Arnold Smith said, 'We all need to learn to share a planet'.[2] By the end of the 1960s, the same wave of decolonisation that transformed the Commonwealth into a multilateral association also took its proportion of the United Nations membership to 23 per cent. Over the next decade this went up to 25 per cent. Ramphal titled his first volume of collected speeches *One World to Share*. From 1979 to 1990 all the new members admitted to the UN were from the Commonwealth, taking the proportion to its highest point at 28 per cent. After that it declined slightly following the break-up of the Soviet Union, Yugoslavia and Czechoslovakia.

Globalisation for the Commonwealth in the 1970s and 1980s implied recognition that many of the problems facing member governments – indebtedness, ethnic conflicts, environmental deterioration, drug trafficking, illegal migrant flows, gender discrimination, protectionism, money laundering – were cross-border, trans-regional and global problems which could never be solved by individual nation-

Table 14.1 Commonwealth percentage of the total UN membership

Year	Membership (COMMONWEALTH in capitals)	UN	Cwlth	%
1945	Argentina, AUSTRALIA, Belgium, BRITAIN, Bolivia, Brazil, Byelorussia (Belarus from 1991), CANADA, Chile, China, Colombia, Costa Rica, Cuba Czechoslovakia, Denmark, Dominican Republic, Ecuador, Egypt. El Salvador, Ethiopia, France, Greece, Guatemala, Haiti, Honduras, INDIA, Iran, Iraq, Lebanon, Liberia, Luxembourg, Mexico, Netherlands, NEW ZEALAND, Nicaragua, Norway, Panama, Paraguay, Peru, Philippines, Poland, Saudi Arabia, SOUTH AFRICA, Soviet Union (Russian Federation from 1991), Syria, Turkey, Ukraine, United States, Uruguay, Venezuela, Yugoslavia	51	6	12
1946	Afghanistan, Iceland, Sweden, Thailand			
1947	PAKISTAN partitioned from India, Yemen Arab Republic (United with Yemen Democratic Republic 1990)			
1948	Burma (Myanmar from 1989)			
1949	Israel	59	7	12
1950	Indonesia			
1955	Albania, Austria, Bulgaria, Cambodia, CEYLON (SRI LANKA from 1972), Finland, Hungary, Ireland, Italy, Jordan, Laos, Libya, Nepal, Portugal, Romania, Spain			
1956	Japan, Morocco, Sudan, Tunisia,			
1957	GHANA, MALAYA (MALAYSIA from 1963)			
1958	Guinea	83	10	12
1960	Benin, Burkina Faso, Cameroon, Central African Republic, Chad, Congo, Côte d'Ivoire, CYPRUS, Gabon, Madagascar, Mali, Niger, NIGERIA, Senegal, Togo, Zaire (Democratic Republic of Congo from 1997)			
1961	Mauritania, Mongolia, SIERRA LEONE, TANGANYIKA (TANZANIA from 1964)			
1962	Algeria, Burundi, JAMAICA, Rwanda, TRINIDAD, UGANDA			
1963	KENYA, Kuwait			
1964	MALAWI, MALTA, ZAMBIA			
1965	GAMBIA, MALDIVES, SINGAPORE			
1966	BARBADOS, BOTSWANA, GUYANA, LESOTHO			
1967	Yemen Democratic Republic (united with Yemen 1990)			
1968	Equatorial Guinea, MAURITIUS, SWAZILAND	127	29[a]	23

Table 14.1 Commonwealth percentage of the total UN membership *(continued)*

Year	Membership (COMMONWEALTH in capitals)	UN	Cwlth	%
1970	FIJI			
1971	Bahrain, Bhutan, Oman, Qatar, United Arab Emirates,			
1973	Vietnam			
1974	BAHAMAS, German Democratic Republic (united in 1990 with German Federal Republic as Germany)			
1975	BANGLADESH, GRENADA, Guinea-Bissau,			
1976	Cape Verde, Comoros, Mozambique, PAPUA NEW GUINEA, Sao Tome, Suriname Angola, WESTERN SAMOA (SAMOA from 1997),			
1977	SEYCHELLES			
1978	Djibouti			
1979	DOMINICA, SOLOMON ISLANDS ST. LUCIA	152	38[b]	25
1980	ST. VINCENT, ZIMBABWE			
1979	DOMINICA, SOLOMON ISLANDS			
1981	ANTIGUA, BELIZE, VANUATU			
1983	ST. KITTS-NEVIS,			
1984	BRUNEI			
1989		159	45[c]	28
1990	Liechtenstein, NAMIBIA			
1991	Estonia, Korea (North), Korea (South), Latvia, Lithuania, Marshall Islands, Micronesia			
1992	Armenia, Azerbaijan, Bosnia-Herzegovina, Georgia, Kazakhstan, Kyrgyzstan, Moldova, Slovenia, Tajikistan, Turkmenistan, Uzbekistan			
1993	Andorra, Czech Republic, Eritrea, Macedonia, Monaco, Slovakia			
1994	Palau			
1999	Kiribati, Nauru, Tonga	188[d]	53[e]	28

Notes:
[a] South Africa was out of the Commonwealth between 1961 and 1994.
[b] Pakistan was out of the Commonwealth between 1972 and 1989.
[c] Fiji was out of the Commonwealth between 1987 and 1997.
[d] Total adjusted to take in to account of the union of the two Yemens and the two Germanys, and the splitting up of Czechoslovakia, the Soviet Union and Yugoslavia.
[e] The 54-member Commonwealth is completed by its non-UN member, Tuvalu, and the accession to membership in 1995 of Cameroon and Mozambique.

states. Ramphal's own awareness of globalisation was fortified by his unique membership of all four of the independent international commissions on global issues in the 1980s on development, disarmament, the environment and South/South cooperation. Ramphal's most quoted remark was: 'The Commonwealth cannot negotiate for the world; but it can help the world to negotiate.'[3] His greatest disappointment was that the Commonwealth's attempt to spearhead a 'New International Economic Order' in the 1970s made so little headway. Indeed, in the last two decades of the twentieth century the gap between rich and poor countries continued to grow.

This became the connotation of globalisation that increasingly dominated Commonwealth discussions as the century drew to a close. As parts of the world solidified into vast trading blocs – the European Union (EU), the North American Free Trade Area (NAFTA) and the Asia-Pacific rim (APEC); as trade and manufacturing became increasingly dominated by multinational corporations; and as finance and technology shifted around the globe with bewildering speed through the new ICT, the majority of Commonwealth countries found it hard to keep up. Increasingly Commonwealth councils, inter-governmental agencies, voluntary organisations and regional associations were preoccupied trying to grapple with the effects of globalisation.

The economic liberalism of the 1990s (which was fortified by the collapse of the Soviet bloc) meant rising faith in the market and free trade and an increasing role for the private sector in the search for solutions. We have seen how the Harare principles of 1991 extolled democracy, good government and the rule of law as the necessary concomitants of sustainable development, freer flows of trade, equal opportunities and human rights. The Millbrook Action Programme of 1995 for implementing these principles implied that sustainable development involved fostering human resources and literacy, and eradicating poverty – especially among women and children. At the same time, 'consensus building' became the Commonwealth's missionary element. The association's unique multicultural and cross-regional linkages would, it was believed, assist the wider international community in 'building bridges across traditional international divides'.[4]

For the last Chogms of the century, where the role of the private sector (to be discussed in Chapter 23) was more overtly extolled, 'globalisation' had been adopted as a new buzzword of the Commonwealth. Indeed, the report of an Advisory Group on the future of small states, chaired by Eugenia Charles of Dominica, provided the first comprehensive definition:

> Globalisation is most easily comprehended as a process of accelerating interdependence which has at its core the liberalisation of trade,

the deregulation of financial markets, the spread of trans-national production of goods and services, and the development of new technologies, particularly information technology. There are also cultural elements to the phenomena associated with the diffusion of consumerist values, environment concerns focused on the protection of seas and habitat, and political issues to do with the effectiveness of the state.[5]

In keeping with the established Chogm habit of issuing declaratory proclamations, the Edinburgh Economic Declaration, *Promoting Shared Prosperity*, was offered in 1997 as a complement to the Harare Declaration on political values. It opened with the words: 'Today's globalised world poses both opportunities and challenges.' Trade liberalisation and market forces were 'engines of growth', but not all countries benefited equally. Care was needed to manage the risks. Peace and prosperity were not possible amid 'deep poverty and growing inequality'. The goal was set for halving 'extreme poverty' by 2015. Consensus was sought for 'an equitable structuring of international economic relations'.[6]

By 1999, the buzzword had been elevated to Chogm theme and also entered the title of the Fancourt Declaration – *On Globalisation and People-Centred Development*. It opened: 'In today's world, no country is untouched by the forces of globalisation. Our destinies are linked as never before.' It declared optimistically that the ICT revolution was creating new opportunities to eradicate poverty. But benefits were not being shared equitably. The Heads of Government called on the global community 'to search for inclusive processes of multilateralism' and give a larger voice to the poorer countries and recognise 'the particular vulnerabilities of small states'.[7]

As the century closed, then, globalisation, facilitated by the new communication technologies, the disciplines of the market, and the freeing of trade and investment were seen as incentives for fostering good government, by democratically elected regimes, based on the rule of law and respect for human rights. The Commonwealth's particular niche in the debate was as the launching pad for a collective voice of the small states.

*

The Commonwealth has, indeed, become the premier small states forum. It has a higher proportion of small-state members than any other worldwide political organisation. This was not always so. On the eve of the Cyprus decision of 1961 which set the precedent for small states, the British Cabinet Secretary said that membership was normally confined to 'significant countries which could expect to exercise some influence in world counsels, to be viable economically, and to be worthwhile partners in some regional defence system'.[8] The Cyprus decision and the break-up of the West Indies Federation two years later changed all that. The way was opened for over 30 small dependencies to become full members. Out of a total of 33 by the mid-1970s, new members with populations of less than one million made up the majority. This was soon reflected in Commonwealth councils.

The Finance Ministers meeting in Barbados in 1977 noted the special characteristics of small-state economies – their dependence on imports, exports and capital inflows, their paucity in natural resources. From 1978, the Chogm communiqués always made reference to small states' needs and the Secretariat created a division to attend to their problems. A new dimension was reached in 1983 when a bloody coup in Grenada led to massive military action by the United States to restore order at the request of the island's Commonwealth neighbours. As a result, the Delhi Chogm of 1983 set up an expert consultative group to advise on problems of small-state security. Its report, *Vulnerability: Small States in the Global Society*, was prefaced by Secretary-General Ramphal with the words: 'The time of "innocence" of the world's smallest states is quietly passing.'[9]

The group held regional colloquia in New Zealand (for the Pacific), Seychelles (for the Indian Ocean and Africa) and Barbados (for the Caribbean). In the light of its origins, the group concentrated on threats to territorial security, though it did not neglect economic and environmental hazards. It produced a useful typology of small states. Defined as countries with a population of less than one million, there were within this total 'mini-states' with less than 200,000 and 'micro-states' with less than 100,000. In the Commonwealth total membership of 45 in 1985, more than half, 29, were in the small state category; of these there were 15 under 200,000 and of these 7 under 100,000. Geographically they were concentrated in the Caribbean (12) and the South Pacific (9).

From the mid-1980s, then, a small states dimension became a significant feature of Commonwealth activities. The Australian government helped to fund a Joint Office in New York to house permanent delegations to the United Nations from four small Pacific states. Over the years, this expanded until the Joint Office housed nine delegations. In 1987 a Small States Exposition was organised in the wings of the Vancouver Chogm, with the help of the Canadian government. Some

30 states mounted export, tourism promotion and information exhibits.

By the 1990s, as the impact of globalisation became the all-pervasive concern, the Secretary-General convened a Ministerial Group on Small States (CMGSS), which first met before the Limassol Chogm in 1993, to discuss concerns about development and security. It was agreed that between Chogms senior officials would form a Consultative Group on Small States (CGSS). At the second Ministerial Meeting in Auckland in 1995, 41 countries attended (small states and their major donors) along with Nauru, the Cook Islands, and Niue and observers from Caricom, and the South Pacific Forum. Here it was agreed that a new study of small-state vulnerability was needed. Dame Eugenia Charles, who as Prime Minister of Dominica during the 1983 Grenada crisis had played a prominent role in calling for American help, was chosen to lead an advisory group of mainly small states composition. Their sophisticated report, *A Future for Small States [Vulnerability II]*, was received at the Edinburgh Chogm in 1997.

Vulnerability II went far beyond the military security preoccupation of the earlier report. In the post-Cold War environment the chief threats had become marginalisation in the global economy and environmental fragility. The group was enjoined to consider six developments since 1985. These were: the role of market forces; the spread of freer trade; regionalisation in the form of 'mega-economic spaces' in Europe, North America and Asia-Pacific; global warming; declining resource flows, and hazardous waste disposal. The group focused on 32 of the Commonwealth's 54 members. Of these there were 15 small states with populations between 200,000 and 1,500,000, five mini-states between 100,000 and 200,000 and eight micro-states. The Group also added four more: (Jamaica, Lesotho, Nauru and Papua New Guinea) with larger populations but lying within the small state regions and having similar characteristics.[11]

Five characteristics were evident. 1) **openness** was shown in the propensity to outward looking and migration, which had some advantage in exploiting new opportunities. 2) **insularity** or **enclaveness**, often accentuated by remoteness, made collective endeavours difficult. By virtue of climate and geography, however, many were well placed for tourism. 3) **resilience** could be found in the 'strong measure of institutional coherence' of many small states. They were often more democratic than many large states. 4) they were **weak** in military capability and could never defend themselves. Neutrality or some sort of collective security were their only options in power struggles. 5) they

Table 14.2 1995 Small member populations

Small (up to 1.5 million)		Plus Regional Neighbours		Mini (under 200,000)	
Bah	276,000	Jam	2,555,000	Sam	165,000
Bar	261,000	Les	1,980,000	Slu	158,000
Biz	216,000	Nam	1,545,000	Svg	111,000
Bru	285,000	Png	4,302,000	Tga	104,000
Bot	1,450,000			Van	169 000
Cyp	734,000				
Fiji	775,000			**Micro**	
Gam	1,113,000			(under 100,000)	
Guy	835,000			Ant	65,000
Mdv	253,000			Dca	73,000
Mri	1,128,000			Grn	91,000
Mlt	372,000			Kri	79,000
Sol	375,000			Nru	8,000
Swa	900,000			Sey	74,000
Tri	1,287,000			Ski	41,000
				Tuv	11,000

Note: For country codes, See p. vii.

were **dependent** on exports and imports, development aid and tourism remittances. All this spelt vulnerability in the global economy. The picture was not entirely negative, but the special needs of the small states needed vigilance at the international, regional and pan-Commonwealth level. This was endorsed once more at the Edinburgh Chogm in 1997, where the Secretariat reported that it was working on a 'Vulnerability Index'.[12]

A measure of the sophistication of *Vulnerability II* was that it bore in mind (and incorporated in its tables) a wider group of small states, within each of the main regions. Thus a total of 49 states came within its purview. These were the UN category known as SIDS – Small Island Developing States. Therefore, in its role of champion of the small states, the Secretariat participated in a Joint Task Force with the World Bank. Its interim report, *Small States: Meeting the Challenge in the Global Economy* was central to the Durban Chogm theme in 1999. Like the Business Forum, the Joint Task Force was concerned about the marginalisation of small states in the process of globalisation. It called on the international community to give special treatment to small states in the transition away from preferential trading systems and to take account of their volatile incomes, susceptibility to natural disasters, and weak infrastructures. The Heads of Government regarded the Task

Force report as a 'landmark document' and endorsed the role of CMGSS as the 'monitoring mechanism'.[13] The strategy that emerged in 1999 was that small states and their sponsors should concentrate their energies on the World Trade Organisation (WTO) where Commonwealth members made up 34 per cent of the membership of 135 at the end of 1999.

*

The first line of defence for small states had long been cooperation with neighbours. All members belonged to regional organisations, which often took priority over Commonwealth or UN membership. Some regional organisations were of long standing, but they underwent changes in the last two decades of the century associated with the emergence of 'open regionalism' and the 'new regionalism'.

Regional organisations were prefigured in the UN Charter and the earliest groupings emerged to cope with the aftermath of the Second World War and the onset of the Cold War. Australia and New Zealand led the way in the Canberra Pact (1944). The North and South American states joined in the Organisation of American States in 1948, initially with no Commonwealth members. Britain and Canada had a major role in the creation of Nato (1949). Australia and New Zealand joined the United States in Anzus (1952), whose three members joined Britain, France, Pakistan, the Philippines and Thailand in the Manila Pact (1954) and Seato (1955). The most successful of all regional organisations began in Western Europe with the Coal and Steel Community (1951) and the Economic Community and Euratom under the Treaty of Rome (1957). Britain at first stood aloof. The European Communities were, at first, seen as rivals to the Commonwealth.

With the transformation of the Commonwealth following the acceleration of decolonisation after 1960, and the simultaneous decline of Britain as a power, regionalism burgeoned. Britain joined the European Communities in 1973, creating potential economic crises for the Commonwealth members, who all, if they had not already done so, joined with their neighbours for military or economic security. In Southeast Asia, Malaysia, Singapore and, later, Brunei joined Asean (1967). In the Americas, Belize and Guyana, the Caribbean island-states, and later Canada, joined the OAS. The African states, one by one, joined the Organisation of African Unity (OAU) formed in 1963. The four West African member countries joined 12 non-Commonwealth members to form the Economic Community of West African States (Ecowas) in 1975.

The two biggest regional organisations were, for a long time, exclusively Commonwealth groupings. These were created by mainly small island states in the South Pacific and the Caribbean. The South Pacific Forum, which emerged from initiatives taken by the Pacific Island Producers Association supported by New Zealand, started in 1971 with seven members and grew to 16. Originally a Commonwealth group, it eventually included the Marshall Islands, Palau and the Federated States of Micronesia. This led to a new name, Pacific Islands Forum, in 2000. In the Caribbean, after the British attempt to create a federal Dominion foundered in 1963, there were continuous endeavours to keep Caribbean cooperation going. The University of the West Indies was not broken up. The Caribbean Community and Common Market (Caricom) emerged in 1973. Membership grew to 15 as all the Commonwealth Caribbean states eventually joined, as did Montserrat and non-Commonwealth Suriname. The British Virgin Islands and the Turks and Caicos Islands became associate members. Within Caricom the six smaller islands of the eastern Caribbean formed the Organisation of East Caribbean States (OECS) in 1981.

In Southern Africa the Front Line States in the fight against apartheid were all Commonwealth members except Angola and Mozambique. They joined together in 1980, to create the Southern African Development Co-ordination Conference (SADCC) to reduce their economic dependence on South Africa. Renamed the Southern African Development Community (SADC) in 1992, it welcomed post-apartheid South Africa in 1994 and, at the same time, created the Common Market for Eastern and Southern Africa (Comesa) in which ten Commonwealth joined eleven non-Commonwealth states.

Reluctance to create regional institutions in South Asia stemmed from the bitter disputes which attended the end of the Raj in India. The partition into India and Pakistan, and subsequent splitting away of Bangladesh from the latter, inhibited cooperation. These problems, and the later separatist campaigns of Tamils in Sri Lanka, led to successive waves of dialogue and stand-off between India and Sri Lanka. Not until 1985 was the South Asian Association for Regional Cooperation (Saarc) created, in which the three larger mainland countries joined Sri Lanka and the Maldives and two non-Commonwealth states, Bhutan and Nepal. Continuing Indo-Pakistan rivalry (not least in the development of nuclear weapons) overshadowed Saarc. In 1995, ten Commonwealth and four non-Commonwealth states met in Mauritius to form the Indian Ocean Rim Association for Regional Co-operation

Table 14.3 Commonwealth members and regional organisations

Trans-Tasman	Australia–New Zealand Agreement (**Canberra Pact**) 1944 Australia–N Z Closer Economic Relations Trade Agreement (**CER**) 1984 Aus., Nzl.
South East Asia	Association of Southeast Asian Nations (**ASEAN**) 1967 Bru, Mas, Sin (and 6 non-Cwlth)
Americas	Organisation of American States (**OAS**) 1948 Ant, Bah, Bar, Biz, Can, Grn, Guy, Jam, Ski, Slu, Svg, Tri (and 23 non-Cwlth) North-American Free trade Area (**NAFTA**) 1993 Can (with USA and Mexico) Free Trade Area of the Americas (**FTAA**) Proposal 2000
Caribbean	Caribbean Community and Common Market (**CARICOM**) 1973 Ant, Bar, Biz, Dca, Grn, Guy, Jam, Ski, Slu, Svg, Tri (and 1 non-Cwlth) Organisation of East Caribbean States (**OECS**) 1981 Dca, Grn, Mts, Ski, Slu, Svg Association of Caribbean States (**ACS**) 1994 Ant, Bah, Bar, Biz, Grn, Guy, Jam, Ski, Slu, Svg, Tri (and 14 non-Cwlth)
Pacific	South Pacific Commission (**SPC**) 1947, Pacific Islands Forum (PIF 200 The Pacific Community (1997) Aus, Bri, Cok, Fij, Kri, Nru, Nzl, Nui, Sol, Tga, Tok, Tuv, Van (and 12 non-Cwlth) South Pacific Forum (**SPF**) 1971, Pacific Islands Forum (PIF) 2000 South Pacific Bureau for Economic Co-operation (**SPEC**) 1973 South Pacific Nuclear Free Zone (**SPNFZ**) 1985 Aus, Cok, Fij, Kri, Nru, Nzl, Nui, Png, Sam, Sol, Tga, Tuv, Van (and 3 non-Cwlth)
Europe	North Atlantic Treaty Organisation (**NATO**) 1949 Bri, Can (and 17 non-Cwlth in 1999) European Coal and Steel Community (**ECSC**) 1951 European Economic Community (**EEC**) 1957 Euratom 1957 European Community (**EC**) 1986

Table 14.3 Commonwealth members and regional organisations *(continued)*

Europe *(contd)*	European Union (EU) 1993
	Bri joined EEC, 1973 (total members of EU in 1999 was 15)
Africa	Organisation of African Unity (OAU) 1963
	Cmr, Gam, Gha, Ken, Les, Maw, Mri, Moz, Nam, Nig, Rsa, Sey, Sle, Swa, Tan, Uga, Zam, Zim (and 35 non-Cwlth)
	Economic Community of West African States (**ECOWAS**) 1975
	Gam, Gha, Nig, Sle (and 12 non-Cwlth)
	Southern African Development Co-ordination Conference (**SADCC**) 1980
	South African Development Community (**SADC**) 1992
	Bot, Les, Maw, Mri, Moz, Nam, Rsa, Swa, Zam, Zim (and 1 non-Cwlth)
	Common Market for Eastern and Southern Africa (**COMESA**) 1994
	Ken, Mau, Mri, Nam, Sey, Swa, Tan, Uga, Zam, Zim (and 11 non-Cwlth)
South Asia	South Asian Association for Regional Co-operation (**SAARC**) 1985
	Ban, Ind, Mdv, Pak, Sri (and 2 non-Cwlth)
Indian Ocean	Indian Ocean Commission (**IOC**) 1982
	Mri, Sey
	Indian Ocean Rim Association for Regional Co-operation (**IORARC**) 1995
	Aus, Ind, Ken, Msa, Mri, Moz, Rsa, Sin, Sri, Tan (and 4 non-Cwlth)

Note: For country codes, see p. vii.

(IORARC) to foster trade promotion, liberalisation and technological exchange.

For most of the Commonwealth members their regional organisations take precedence over the Commonwealth or United Nations – although Britain tries to maintain a balance. At the Edinburgh Chogm in 1997 Tony Blair spoke in Churchillian terms of Britain being pivotal in three spheres, Europe, the North Atlantic and the Commonwealth. For the majority of the Commonwealth members – mainly, of course, small states – regionalism became, in the words of *Vulnerability II*, 'a process feeding the globalisation process, not contradictory to it'. In face of what it called the 'open regionalism' practised by the three great trading blocs – EU, NAFTA, APEC – which is based on free-market capitalism, but endeavours not to disadvantage the rest of the world, the smaller countries turned to 'new regionalism', similarly imbued with liberal principles and less inward-looking than in earlier days when preferential treatment was the chief aim.[14]

Under the Lomé Conventions, which began in 1975, developing countries created the large grouping of 71 African-Caribbean-Pacific States (ACP) to negotiate trade and aid relations with the European Community. Preferential access to the European market was negotiated, but the group encountered increasing 'conditionality' in respect of good governance, the rule of law and respect for human rights. Lomé IV, 1989, expired at the end of 1999. After more than a year of negotiations, a new convention was agreed, to last for 20 years. However, by 2008 trade preferences were to be progressively reduced for all but 38 of the poorest countries. The new agreement, to be known as the Suva Convention, was scheduled for signing in a Commonwealth country, Fiji, in June 2000, but was diverted to Cotonou, Benin, because of the armed coup in Suva in May.

As Commonwealth countries endeavoured to fulfil the Harare principles, the regional organisations, and the NGOs with their own regional branches, were given a greater role. As the private sector took a more prominent part, the Commonwealth Private Investment Initiative (CPII), launched in Auckland in 1995, built up four regional funds. The Commonwealth Youth Programme works through regional youth centres in Guyana, India, Solomon Islands and Zambia. The Commonwealth of Learning appointed Regional Advisors to the President in 1997. A regional dimension is increasingly evident in all Commonwealth endeavours.

*

In delineating the Commonwealth's particular niche in world affairs, it is important to emphasise its trans-regional character. It is, however, not unique in this regard. The ACP Group has been mentioned. Over half (39 out of 71) of its members are from the Commonwealth. If, at the rich-nation end of the spectrum, Britain and Canada are part of the Group of Eight industrialised countries, more than half the

Commonwealth members are involved in the Group of Developing Nations in the United Nations (G77), and in the Non-Aligned Movement. Commonwealth members also make up 34 per cent of the members of the World Trade Organisation.

Nine Commonwealth countries are also members of the 52-strong Francophone Community. Building on meetings of French-speaking education, youth and sports ministers, and the associations of French-language universities and parliamentarians, started in the 1960s, L'Agence de Co-opération Culturelle et Technique (ACCT) was formed in 1970. But in 1997 the fully and partially French-speaking countries created a more politically focused grouping with a Secretariat and Secretary-General. Titled L'Organisation Internationale de La Francophonie (OIF) it approved a new charter at the Francophone Summit in Moncton, New Brunswick, in 1999. The Commonwealth members are Cameroon, Canada (and also Quebec and New Brunswick), Dominica, Mauritius, Seychelles, St. Lucia and Vanuatu. As well as promoting cooperation, La Francophonie is designed to defend usage of the French language.[15] Thus, as it tackles the familiar challenges of globalisation, it provides a window to a world that is an alternative to 'Americanisation'. In January 2000 the Commonwealth and La Francophonie held their first joint colloquium, in Yaoundé, Cameroon, on 'Democracy in Pluralistic Societies'.[16]

Compared with all these regional and trans-regional organisations, the Commonwealth has characteristics that are becoming increasingly sought after. Canadian diplomat, Charles van der Donckt, told a pre-Chogm seminar in Johannesburg in 1999: 'It is a flexible and decentralised instrument which does not demand constant political attention; it is a cost-effective co-operative framework which does not engulf vast amounts of public funds; and it does not suffer from major structural characteristics which can paralyse its functioning under adverse political conditions... . Succinctly put, leaders of democratic nations want to belong to institutions that tackle real world problems.'[17] Above all, the Commonwealth is marked by its unique mix of cultures, its small-state majority and, above all, by the width and depth provided by its IGO and Vippso infrastructures, which will be discussed in Parts V and VI.

Part V
Official Commonwealth – IGOs

15
The Secretariat and the CFTC

For all its ivory tower isolation in Queen Anne splendour, behind high walls and security guards off Pall Mall, the Secretariat is the hub of the contemporary Commonwealth. The first three Secretaries-General from 1965 to 2000, each, in his own manner, made particular contributions to the Secretariat's evolution while serving the Heads of Government collectively. The profusion of Commonwealth meetings, from the Chogms to the *ad hoc* groups and taskforces, are coordinated from Marlborough House. However one responds to the architectural and regal symbolism of the venue, understanding ComSec (to use the argot) is essential to any appreciation of the contemporary Commonwealth.

We have seen how the agreed memorandum on its establishment enjoined modest beginnings, but permitted pragmatic growth. Funding was to be by assessed contributions calculated according to the UN model. Initially, Britain paid 30 per cent, followed by Canada 28.8 per cent, India 11.4 per cent, Australia 10.4 per cent, New Zealand 2.5 per cent and Pakistan 2.4 per cent and the rest of the original 21 paid 1.5 per cent. The ABC members – Australia, Britain, Canada – would together always pay more than half. Arnold Smith appointed two deputy secretaries-general (Political and Economic) and began with three divisions, Administrative, Economic and International Relations. The expenditure for the first year was a mere £175,000 and 41 staff were appointed.

An early task required by the Heads of Government was a comprehensive review of existing intra-Commonwealth organisations concerned with economic and related affairs to determine whether there was any overlapping with other agencies and to decide what should be absorbed into the Secretariat. A group of eight senior officials undertook this review in 1966 under the chairmanship of Lord Sherfield of Britain (better known as Sir Roger Makins), whom Arnold Smith found to be a 'superb' chairman.

Out of a total list of 253 organisations based in Britain, the committee concentrated on 13 and reviewed ten of these in detail. Some were long-established technical organisations; others were fairly recent origin.

1. *The Commonwealth Liaison Committee* (CLC) had been created in 1948 to inform member governments about the European Recovery Programme and had developed into a bi-monthly forum, at the official level, for the exchange of economic information.
2. *The Commonwealth Economic Committee* (CEC), which had its own secretariat, dated from 1925. After 1958 it met quarterly as the coordinating machinery of the Commonwealth Economic Advisory Council, a product of the Montreal Economic Conference, and involved Finance and Economic Affairs Ministers. The CEC published regular commodity and trade reports.
3. *The Commonwealth Education Liaison Committee* (CELC) was another by-product of the 1958 Montreal Conference. It had come into being, after the subsequent Oxford Education Conference in 1959, as a forum for advancing projects arising from that, and later, educational conferences. It too had its own Secretariat in the Commonwealth Education Liaison Unit (CELU) created in 1960.
4. *The Commonwealth Institute*, formerly the Imperial Institute, originated as a memorial to the Jubilee of 1887. Relocated from South Kensington in 1962 to a purpose-built exhibition building in Holland Park, its role was promoting knowledge about the Commonwealth in Britain by exhibitions, lectures, films, study conferences and courses.
5. *The Commonwealth Agricultural Bureaux* (CAB) was created in 1929 as a grouping together of earlier foundations – institutes conducting identification services and research, and bureaux that were clearing houses for research data, in specialised fields of agricultural science. (CAB is the subject of Chapter 18.)
6. *The Standing Committee on Commonwealth Forests* provided continuity and linkages between periodic forestry conferences.
7. *The Commonwealth Aeronautical Advisory Research Council* (CAARC) was formed in 1946 and held triennial meetings to avoid research duplication.

8. *The Commonwealth Telecommunications Board* (CTB) in 1949 succeeded an earlier imperial organisation dating from 1925, to co-ordinate activity under the Commonwealth telegraph agreements.

9. *The Commonwealth Air Transport Council* (CATC) was created in 1945 to review progress in civil aviation.

10. *The Commonwealth Science Council* (CSC) began in 1946 as the Standing British Commonwealth Scientific Officers Conference and held biennial meetings to encourage co-operation between government civilian scientific organisations.

Three other organisations given brief scrutiny were the Commonwealth Forestry Institute, which was incorporated within the Department of Forestry at Oxford; the Commonwealth Defence Science Organisation (CDSO), which was very modest in scale, and the Commonwealth Foundation, which had emerged from the same PMM as the Secretariat. It had an already determined administrative relationship with that body and is the subject of the next chapter.[1]

The Sherfield Committee's conclusion was that the economic and educational bodies should be absorbed into the Secretariat, but that the organisations concerned with agriculture, forestry, aviation, science and telecommunications were technical and so well established in their specialist fields that they should continue to stand alone. The CLC had already been absorbed into the Secretariat. Over the next year, the CEC with its 91 staff became the Trade and Commodities Division and the CELU became the Educational Division. The Executive Secretary of the CSC became the Secretary-General's scientific adviser. These amalgamations increased the Secretariat staff to 160. During Arnold Smith's years, other developments were the appointment of a Medical Adviser (1968) and new divisions for Law (1969), Information (1971), Export Market Development (1972) and the Youth Programme (1973). At its tenth anniversary the ComSec staff totalled 279.[2]

Arnold Smith's chief institutional innovation was the Commonwealth Fund for Technical Cooperation (CFTC). This was created in response to evident needs under a rubric in the agreed memorandum of 1965 which provided that the Secretariat could play a valuable part in assisting member governments in advancing development projects and obtaining technical assistance on a multilateral Commonwealth basis. A proposal was put to the September 1996 Chogm for a scheme of what Smith called 'third-party technical assistance'. The idea was that a member country's contribution would go into the Fund, which would facilitate work by an expert from another country giving assistance to a third country. The proposal was referred to a meeting of senior officials in Nairobi in 1967, where caution was voiced especially by Australia, Britain, and New Zealand about overlapping with existing bilateral programmes. There was also some suspicion of the multilateral concept. However, Philip Ndegwa, Permanent Secretary of the Kenya Ministry of Economic Planning and Development, castigated the richer members for their rigidity. A modest multilateral technical assistance programme started in 1968. After review by the Finance Ministers in 1969, the CFTC was finally approved by the Heads of Government in 1971. It was intended as the Secretariat's agency for providing experts, consultancy services and training.

The Fund was based on voluntary (not assessed) contributions from member governments and began with a modest goal of £250,000. Britain contributed half. The Fund reached £1,000,000 in 1973. After peaking at £25,000,000 in 1986–7, it declined by the end of the century to about £20,000,000. Experts were provided under the Fund on long-term and short-term contracts. Starting with about 50, the scheme reached 300 in 1979; it averaged about 250 a year in the 1980s, but was down to 119 in 1997. Over the years 1997–9 there were 580. Under General Technical Assistance individual experts were provided to advise on planning, feasibility studies, legislative drafting and administrative reform. A Technical Assistance Group provided a consultancy service (dubbed the 'fire brigade') to help with statistical services, budget monitoring and trade promotion. There were also training and export development programmes, later joined by industrial and agricultural development units. Although the Fund was, by international standards, very small, it was cherished for its flexibility, comparative speed of response, and pioneering of South/South cooperation in use of experts – later labelled TCDC – technical cooperation between developing countries.[3]

The second Secretary-General from 1975 to 1990 was Shridath (Sonny) Ramphal, a Guyanan lawyer and politician, who had had considerable experience of Chogms as foreign minister and had a high profile as a former Vice-President of the UN General Assembly. (He was later a candidate for the UN Secretary-Generalship.) Ramphal was a much more flamboyant personality than Arnold Smith, with a background not in Cold War and East/West tensions, but in the Third World and the North/South dialogue. He became renowned for an oratorical style of alliterative antithesis well illustrated by his statement to senior officials in 1976: 'I assume that what governments want is a Secretariat that is effective without being expansive, that is dynamic without being diffuse, that can grow without being grandiose.'[4] A necessary part of that growth he said was 'to dissolve the residual film of anglocentricity that was distorting its image and to support its functional dynamism'.[5] His best-known aphorism was that: 'The Commonwealth cannot negotiate for the world; but it can help the world to negotiate.'[6]

Ramphal made two issues into something like a crusade – these were rectifying economic inequalities and combating apartheid. This led, as we have seen, to coolness from Britain, especially from Mrs Thatcher. The Secretariat reached its peak of personnel at 411 in the mid-1980s. The CFTC was more closely woven into the Secretariat's work; Ramphal called it ComSec's 'operational arm'. At the same time, new divisions concerned with Science, Economic Affairs, Export Marketing, Food Production, Rural Development and Human Resources were created. Gender equality and environmental degradation also became new preoccupations. Ramphal himself was the only person to serve on all four of the independent international commissions on global issues in the 1980s – Brandt on development in 1980, Palme on disarmament in 1982, Brundtland on the environment in 1987, and Nyerere on South/South cooperation in 1990.[7] The Secretariat also helped in servicing some of these commissions. Thatcher once quipped, at the 1987 Chogm, that 'the Secretariat fiddles while Ramphal roams'. There was probably relief in Britain at the election as the Secretary-General in 1990 of Chief Emeka Anyaoku of Nigeria.

'The Chief', as the new Secretary-General was referred to by colleagues, was a Secretariat man. A former classical scholar, he had joined as a young official from the Nigerian diplomatic service in 1966 and was regarded by Arnold Smith from the start as a high-flyer. He was secretary of the Sherfield Committee on intra-Commonwealth organisations. In spite of his potentially tricky situation as an Igbo, he became an important assistant to Arnold Smith during his mediation attempts during the Biafran war. Apart from a brief period as Nigeria's Foreign Minister in 1983, Anyaoku served in the Secretariat from its first year of operations. His experience ranged from overseeing Gibraltar's referendum of 1967, to the re-establishment of British rule after Anguilla's secession from St Kitts in 1969, and serving as secretary of the EPG in South Africa in 1986. His first year as Secretary-General was dominated by the H-Lag and the background work for the Harare Declaration. Chief Anyaoku regarded the Commonwealth's chief achievement as its role in the ending of apartheid and South Africa's return to membership in 1994 in which he played a significant personal part.[8] Within the Secretariat, however, the Anyaoku years will be remembered for a restructuring in the manner of many contemporary bureaucracies, but was consistent with the ideology of the Harare Declaration.

Much of the spirit of this restructuring – termed 'management of change process' – reflected the new corporate business approach, which came to dominate organisational management in the 1990s. There was a 'downsizing' of staff from over 400 to 320 by 1999. There was a new funding pattern based on three-year cycles from 1 July 1993. Budgets and expenditures became subject to the scrutiny of Scoso, the triennial Steering Committee of Commonwealth Senior Officials. The entire work of ComSec became 'programme-based' and a Strategic Planning and Evaluation Unit was created. The Secretariat also sponsored new professional associations to help further the Harare principles. The Commonwealth Association for Public Administration (CAPAM) was formed in 1994 and went on to organise international innovation awards. The Commonwealth Local Government Forum (CLGF), also launched in 1994, fostered democracy and good governance at the local body level.

Professional consultants were hired from outside to review both policy and administration and a change management officer was appointed. The whole of the technical assistance, economic and social programme areas were subjected to rigorous analysis using contemporary corporate theory by two academics from the Institute of Development Studies of the University of Sussex.

Professor Mike Faber reported on 29 April 1994 on the Secretariat's 'C' programmes – those largely funded by the CFTC. Faber (a former Director of the Technical Assistance Group of the CFTC in 1972–5 and 1978–83) emphasised that the Fund was a very small one by international standards. It accounted for less than 1 per cent of the total aid programmes of the three ABC donors and developing member countries got only 2 per cent of their technical assistance from the Fund. Therefore, to make an impact, he insisted that the Fund needed to take initiatives that had a distinctive character. 'Do Different' was the motto he preached. Heads of Government also took the same view when at Limassol in 1993 they called for concentration on areas where the Fund had a 'demonstrable comparative advantage'.

Faber accepted that a mix of 68 per cent on national projects, 22 per cent regional, and 10 per cent pan-Commonwealth was about right.

But he suggested that the CFTC had evolved too large a range of 'products'. These were: General Technical Assistance, the Fellowship and Training Programme, the Industrial Development Unit, the Technical Assistance Group and Export Market Development. Since these had developed in the 1970s, times had changed. Faber insisted, 'the product mix strikes me as being quite simply wrong' when judged against the criteria of relative need, cost-effectiveness and comparative advantage. For a major company to survive it needed to adjust its products to the demands of the market.

He felt the Fund should concentrate on general technical assistance, training, and its economic and legal advisory services. He found that technical assistance from the Fund was more cost-effective than that from most multilateral organisations. The Fund could respond quickly and flexibly to needs. It was better than the huge Washington-based institutions, the IMF and World Bank, which, he found, were too theoretically based, remote from actual needs and attuned to OECD concepts. The CFTC, small though it was, stood apart from the Washington consensus. It was especially sensitive to the needs of small states. He found that everywhere he went the activities of the CFTC were viewed as 'a valuable advantage of Commonwealth membership'. He therefore regretted its 'invisibility'. The Commonwealth, he said, ought to celebrate the strengths of the association.[9]

The rest of the economic and social programmes of ComSec were evaluated in a report of September 1995 by Professor John Toye, also from the Sussex Institute. Judged by the Harare Declaration's tenet about sustainable development, the Limassol Chogm's call for 'demonstrable comparative advantage', and a call from the 1994 SOM for a balance between the political and ecosoc aspects of the Secretariat's work, Toye suggested that restructuring had not gone far enough. He found that, notwithstanding the new programme-driven decision-making structure, 'a supply-side culture' was still in evidence. A 'demand-driven culture' would look different. He applied the now familiar corporate philosophy to the Secretariat's activities.

Toye, like Faber, emphasised that the ecosoc programmes were, in comparative terms, 'extremely tiny'. They were, however, valuable, especially for small states that lacked expertise to make their own economic analyses. Also like Faber, Toye criticised the spread of 'products'. So little money, spread over so many programmes, ran the risk of making too small an impact. Practical proposals made by Toye included eliciting member preferences; appointing an ambassador-at-large to maintain face-to-face contacts; improving statistical services for small states; maintaining concentration on gender equality; and building on absolute advantages displayed by the Commonwealth Youth Programme. He suggested moving the Secretariat's aid to sport to the CYP. His main message was that the Secretariat should discourage the remnants of supply-driven behaviour and make 'a clearer division of organisational responsibilities between those within the COMSEC who are "purchasers" of services (e.g. top-level management) and those who are "providers" (e.g. COMSEC Divisions)'.[10]

With the advice of the independent consultants, the priorities established by the Heads of Government, and the detailed adjustments recommended by Scoso, the CFTC was now fully integrated into the Secretariat structure. All ComSec work was placed under supervision by one of three deputy secretaries-general. All activities were rationalised into 11 broad programmes (with 22 sub-programmes) grouped under four heads: (A) Political, (B) Development, (C) Gender Equality and (D) Secretariat Governance and Management. As revised in 1997 these were:

Political	A1	Promoting Fundamental Political Values
Development	B2	Economic Development
	B3	Human Development
	B4	Commonwealth Youth Programme
	B5	Public Sector and Public Service Reform
	B6	Capacity-building
	B7	Science and Technology for Sustainable Development
Gender Equality	C8	Gender Equality: The Commonwealth Plan of Action and Gender Policy Formulation and Implementation on Critical Political, Legal and Developmental Issues
Secretariat Governance and Management	D9	Secretariat Governance, Executive Direction, Strategic Planning and Evaluation.
	D10	Information and Public Affairs
	D11	Administrative, General Services, and Information Technology[11]

In budgeting terms the ecosoc programmes took up three-quarters of the Secretariat's funds, which in 1997 totalled £38,300,000. But, as Professor Faber regretted, much of this was invisible. John Thaw's 'Commonwealth stories' before the Edinburgh Chogm publicised some vivid examples, but could hardly redress the balance.

To fulfil the new goals Anyaoku issued a 'culture statement' on the Secretariat in April 1997. In phrases which almost caricatured political correctness, he said, 'The Secretariat culture should be an open, transparent, flexible, caring and creative organisation which satisfied the requirements and expectations of governments and is efficient, achievement orientated, gender aware and uses the multi-cultural background and skills of staff to its advantage.' To little avail! Two years later, the change management officer, reported that the culture was 'characterised more by turf and boundary protection, a fear on the part of many to express themselves freely, and cross organisational communication'.[12]

By contrast, the political side of the Secretariat's work was the part that provided the headlines. From 1995 the Secretary-General's authority in this area was considerably enhanced. As related in Chapter 10, the Millbrook Programme of Action dealt first with 'Advancing Commonwealth Fundamental Political Values'. As a response to violations of Harare principles, the Secretary-General was supplied with a raft of options. These included public expressions of the Commonwealth's disapproval of infringements; contacts and the use of good offices with *de facto* governments; encouraging bilateral regional links; the sending of envoys or eminent person groups; the setting of deadlines for the restoration of democratic rule; exclusion of errant regimes from Commonwealth meetings; suspension of errant regimes from assistance programmes; and consideration of other bilateral and multilateral sanctions on contacts.[13] This list amounted to discretions and opportunities which went far beyond the cautious mandate of 1965. They accorded well with the aspirations of Arnold Smith at that time.

Anyaoku retired in 2000 having presided in Marlborough House through the Secretariat's most intensive period of change. His part in the Commonwealth's renaissance was influential on many fronts. His successor, Don McKinnon, former Foreign Minister and Deputy Prime Minister of New Zealand, brought considerable experience of Commonwealth affairs, not least a small state perspective. As the first deputy chair of the C-Mag and broker in the peace negotiations between Papua New Guinea and Bougainville, he was in touch with the problem of the errant states and the poor island states. Bringing a New Zealand brand of low-key informality to political discourse, he surprised the reporters at his post-election press conference in Durban by giving informative answers to their questions. A Secretariat official quipped: 'He will have to be trained.' When he assumed office in April 2000, there was a Maori welcoming party in the garden. As they swarmed up Marlborough House's grand staircase to the Secretary-General's office clad in their flax piupius, did they presage a more relaxed atmosphere within the austere portals?

16
The Commonwealth Foundation

Housed within the Secretariat complex, in the west wing of Marlborough House, is the Commonwealth Foundation. With a staff of scarcely more than a dozen and an income of only £2,600,000, the Foundation is on an altogether smaller scale than its co-tenant. But the Foundation, an autonomous inter-governmental body, funded by voluntary subscriptions and answering to a Board of Trustees, has been the catalyst for an astonishing growth and increasing involvement of the voluntary and non-governmental organisations of the Commonwealth. Its origins preceded the Secretariat, since the idea of a foundation to foster professional linkages had been mooted in the early 1960s and was part of the *Way Ahead* package presented to the 1964 PMMs. Although 'overtaken' by the Secretariat, the Foundation was considered and approved by exactly the same procedures, which brought forth the Secretariat during 1964 and 1965. After Arnold Smith commenced work as Secretary-General in August 1965, the Foundation's first Director, John Chadwick, followed on 1 March 1966.

The Foundation's mandate was, at first, clear and simple. The agreed memorandum approved in July 1965 established the Foundation to '**administer a fund for increasing interchanges between Commonwealth organisations in professional fields**'. The initial goal for the fund was £250,000 for which Britain agreed to pay half. After the first decade, the total was raised to £450,000 and Britain's contribution became 30 per cent. The fund did not top £1,000,000 until the 1980s, after the mandate had been considerably widened. It passed the £2,000,000 mark in 1991–2, fluctuated through the 1990s and did not go beyond £2,500,000 until 1998–9. Thus, beside the great international foundations and even the CFTC, the Commonwealth Foundation is minuscule. But John Chadwick, Director from 1966 to

1980, was told when visiting the Rockefeller Foundation that money could not create ideas, that there was 'no substitute for brains'.[1]

The Foundation's original mandate was dubbed the 'seven commandments'. They were:

1. to support fuller representation at professional conferences;
2. to assist professional bodies to hold more of their own conferences;
3. to facilitate professional exchanges and study visits;
4. to stimulate the exchange of professional information;
5. to assist, on request, the setting up of new national associations;
6. to promote the growth of Commonwealth-wide or regional associations; and
7. to consider exceptional requests to help associations or individuals outside the professional field but within the general ambit of the Foundation operations.[2]

In the early years, the Board saw its role as breaking down the isolation and boosting the morale of middle-ranking professional people in developing member countries. As Chadwick put it, 'a small travel grant, judiciously applied, could earn dividends far in excess of funds actually laid out'.[3] Grants were made to assist conference attendance, to help the production of professional bulletins and journals, or to build professional libraries.

The two main contributions in the first decade were financial help in the formation of new professional associations, (some 40 of which were eventually founded as discussed in Chapter 19) and the creation of Professional Centres, where groups of national professional bodies could share common premises. Seventeen of these were founded. Such widespread largesse with comparatively small sums was not without critics. The first Canadian Trustee, former diplomat Escott Reid, resigned because he thought the Foundation should, as he put it, 'stick to its knitting'. He felt that Chadwick was advancing too many worthy causes without increasing professional interchanges. He thought the Foundation should concentrate on about ten professions over an agreed period.[4] As opposed to focusing in this way, however, the Foundation's scope was to be considerably widened.

It was realised by the mid-1970s, after the Secretariat and the Foundation had existed for a decade, that there were many areas where the official and unofficial elements of the Commonwealth could cooperate more fruitfully. Yet governments were wary of the non-official bodies, which often had to adopt an adversarial stance to get attention for their concerns. Chadwick, who was a former CRO official, wrote: 'Any honest civil servant will admit that news of an approaching NGO delegation would often create "that sinking feeling".'[5] In 1975, seminars were held in London by the Royal Commonwealth Society and in Jamaica by the Foundation to consider official/non-official cooperation, and in 1976 a major conference was held on this theme at Dalhousie University, Halifax, Nova Scotia. Here it was realised that, as well as the professions, there were numerous other voluntary and unofficial organisations at work in the development field, and also in education, parliamentary government, the arts and sport. The Dalhousie Conference recommended that governments should formally encourage the work of voluntary bodies, widen the mandate of the Foundation, encourage the Secretary-General to include NGOs in the Secretariat's work, and should reassess the information, educational and cultural programmes. It proposed that up to 3 per cent of official development aid should go through Commonwealth multilateral channels, and that the Foundation should be given more money.

These proposals found scant support at the 1977 Chogm, but the Canadians ensured that an Advisory Committee was appointed to consider relations between the official and unofficial Commonwealth. This committee's report, entitled *From Governments to Grassroots* (1978), indicated that the growth of the unofficial sector had been uncoordinated and haphazard. It proposed, specifically, two things: 1) that the Foundation's mandate should be expanded to take in (a) culture, information and the media, (b) social welfare and the handicapped, (c) rural development, and (d) the role of women; and 2) it suggested that governments should create a unit or liaison body to foster and consult with national NGOs, and that the Secretariat should create an 'NGO desk'. These proposals were endorsed, in part, by the 1979 Lusaka Chogm and the level of subscriptions to the Foundation was raised to £1,100,000, a total not actually reached until 1982–3.[6]

At the end of 1980, the Board of Trustees adopted a vastly enlarged list of areas of interest stemming from the Dalhousie initiatives. These were:

- *Food production* – rural development, agriculture, veterinary science, forestry and fisheries.
- *Health* – medical and paramedical services, pharmacy, dentistry and services to the handicapped.
- *Education*.

- *Social welfare* – social services, community development, women, youth, minorities, family planning.
- *Science and technology* – appropriate technology and building science.
- *Culture* – the arts, literature, libraries, museums.
- *The media.*
- *Public administration and the law.*[7]

After a decade of concentration on professional linkages, and operating within the legal framework of a charity in British law, the Foundation moved on. It adopted the legal status of an international organisation, with a comprehensive new social, economic and cultural mandate. It was not, however, given large sums of money.

During the 1980s, there was a virtual explosion of voluntary activity. New associations were founded, international agencies began to take note, and some cooperation between governments and NGOs began, including some specialist non-official input into international conferences.

To facilitate cooperation between the Commonwealth associations and to increase the flow of information, the Foundation (though not the Secretariat) took up the *Grassroots* report's idea of liaison units. The notion of a key national organisation acting as NGO Liaison Unit in a country was explored in regional seminars by Inoke Faletau, Foundation Director 1985–93. Coming himself from Tonga, his first consultations were in the Pacific, at Apia, in 1986, and the first liaison units – now styled 'Commonwealth Liaison Units' (Clus in the argot) began in the Pacific Islands. The other regional seminars were held in Bombay, Grenada and Malta (1987) and Mauritius (1988). By 1993, when the Foundation's fund was being supported by 40 member governments and the Foundation had assisted 35 new associations, 40 Clus had come into being.[8] Only at this point did the Secretariat create its own NGO Liaison Officer, to maintain contacts with this burgeoning area. The Clus were, in many cases, aided with grants from the Foundation of up to £4,500 to acquire communications equipment such as computers and fax machines. **The role of a Clu was to foster inter-NGO exchanges of information and cooperation at the national, regional and pan-Commonwealth levels.** The magazine *Common Path* was distributed by the Foundation to disseminate news of its activities.

In 1991 the Foundation moved on from regional consultations to hold the first 'Commonwealth NGO Forum', in Harare, a few months before the Chogm. From this forum arose the call for an NGO charter.[9] The result, instead, was the first attempt to survey the growth of the voluntary movement, to define its characteristics and to recommend ways forward. Consultants Colin Ball and Leith Dunn started work in 1992; their draft was considered at the second NGO Forum in Wellington in 1995 and published for the Auckland Chogm later in the year. Rather than a charter, Ball and Dunn produced *Non-Governmental Organisations: Guidelines For Good Policy and Practice*, which was later translated into five languages. It was described by the Foundation's Director, Humayun Khan, as 'a Geneva Convention for NGOs'.[10]

The *Guidelines* demonstrated clearly the change in the focus of the Foundation from its early years. In place of the original priority placed on professional linkages, the concentration was now on organisations for working with people to improve their social and economic position. Indeed, the authors deliberately excluded professional organisations from their definition of an NGO. Their four-part definition for such a body was that it must be: **voluntary, independent, not-for-profit, and not self-serving**.[11] Presumably, the last would not be met by professional organisations, which, by their nature were self-serving, in the sense that they existed for the benefit of their members by fostering professional standards, and in some cases controlling professional accreditation. The organisations covered by the *Guidelines* were largely in the care and welfare or development categories. **They worked with people to encourage emancipation from dependency, the alleviation of poverty, and advancing human development**. There were also the rising issues of environmental degradation, globalisation, population limitation and HIV/AIDS.

Although there had been a rapid growth of bodies labelled NGO, some were not deemed 'true NGOs' by virtue of funding control by governments or businesses or political organisations. Some were arrogant, even 'neo-colonial'; some were simply fraudulent. The conclusion was that, if governments and NGOs were to work in partnership, there had to be accountability, mission statements, efficient management, equal opportunities for women and better information exchanges. There had also to be appropriate legal frameworks for the recognition, operation and audit of organisations. 'In order to create an enabling environment for NGOs, governments should promote voluntarism generally and acknowledge the validity of the role of NGOs in civil society. Governments should also have appropriate legislation and official procedures for the registration and public accountability of

NGOs.' For the next few years, much of the work of the Foundation was directed at implementing these *Guidelines*.

Under Deputy-Director Don Clarke from New Zealand (1995–8) the Foundation's work was reviewed and restructured. An 11-member NGO Advisory Committee was created in 1996. Regional seminars were held in 1996–7 to consider NGO/government relations in the light of the *Guidelines* and a training kit was issued. During the Commonwealth Forum in Edinburgh, during the 1997 Chogm, their studies were brought together in a pan-Commonwealth seminar on the theme: 'Common ground for development'. From this seminar came the call that the distinctive purposes of NGOs should be recognised; formal mechanisms for NGO participation in official policy-making created; legal frameworks and regulatory arrangements for NGO participation in open government achieved; and that all such moves should reflect their great diversity. It was also agreed that action to improve the viability and sustainability of NGOs was needed.

At the same time, the Foundation appointed a consultant, Heather Acton of Economic Planning Associates, to review the Clu network. Reporting in September 1997, the consultant found that the title 'Commonwealth Liaison Unit' had created misunderstanding, that NGO development was very uneven, and that the concept of the Foundation having a single contact point in a country was inflexible. There were also regional variations. In the Pacific, the Clu network was valued and fruitful. In Africa and the Caribbean, there were suspicions about the Foundation's relationships with regional organisations. Following up on the review, the Director addressed all Clus on 18 March 1998. He told them that it had been decided that the system of using a single umbrella organisation as national contact point would not be continued, that the Clus should be phased out, and a new concept of 'network NGOs' would be adopted. The Foundation would have more flexible arrangements with national NGOs, and the essence of these relationships should be a two-way flow of information. There would be Memoranda of Understanding between these contact points and the Foundation and provision for monitoring indicators, annual reporting, regular reviews and external assessment. Unsatisfactory arrangements would be dismantled.[12]

The Foundation produced a Strategic Plan for the period 1997–2001. The mission was now stated with great clarity as: to **'promote people-to-people interaction and collaboration within the non-governmental sector of the Commonwealth'**. The Foundation would continue to support professional associations and cultural activities. Among the latter were Commonwealth prizes for fiction and poetry, competitions for short stories and photography, and arts and crafts awards. Support for Arts and Cultural Festivals at the time of the Commonwealth Games would continue. The Foundation would support the Commonwealth generally by a new publication pro-gramme, study fellowships and young journalist scholarships to facili-tate participation in key NGO events. It would cooperate with the recently founded Secretariat-sponsored NGOs in the fields of public administration and local government to press for a bigger non-official role in Commonwealth ministerial meetings. The four priorities were now to promote (1) inter-country networking; (2) training; (3) capacity building; and (4) information exchanges. These were largely directed at improving the viability and effectiveness of the voluntary organisa-tions and their relations with governments.[13]

The specific end-of-century goals of the Foundation were three-fold. First, it facilitated NGO representation at the Youth Ministers' and Health Ministers' meetings in 1998, and the Women's Affairs and Education Ministers' meetings in 1999. Second, the Third NGO Forum was held in collaboration with the South African NGO Coalition, Sangoco, before the 1999 Chogm in Durban. Third, a taskforce was appointed, on the initiative of the Advisory Committee, to produce a new study about *Civil Society in the New Millennium*. The aim of all these activities was to strengthen the whole area of citizen initiative for fur-thering the 1991 Harare principles of democratic pluralism, good gover-nance, human rights, combating poverty and protecting the environment.

The *Civil Society* project was the largest ever undertaken by the Foundation. Over 200 researchers and 60 partner organisations inter-viewed over 10,000 ordinary citizens in 47 member countries. The purpose was to find out what ordinary people thought of the role of governments and non-governmental organisations. Three remarkably sophisticated questions were put to the participants:

Q.1. What is your view of the 'good society' and to what extent does such a society exist today?

Q.2. What roles are best played by citizens and what roles are best played by the state and other sectors in such a good society? What limits the playing of such roles in today's society?

Q.3. What would enable citizens to play their role in the develop-ment of society more effectively in the future?[14]

The report was completed ahead of schedule by September 1999 and titled *Citizens and Governance: Civil Society and the New Millennium*. It was considered by the Third NGO Forum meeting in Durban in November 1999 shortly before the Chogm and then presented to the Heads of Government. It was, in part, an extremely moving document by virtue of over 40 pages of quotations from citizens around the Commonwealth.[15] It was also a somewhat frustrating document in that its conclusions were embodied in a series of triangular diagrams depicting models for state/citizen/intermediary organisation interaction.

The conclusions were surprisingly clear and simple and ran counter to the free market, user pays orthodoxy of the Cold War victors – even the tenets of the Harare Declaration. The respondents showed themselves very concerned about **basic needs** (economic security, social services, physical security and peace); they wanted **association** in their communities (including respect for culture, sharing and caring), and expected to **participate** (in responsive and inclusive governance, equal rights and justice). It was also clear that women and young people felt excluded; men felt included but threatened. The overall conclusion was that, contrary to the privatising trends of the developed countries, many people around the Commonwealth envisaged significant roles for the state as **provider** of services and law, **facilitator** of citizenship participation, and **promoter** of equal rights and justice. The report ends: 'The journey to create a good society throughout the Commonwealth must now begin.'[16]

In forwarding the report to the Chogm, the NGO Forum spoke for the hundreds of millions who make up the mainstream of the Commonwealth. The accompanying preamble was stark and eloquent: 'Poverty is still the reality for most people in the Commonwealth .... Globalisation not only disempowers; it further impoverishes the many whose daily life is a daily struggle to survive.' The Forum recommended to the Chogm the development of 'meaningful partnerships among civil society organisations and between civil society, government, and the corporate private sector' to deal with the harmful effects of globalisation.[17]

Heads of Government were not, one suspects, ready for the *Civil Society* report. They merely 'noted' it in their Durban communiqué. They accepted, somewhat flatly, the significance of civil society for 'empowering people to benefit from globalisation'. They enjoined the next SOM in 2000 to study the possibility of the Forum presenting its views to the Brisbane Chogm in 2001. Meanwhile the Foundation turned from publication to practicalities and looked for ways to foster a civil society agenda within Commonwealth institutions and member countries. The NGO Advisory Committee was replaced by a new Civil Society Advisory Committee. Plans were outlined for a 'Citizens and Governance Programme of the Foundation'. A tri-sector forum of business, government and civil society leaders was envisaged for the Brisbane Chogm in 2001.

The appointment, in 2000, of Colin Ball, joint-author of the *NGO Guidelines*, added long-standing expertise in the development and welfare fields, and Gracia Machel's selection as chairperson elevated the international profile of the Foundation. Yet, with less than £3,000,000 per year at its disposal, the Foundation's mission looks, on the face of it, impossible. Britain's annual £500,000 contribution amounts, per head of population, to less than a penny – a scarcely visible fraction of the sum spent on, say, the Millennium Dome. The first Director may have been convinced that the value of a small sum can be out of all proportion of its value, but there is a limit to the number of bricks that can be made without straw.

17
The Commonwealth of Learning

In a quiet suite of offices in Vancouver, BC, the Commonwealth's least-known major agency may be found at work in comfortable, if remote, surroundings. The Commonwealth of Learning (COL in the argot) came into being in 1989 to fulfil one of the most visionary proposals ever put before the Heads of Government. It remains outside the purview of most people, partly because of its physical remoteness, but also because of its somewhat grandiose and ambiguous title, which does not really convey the intentions of its progenitors. The name derives from the short title of a report which proposed something different.

The report by an expert group and approved by the 1987 Chogm, was about cooperation in distance education and open learning. Subtitled *Towards a Commonwealth of Learning*, it actually proposed the creation of a 'University of the Commonwealth for Cooperation in Distance Education'. This title described the practical intention. If it had been adopted, the COL's profile might have become greater.

As with so many of the developments we have discussed, the idea arose out of crisis – in this case crisis caused by economic restructuring in the wealthier member countries. Literacy, education and training, especially in technical and professional fields, had long been accepted as vital keys to development. The founding fathers of the new Asian-African-Caribbean nations had nearly all been students in Britain or North America at one time. Founding university colleges in Africa had been an important postwar British policy. Increased assistance for higher education and professional training had been part of the *Way Ahead* proposals in 1964 which led to the creation of the Secretariat and the Foundation. Prestigious scholarships, such as those at Oxford awarded by the Rhodes Trust, or those from the Cambridge

Commonwealth Trust, and the wider Commonwealth Scholarship and Fellowship Plan had become badges of personal achievement and advance for generations of professional leaders.

Student mobility and, more importantly, the life-long contacts so generated, were a very significant part of the social and professional cement of the Commonwealth's élites. Much of this was put at risk when the developed member countries – the Meccas for advanced students – began to introduce full cost-recovery fee regimes for foreign students. Starting with Britain in 1980, the practice soon spread to Canada, Australia and New Zealand, which all began to view higher education as a profitable service export rather than a part of a national influence-enhancing diplomacy. For several years a Commonwealth Committee on Student Mobility monitored the problem and ritually urged Education Ministers and Heads of Government to favour more generous fee regimes for Commonwealth students.

A new approach was sought at the 1985 Nassau Chogm. The Secretary-General was instructed to investigate the potentiality of distance education for bridging the widening education gaps.[1] Accordingly, in October 1986, Ramphal gathered a group of experts chaired by Lord Briggs (better known as the historian Asa Briggs) who was Provost of Worcester College, Oxford, and Chancellor of Britain's Open University, founded in 1969 as the first university purposely created on the distance learning principle. The group included Dr G. Ram Reddy, Vice-Chancellor of the Indira Gandhi National Open University, Delhi, founded in 1985, the largest such institution in the Commonwealth. The Briggs Group surveyed the considerable wealth of distance education experience in the Commonwealth dating from nineteenth century correspondence schools for pupils in remote areas of the old Dominions. The report defined '**distance education**' as a process in which a significant part of the teaching was by someone removed in space and time from the learner. '**Open learning**' was defined as a process of learning, openly available to learners no matter whom or where they were and when they wished to study. Open learning institutions might use distance education techniques, but not necessarily.[2] The Briggs Group realised that huge advances could be made in the area of part-time study by using distance education, for which the technology was becoming more readily available and the costs falling. The Open University was already enrolling more students than any other British university outside the federal University of London. The average cost per graduate was relatively lower than elsewhere.

To provide for the needs of Commonwealth countries, the Briggs Group identified four options: 1) an **information service** to share distance education information; 2) a **brokerage service** to share information and also foster cooperative activity between distance teaching institutions; 3) an **agency** with wider functions, able to undertake activities in the development of learning materials and in institutional development; or 4) a **Commonwealth Open University** to enrol and teach students. The group recommended the third option – an institution, which would work with and through existing colleges and universities, but not enrol its own students. It suggested a **University of the Commonwealth for Co-operating in Distance Education** to assemble materials and courses from existing institutions and make them more widely available. It envisaged starting with a small professional staff of about 20 at an initial annual cost of about £2,400,000. It put forward as the long-term aim: 'that any learner, anywhere in the Commonwealth, shall be able to study any distance-teaching programme, available from any bona fide college or university in the Commonwealth'.[3] Secretary-General Ramphal prefaced the report with one of the superlatives for which he was renowned: 'seldom ... has a group of the great and the wise produced a Report which is so visionary as well as practical'.[4] At the Vancouver Chogm in 1987, general pledges of support were forthcoming, especially from Brunei, Canada, India and Nigeria. An additional sum from the Province of British Colombia secured Vancouver as the site for the new institution. This came into being with remarkable despatch.

After a feasibility study by the principal of one of Canada's leading distance education universities, the Commonwealth of Learning (COL) was created as an international agency under a Memorandum of Agreement of 1 September 1988, and an agreement granting tax exemptions was signed with the Canadian government at an inauguration ceremony on 14 November 1988. The COL started work on 1 January 1989. At the time of the Kuala Lumpur Chogm later that year, the Queen saw a laptop computer which already could access information on 8,000 distance education courses from 200 institutions.[5] She expressed surprise that the COL was up and running so soon.

The first Principal, Dr James Maraj, came from a background which included service as Assistant Secretary-General in the Secretariat supervising the Commonwealth Youth Programme and as Vice-Chancellor of the University of the South Pacific. After the first full year he reported the COL's concentration on six main areas. These were 1) training in distance education techniques, 2) providing an information and advisory service, 3) acquisition and development of learning materials, 4) telecommunications technology, 5) continuing professional education, and 6) special emphases on teacher education, environmental issue and the role of women in development.[6] The main initial source of funding came from grants of Cdn$6,800,000 from Brunei, $4,250,000 from Canada, $1,200,000 from Nigeria, and $1,000,000 from India. Maraj, however, was a controversial figure, who fought for the independence of the COL and excited suspicions of empire-building. By the mid-1990s the COL faced a severe funding crisis. The largesse of the Sultan of Brunei dried up. The British put most of their initial contribution towards an international information service and credit transfer system to be spent in Britain and based on their own Open University.

In 1993 the COL was reviewed by Dr Ian MacDonald, of Trent University, Ontario, who became chairman of the Board of Governors in the following year. After Maraj's retirement, there was a temporary president until Professor Raj Dhanarajan, of Malaysia, from the Open University Institute of Hong Kong, was appointed in 1995. As the COL was restructured in the mid-1990s and began to seek a steadier income, there was pessimism about the 'any learner anywhere' vision ever being fulfilled. The COL reported to Heads of Government that it was having to turn down requests from governments for its services.

The vision was clearly still there. In a 'Strategy for Success' produced in 1995; the COL was touted as 'a building-block for social transformation on a global scale'. It listed Commonwealth-wide systems of educational broadcasting; credit transfer; quality assessment and accreditation of institutions; and learning centres and joint-venture partnerships as 'all just around the corner in the work of the COL'.[7] But in the report for 1994–6 it was admitted that the COL needed to move in 'a slightly different direction'.[8] The stress was now on technical and vocational training, continuing education and professional development, open schooling, non-formal education, and a renewed emphasis on gender equality. One of the most successful projects was a module-based technical and vocational training joint curriculum assembled by the COL for use in 14 Caribbean countries. Over 40 modules (all already in use somewhere, some of the best being from Australia) were assembled by the COL in Vancouver for the Caribbean participants. Limits to this sort of sharing, however, were evident in the growing tendency for knowledge – 'intellectual property' – to be treated as a commodity of trade and profit.

The report presented to the 1997 Chogm at Edinburgh listed some of the practical manifestations of this redirection. A master's degree course in distance education through the Indira Gandhi Open University had produced its first graduates. An open learning project had commenced in association with the Allam Iqbal Open University of Pakistan. A pilot scheme for technical assistance in primary teacher training was being funded by the Asian Development Bank. Distance learning courses had been arranged in legislative drafting and teacher training. There was a shift away from emphasis on the traditional tertiary sector into five new areas 1) open schooling especially for girls and women, 2) technical and vocation education and training, 3) non-formal education, 4) continuing and professional education especially for teachers, and 5) removal of barriers to educational access by women. Another area with great potential was the use of distance education in sports coaching training, in association with three Canadian sports bodies.[9]

To ensure continuity, annual funding of Cdn $5,000,000 was sought for three-year cycles. Contribution pledges were now made at the triennial Conferences of Commonwealth Education Ministers. The Three-Year Plan for 1997–2001 was approved by Education Ministers in Gaborone in 1997. A graded contribution scale was accepted. In Tier 1 were countries who would pledge, as a group, Cdn $4,000,000 in each of the following three years: these countries were Australia, Britain, Canada (both Federal and BC governments), India and New Zealand. Tier 2 countries who would contribute, as a group, $1 million over the same period – Brunei, Malaysia, Nigeria, Singapore and South Africa. Tier 3 would consist of a further 43 countries that would, as a group, contribute $1,000,000 per year. Thus $5,000,000 was secured in 1997 and any additional money would have to be gained from special contracts or collaborative projects. The other main change was the arrangement of a 'regional presence' for the COL. As in so many other spheres of activity, the Commonwealth was divided into nine distance learning regions and Regional Advisers to the President were appointed.[10]

By the end of the century, the COL was confident of its place as an 'apt and agile agent for the Commonwealth' especially in the rising realms of the information and communications technologies (ICT). It collaborated with the World Bank in creating the Global Knowledge Partnership. It celebrated its tenth anniversary by organising the first Pan-Commonwealth Forum on Open Learning held in Brunei during March 1999. Following this it was agreed that the Federation of Commonwealth Open and Distance Learning Associations (FOCODLA) would take responsibility for a second forum in 2002. With help from the British government it investigated the prospects for 'virtual education via the net'.

For its tenth anniversary report to the 1999 Durban Chogm, the COL refined a four-fold mission as **catalyst for collaborative action, capacity builder, training resource,** and **provider of information**. The new emphasis on open schooling, especially for females; technical and vocational training and non-formal education; and continuing professional, especially teacher education was a response to what Chairman Ian Macdonald called 'a chilling fact of life'. Rhetoric by governments about eliminating illiteracy by the end of the century had foundered. As COL President Gajaraj Dhanarajan put it, the Commonwealth was 'home to the world's largest source of illiteracy, under-education and under-provision for learning'. To meet these challenges the COL sought funding of Cdn$9,000,000 per year. It also created COL International in 1999 as a not-for-profit corporation to fund activities by fees-for-services under contract. The aim was to create 'a seamless canvas with respect to training; providing services, developing courses and programmes, training teachers, supporting and encouraging policy development, facilitating accreditation and credit transfer'.[11] In the tertiary sector, the Commonwealth executive masters' degrees in Business Administration and Public Administration continued, and a 'credit bank' to facilitate transfer of courses credit was started. The COL's distance education programme for legislative drafters jointly organised with the Secretariat was adopted by universities in the South Pacific and South Africa.

In spite of the financial crisis of the mid-1990s and the changing emphasis in the direction of very practical, vocational, and non-formal education, the original 'any learner anywhere' vision was not forgotten. The COL was, in reality, the Commonwealth's University for Co-operation in Distance Education and Open Learning. Both the vision, and the valuable services and institutional development deserve to be better known. Yet this 'invisibility' is something shared by all the Commonwealth's major IGOs.

*

The official Commonwealth, as we have seen in Chapter 13, has not been energetic enough in projecting itself. The Secretariat exists in its splendid premises hidden behind high walls, and the Secretaries-General have become public personalities in their own right, well recognised on the international stage. Marlborough House seems a bureaucratic mystery. The Foundation has so small a staff and such limited funds that it cannot expect a high profile. Thousands of voluntary organisation workers are grateful for their share of its meagre funds. Those concerned with the alleviation of poverty no doubt appreciate the recent disclosure of ordinary people's views of 'good governance', which may serve to temper the rising fashion for public-private partnership as a panacea. But by couching its argument in the concepts and language of 'civil society', the Foundation may be in danger of appearing an élitist and somewhat academic body. The COL probably suffers from its remoteness in the Pacific Northwest; from the rivalry of established distance learning institutions; and from the inherent difficulties of its brokerage role in an increasingly commercialised educational world. Thus, all the IGOs have their critics, and the member governments are reluctant to provide adequate funds. In such an atmosphere, the undoubted on-going expertise to be found in the IGOs gets forgotten. Their work deserves to be better known, more appreciated and more generously funded.

18
Outgrowing the Commonwealth – The Case of Cabi

The oldest and largest of the inter-governmental organisations was not listed, for the first time, along with the other leading IGOs, in the 1998 *Commonwealth Yearbook*. It appeared, but only within a list of some 130 organisations under the heading 'Commonwealth Network'. This list included IGOs, regional organisations, and certain international organisations that had their roots in the Commonwealth, but had later spread their wings more widely, like Sight-Savers International and the World Scout Movement.

The Commonwealth Agricultural Bureaux, began as a group of four research institutes and ten 'clearing houses' for research information covering the whole field of agricultural, veterinary, forestry and food production sciences. It changed its name in 1986 to CAB-International, later to CABI, pronounced 'Cabi'. It became a new type of international, not-for-profit inter-governmental organisation, open to all countries, based on treaty-level agreements with governments and self-financing from charges for its publications and services. This transition well illustrates the growing globalisation of many areas once handled 'in family' and also the restructuring brought on by the user pays, free market philosophy of the 1990s. However, the creation and growth of Cabi is instructive of how services could evolve from colonial mechanisms to provide some of those continuing benefits which enabled the Commonwealth to survive the crises of decolonisation.

The origins of Cabi went back to before the First World War. To coordinate research into West African insects 'helpful and inimical to man', the Colonial Office set up a research committee in 1910 with half the cost met by the British government and half by its West African colonial governments. The committee's scope was extended to all colonies by the 1911 Imperial Conference and in 1913 the Imperial

Bureau of Entomology was created. During the First World War, the need to protect food supplies led to concerns about fungi and plant diseases so in 1916 it was suggested that a Bureau of Mycology should be created and the two bodies be incorporated in an Imperial Bureau of Phytopathology. But instead, the 1918 Imperial War Conference recommended a separate Bureau of Mycology, which started at Kew in 1920. By the time of the 1926 Imperial Conference there were calls for new specialist bureaux and, after an Imperial Agricultural Research Conference discussed the matter in the following year, a series of 'clearing houses' for collating and disseminating research information was mooted, with costs to be shared by participating governments.

'The Scheme', as it was called, envisaged new bureaux for soil science, animal nutrition, animal health, animal genetics, plant genetics (herbage plants) plant genetics (other than herbage plants), and food production. Thus in 1929 the Imperial Agricultural Bureaux (IAB) became the umbrella organisation for all these institutions, with a headquarters at Farnham Royal. The old entomology and mycology bureaux were elevated to become research institutes (by virtue of their specimen identification and research roles, as distinct from the information 'clearing house' role of the bureaux). New bureaux for soil science and forestry were added in 1938 and agricultural economics in 1966. The biological control laboratory of the entomology institute went to Canada as the Imperial Parasite Service in 1940. It became the Bureau of Biological Control in 1947, and became the fourth institute in 1950. The overall name changed to Commonwealth Agricultural Bureaux (CAB) in 1948.

The original contributors to the IAB were England & Wales, Scotland, Northern Ireland, Canada, Australia, New Zealand, South Africa, the Irish Free State, Southern Rhodesia, India, and the Colonial Office representing the other colonies and protectorates. The ABC members (Australia, Britain and Canada) were – as always – the major contributors. Until 1972 government subscriptions were the chief source of income. Each member government sent nominees to the executive council. After the Second World War a system of quinquennial (later triennial) review conferences was evolved to bring the component parts of CAB and the member governments together to receive reports and set new aims.[1]

Membership gradually increased with decolonisation and the newly independent governments could be more critical than the old colonial governments. At the time of the Sherfield Committee's review of intergovernmental organisations in 1966, CAB had a staff of 338 and an annual income of £713,280. Ireland was an associate member. Duplication with the FAO or UNESCO was avoided. CAB's 18 abstracts journals and its identification services were used worldwide. Already 67 per cent of income from publications came from non-Commonwealth sources, mainly the United States and Western Europe. The Sherfield Committee was impressed by the CAB's efficiency and considered its role so specialised that it could not be usefully integrated into the Secretariat.

CAB, however, was not averse to using the good offices of the new Secretariat. Sir Thomas Scrivener, the Director, sought Arnold Smith's support to resolve a potential funding crisis. This stemmed from a decision by the 1965 CAB review conference to adopt the UN formula for calculating subscriptions, which adversely affected several members. The British subscription rose from 28 per cent of the total to 45 per cent and Canada, India and Pakistan also faced increases. The Indian subscription quadrupled. Canada reserved its position, but later accepted the increase. Britain pegged its subscription to 30 per cent of the total (as with the Secretariat) but made additional *ad hoc* grants. Pakistan continued to pay at the old rate and India held back £20,000. Malta decided to leave. Scrivener asked the Secretary-General to use his influence with the High Commissioners from defaulter countries on the grounds that if CAB had to reduce its services, this might be damaging for the Commonwealth. He said CAB was 'one of the few, perhaps the only Commonwealth organisation, that is genuinely international in the scope of its operations'.[2] He said it was the only comprehensive information service for agricultural sciences in the world and many people relied on it.

Twenty years later, at the 1985 review conference, the decision was made to go further and become a full international organisation open to non-Commonwealth countries since many were already using its services. From 1 January 1986 the organisation became CAB-International. Thus Fiji could remain a member when its Commonwealth membership lapsed in 1987. Ireland, Pakistan and Myanmar (former Commonwealth countries) could be members. In 1988 Hungary became the first non-English-speaking, or ex-empire, member. CAB-International also decided that income should be derived chiefly from fees for services and publications and there would be a phased reduction of membership subscriptions.

In 1990 CAB-International's services were grouped into three main areas. These were: (1) biosystematics – the long-established identification and classification services of the three original international Institutes of

Entomology, Mycology and Parasitology; (2) the Institute of Biological Control – for controlling pests and pathogens by environmentally friendly methods; and (3) dissemination of science-based information.[3] The last of these tasks was the work of the ten bureaux that retained their old names until the mid-1990s. Then, in 1996, all this work of the bureaux was grouped under a new, fifth institute, the Cabi Information Institute, sited at Wallingford, and known initially, as Cabi-II.[4]

As membership grew, from 29 countries in the mid-1980s to 40 in 1999, the newcomers included Chile, China, Colombia, Indonesia, Myanmar, the Philippines, South Africa and Vietnam. New Zealand, one of the founding members, pulled out in 1998 because government restructuring removed the old link organisation, which was never satisfactorily replaced. Subscription income, which was 21.7 per cent of total income in 1984, fell to 8.4 per cent in 1993, and to about 2 per cent in 1997. To emphasise its international nature and attract new members the new organisation endeavoured to present a corporate image, which involved some break with its former Commonwealth affiliation.

The reputation of CAB had become so well established that the idea of a completely new name was problematical. Reversion to IAB – as International Agricultural Bureaux – was, it seems, not attractive and CAB-International was chosen partly for tradition. While the corporate strategy adopted in 1990 suggested that the historical association with the Commonwealth was 'a strength that should not be discarded',[5] the 'Mission, Mandate, and Image' statement in 1993 had to admit that it had disadvantages.

> The identification of CAB INTERNATIONAL with the UK and the Commonwealth in the minds of many of those who know it imperfectly will remain a continuous source of concern, not least because in some cases it may deter membership or financial support. CAB INTERNATIONAL will take every opportunity to project itself as an international organization, which, while benefiting from its historical roots and continuing links with the Commonwealth, nowwelcomes all countries to membership.[6]

This truly international image was regarded as the key to future expansion. The simplified acronym was now spoken as a single word – Cabi – and at the same time a new logo was adopted rendering Cabi as simple, bold lower case initials making a roundel and surrounded by the legend 'International Centre for Agriculture and Biosciences'. A new mission statement declared that Cabi was 'dedicated to improving human welfare worldwide through the dissemination, application, and generation of scientific knowledge in support of sustainable development, with emphasis on agriculture, forestry, human health, and management of natural resources, and with particular attention to the needs of developing countries'.[7] Although now connected to the Commonwealth only by virtue of the fact that 80 per cent of its members were Commonwealth countries, Cabi had aims which paralleled many aspects of the Harare Declaration. To assist developing members who could not afford certain services a Partnership Facility was started in 1991 as a channel for development assistance. In this, the ABC countries were the first contributors.

Cabi became a self-financing, not-for-profit, organisation, which embraced comprehensively the new information and communications technology. BioNET-International began to make bioscience expertise available. *CAB Abstracts* and *Cabi Health* also produced databases available on CD-ROM. A *CAB Thesaurus* was published, and the Publication Division, via a marketing arrangement with Oxford University Press, became a major revenue earner. Cabi also ran training courses, 22 of which were offered in 1995. A British initiative led to Darwin Fellowships being made available tenable at the Cabi Institutes.

The corporate plan for 1998–2000 restated the mission in terms of a commitment to excellence as an international science publisher and provider of specialised services in information science, biosystematics, ecology and biological control. Cabi's organisational restructuring was completed in 1998 when the four institutes of Entomology, Biological Control, Mycology and Parasitology were brought under the aegis of CABI Bioscience and consolidated at two sites in Ascot and Egham. Overseas field stations were designated as Regional Bioscience Centres in Kenya, Pakistan, Malaysia, Trinidad, and Switzerland.

By the twentieth century's close Cabi consisted of three divisions. Priority was given to pest management in agriculture. CABI Bioscience was concerned with tackling a range of global challenges:

> raising agricultural productivity in sustainable systems; conserving and making better use of the world's vital biological resources; reducing habitat destruction and ecosystem deterioration; developing capabilities to tackle natural resource management challenges; and improving the livelihoods and well-being of the resource-poor in the developing world.[8]

CABI-Publishing had become a front-line activity. As well as new-format periodicals, it published over 50 book titles annually. An office was opened in New York in 1998 to serve its largest market. CABI Information was dedicated to the collection, organisation and dissemination of information in the fields of agriculture, forestry, natural resource management, and human nutrition and health. Operation of the Information for Development Programme, BioNET International, and numerous other databases were part of the mandate.

All of these activities represented contributions on the global science stage, but the main focus was on the same social aims as many of the Commonwealth agencies and NGOs. Commonwealth organisations like the Foundation, the CFTC, and some regional organisations participated in Cabi conferences as observers. After a decade of change, Cabi was well established as a separate global actor. Over the span of 80 years, a colonial pest identification service had grown to be a world leader in information science, scientific publishing and ecological health.

Part VI

People's Commonwealth – VIPPSOs

19
Professional Associations

In his final report as Secretary-General in 1999 Chief Anyaoku mentioned what he called the 'people's Commonwealth'. It was a dimension he had cherished throughout his term. His first review, in 1991, was not, he then said, 'just of inter-governmental cooperation, but of the whole Commonwealth'. In 1993, his appointment of an NGO Liaison Officer recognised the significance of 'the "people's Commonwealth" of non-governmental organisations'.[1] The liaison officer was describing his role in 2000 as working with the voluntary organisations that 'form an important part of what is called "the people's Commonwealth" ... an association of peoples linked by ties of friendship and mutual support'.[2]

The concept – even the appellation – was not new. As far back as 1920, Duncan Hall, in his seminal book, *The British Commonwealth of Nations*, provided an appendix on inter-imperial voluntary associations. In 1963, a fellow Australian, Lord Casey, called for an 'organised system of personal contacts'. In the following year the Royal Commonwealth Society (RCS) convened a seminar for nearly 40 organisations which sent a manifesto to Heads of Government reminding them that 'Far too little is known about existing links uniting the governments, the professions, the universities, commerce and industry throughout the Commonwealth.'[3]

The creation of the Commonwealth Foundation in 1966 was the first serious attempt to foster these linkages. The American political scientist Margaret Ball, in her valuable book *The 'Open' Commonwealth* (1971) admitted she found the voluntary network so extensive 'as to defy description'. Yet Professor Bruce Miller (another Australian) attempted in his 1974 'Chatham House Survey' to do justice to the Commonwealth 'as an assembly of peoples as well as an association between governments'.[4] The Dalhousie conference in 1976 recommended greater recognition for the practical value in 'the totality of non-governmental relations'. This was taken up cautiously in 1978 in the advisory committee report *From Governments to Grassroots*, which recommended NGO liaison desks in the Secretariat and in member foreign ministries – an idea not acted on for 15 years. Meanwhile the RCS again grasped the nettle with a paper in 1985 titled *Towards a People's Commonwealth* extolling 'a vast and so far not properly recognised body of people and expertise ... '.[5]

The concept finally came into its own in the 1990s. In Edinburgh there was the 'Commonwealth Centre' in the wings of the 1997 Chogm; two years later, in Durban, it was labelled 'Commonwealth People's Centre'. In 2000, Terence Dormer, the Secretariat Desk Officer for NGOs, noted that there were about 70 recognised pan-Commonwealth organisations and he provided a typology with examples:

- professional associations (Commonwealth Nurses Federation),
- charities (the Commonwealth societies for the blind and the deaf),
- campaigning groups (Commonwealth Human Rights Initiative),
- religious bodies (Commonwealth Jewish Council),
- youth organisations (Commonwealth Youth Exchange Council),
- health (Commonwealth Medical Association),
- education (Council for Education in the Commonwealth),
- academic institutions (Association of Commonwealth Universities),
- law (Commonwealth Lawyers Association),
- trade (Commonwealth Business Council),
- environment (Commonwealth Human Ecology Council),
- sport (Commonwealth Games Federation),
- Commonwealth friendship (The Royal Commonwealth Society),

He said these constituted an 'impressive bank of skills and goodwill'.[6]

Yet, it is worth asking how far there is a 'People's Commonwealth' as something tangible – an existence beyond the rhetoric? At the most obvious level, 'People's Commonwealth' is simply a label embracing non-governmental activities. It covers citizens' endeavours, voluntary organisations, sporting activities. A great deal has grown up. But how coherent is it? A glimpse at the scope and variety of the activities will be attempted in this and subsequent chapters, starting with the professional associations.

*

Administering a fund for increasing 'interchanges between Commonwealth organisations in professional fields' was the original mandate of the Commonwealth Foundation. To do this it would assist conference attendance and exchanges and promote new organisations. To avoid the risk of duplication, it was to assume no role in regard to cultural activities or the press. The one existing organisation singled out for the development of informal contacts was the Commonwealth Parliamentary Association (CPA). This was one of a trio of influential bodies that had evolved from empire organisations dating from before the 1914–18 war.

The earliest was the **Press Union (CPU)** founded in 1909 and, at one time, dubbed the 'Parliament of the Press'. An association of proprietors, publishers, editors and managers, the Union fought for press freedom, improved communications and high standards of journalism.[7] In 1979 the CPU executive met in Lusaka at the time of the Chogm and successfully urged the Secretary-General to support a proposal for a Commonwealth Media Exchange Fund. The CPU's corporate membership of over 500 is located in 47 countries, but is concentrated where the largest collection of newspapers can be found namely in Australia, Britain, Canada, India and New Zealand.

The **Parliamentary Association (CPA)**, founded in 1911, is a much larger body being made up of all members of legislatures. Beginning with Britain and the old Dominions, its membership expanded with the spread of decolonisation. The legislatures constitute the branches, with speakers and presiding officers as presidents and the clerks as secretaries.[8] The number of CPA branches far exceeds the membership of the Commonwealth, since the British off-shore islands are represented as well as the Westminster Parliament, and in federal states central and provincial legislatures are represented, as are the assemblies of certain dependencies. The Secretary-General of the CPA, Arthur Donahue of Nova Scotia, told the London Institute of Commonwealth Studies jubilee seminar in 1999 that, by the onset of the new century, there would be approximately 14,000 members in 142 branches. Recent newcomers ranged from small island territories, to states re-admitted after years of military rule, and new members of the Commonwealth. These were as diverse as Anguilla, Cameroon, Ghana, Mozambique, Seychelles, South Africa (with its nine provinces), Uganda and Fiji. He also included Pakistan (with its four provincial assemblies), which was suspended a few months later. The return of Nigeria later in 1999 meant reconstituting a federal branch and 36 state branches. New members also included the Scottish Parliament, the Welsh Assembly and the Legislative Assembly of the Indian Territory of Nunavut, in the Canadian far north.[9]

Annual conferences of the CPA mirror the Chogms in the issues they cover. Since 1981 the association has also held Parliamentary Conferences of Small States, a development in keeping with special attention given to this dimension in all Commonwealth endeavours. In common with many other associations, the CPA pays considerable attention to the professional development of its members by holding seminars on parliamentary procedure; the role of MPs; the role of the Opposition; managing the executive/legislature interface; the independence of the judiciary; and relationships with the media. As would be expected, the preoccupations at the end of the century were globalisation, information and communications technology, and civil society involvement in decision-making. The CPA increasingly interacts with other professional bodies and the Secretariat. Although in 1966 an Australian minister tried to prevent the first Secretary-General, Arnold Smith, from speaking, on the grounds that he was only supposed to be a post-boy and was not an MP, in subsequent years the Secretary-General has been invited to deliver major addresses at CPA conferences. Both Sonny Ramphal and Don McKinnon were familiar with the association having been members themselves in their capacities as MPs and ministers.

The third pre-1914 organisation is the **Association of Commonwealth Universities** (ACU) which began as the Empire Universities Bureau in 1913 following an inter-university conference in London. Starting with 53 member institutions, the membership expanded rapidly with the growth of higher education after the 1939–45 war. In 1998 there were 487 member institutions (463 of which were universities). India, with 104 institutions has the most members. Britain's members nearly doubled at a stroke in 1992 with the designation of polytechnics as universities. Hong Kong's four members opted to stay with the ACU after the reversion to Chinese sovereignty in 1997.

The role of the ACU – once called 'perhaps the most influential of all non-governmental bodies in the Commonwealth'[10] – is to assist members building up staff, contribute to mobility among staff and students, to disseminate information about higher education issues, and to host consultancy services in higher education management. From 1912 to 1993 the ACU held quinqennial congresses, but at the fifteenth Congress in Swansea it was recognised these gatherings had become so vast and costly that it was decided to hold two smaller conferences in each quinquennium. One would be attended only by executive heads; the other to include a second representative. The first of the new-style General Conferences was held in Ottawa in 1998 on the subject of 'Leadership and the Management of Change'. It listened to a witty and challenging address by Julius Nyerere, only just over a year before his death, in which he castigated the free market orthodoxy of the 1990s and what he called the 'dogmatic democracy' and 'dogmatic capitalism' being foisted on the poor majority of the world.[11]

The continuing work of the ACU involves providing services for member institutions. Staff recruiting is assisted by the advertisement of vacancies and, in some cases, interviewing of candidates. Student mobility is fostered by the Commonwealth Scholarship and Fellowship Plan (CSFP), which is administered in Britain by the ACU on contract to the government. It also administers certain other fellowships, and bursaries. It hosts the Commonwealth Higher Education Management Service (CHEMS) started in 1994, which provides consultancy services in management on a fee-charging basis. Not least of the benefits of membership are the ACU's publications. The *Commonwealth Universities Year Book* became so large at one point that it was produced in a box of four volumes. By 1999, it managed to compress a total of 2,200 pages in a two-volume format including additional information. As well as details of all the faculties and departments of member institutions, country by country, it included brief introductions to national tertiary policies, profiles of each member, national degree guidelines, admission procedures, awards and indications of research strengths. At the news level, the ACU's bulletin has five issues per year titled *ABCD – the a.c.u. bulletin of current documentation* giving up-to-date information on senior appointments, reviews of national tertiary developments, and includes opinion pieces about current issues. From a rather austere modified A5 format, it was transformed in time for reporting the first General Conference in 1998 into an A4-sized glossy magazine with more generous layout and, in 1999, adopted the *double entendre* subtitle: 'simply put, higher education matters'. In common with the Secretariat and other Commonwealth bodies, the ACU has given increasing attention to gender issues, with a women's programme to enhance the role of women in the institutional development of members.

The pre-1914 trio are well established and influential non-official bodies that work closely with the inter-governmental bodies. They were joined soon after the war by organisations for teacher exchange (1919) and forestry (1921).

*

A further trickle of professional organisations arose after the 1939–45 war starting with the Commonwealth Broadcasting Conference in

1945. Six networks – in Australia, Britain, Canada, India, New Zealand and South Africa – made up the conference (renamed Commonwealth Broadcasting Association from 1974). It grew with decolonisation and also began admitting self-governing territories. In the 1970s it joined with the Press Union and the journalists in the Media Exchange scheme. From the same period came the Commonwealth Engineering Conference, begun in 1946 with the same six members. The Commonwealth Engineers Council dates from 1975 and members grew in step with decolonisation. The Royal Agricultural Society of the Commonwealth, as a federation of national agricultural societies, was founded in 1957. Also in the 1950s organisations for the blind (1950) and the deaf (1959) were founded.

A virtual explosion in the professional organisations, however, began in the 1960s. The Foundation received its first application for support in 1966 from the Commonwealth Association of Architects (CAA), founded in the previous year. Support was also given to the Commonwealth Medical Association (CMA), which had started earlier in 1962, and marked a recognition in the medical profession of the changing political Commonwealth. There had long been powerful branches of the British Medical Association in the colonies and Dominions. In 1947 the BMA had created a Commonwealth Council to monitor contact with overseas branches. Thousands of doctors appeared in the Commonwealth List of the British Medical Register. But increasingly, national medical associations were created to represent doctors and the CMA membership was made up of these national associations.

*

Over the next 30 years some 40 new professional bodies were created, often with Foundation assistance. Some years saw three new bodies (see Table 19.1). The Foundation also gave support for the creation of 17 professional centres where groups of national associations could share premises for meetings, secretarial support and libraries. These, in turn, created their own organisation. The Commonwealth Association of Professional Centres (CAPC) was inaugurated in Canberra, Australia, in 1996.

These professional bodies, involving hundreds of thousands of qualified people around the Commonwealth, have many characteristics in common. Membership usually consists of national professional bodies. Most organisations have regional groupings, which hold regional seminars. They are governed by representative assemblies or councils; they have executive committees for continuity of decision-

Table 19.1 The growth in professional associations

Date	Acronym	Profession
		Imperial NGOs
1909	CPU	Press Union
1911	CPA	Parliamentary
1913	ACU	Universities
1919	LECT	Exchange Teachers
1921	CFA	Forestry
		Post-1945 NGOs
1945	CBA	Broadcasting
1946	CEC	Engineers
1946	CSC	Science Council
1950	RCSB	Blind – Sight-Savers International
1957	RASC	Royal Agricultural Society
1959	CSD	Deaf – Sound Seekers
		The New Associations
1962	CMA	Medical
1965	CAA	Architects
1966	ACLALS	Literature and Language Studies
1968	CLA	Lawyers
1968	CVA	Veterinary
1968	CGB	Geographic Bureau
1969	CASLE	Surveying and Land Economy
1969	CPA	Pharmacists
1969	CHEC	Human Ecology Council
1970	CMJA	Magistrates and Judges
1970	CCEAM	Education Administration and Management
1970	CYEC	Youth Exchanges
1971	CCPA	Postal Administration
1971	CLEA	Legal Education
1971	CAP	Planners
1972	COMLA	Librarians
1973	CNF	Nurses Federation
1974	CAM	Museums
1974	CASTME	Science, Technology and Maths Educators
1974	CLT	Linking Trust for Schools
1978	CJA	Journalists
1978	CASAS	Scientific Agricultural Societies
1978	CATA	Tax Administrators
1979	CTUC	Trade Union Council
1983	CLA	Lawyers
1983	CALC	Legislative Counsel

Table 19.1 **The growth in professional associations** *(continued)*

Date	Acronym	Profession
		The New Associations (contd)
1983	CAMHADD	Mental Handicap and Development Disabilities
1984	CAHE	Hansard Editors
1984	CAPGAN	Paediatric Gastroenterology and Nutrition
1984	ACARM	Archivists and Records Managers
1985	CAEJC	Education in Journalism and Communication
1985	CAEA	Education of Adults
1987	CAPL	Parliamentary Librarians
1987	CHRI	Human Rights Initiative
1988	CAD	Association for Development
1989	CHS	Historians
1991	CDA	Dentists
1993	CUSAC	University Study Abroad
1993	CAPAM	Public Administration and Management
1994	CLFG	Local Government Forum
1996	CAPSL	Public Sector Lawyers
1996	CAPC	Professional Centres
1998	CACG	Corporate Governance
1998	ACEAB	Examination and Accreditation
1999	CEJA	Environmental Journalists

making. They are managed by secretariats or bureaux, usually located in London, but a few notable cases are run from Commonwealth centres as diverse as Canada, Jamaica, India, Malaysia and New Zealand. They hold periodic congresses or conferences. They are valued for their publications – yearbooks, newsletters, membership directories, professional handbooks and a few scholarly journals. Some of them monitor standards of professional qualifications.

Some associations are well supported and influential, others struggle to make ends meet or even enunciate a clear mission. There was an attempt in the 1980s to coordinate their activities in an informal grouping called, initially, Commonwealth Professional Associations (CPAs) hosted by the lawyers' association. To avoid confusion with the parliamentarian CPA, they changed the name to Organisation of Commonwealth Associations (OCA) in 1989 when the hosting was transferred to the Royal Commonwealth Society. The CMA took them under its wing in 1997, but the group lapsed for want of a common goal.

*

In its strategic plan covering the opening of the new century, the Commonwealth Foundation undertook to review its support for the pan-Commonwealth professional associations and to continue its grants where appropriate. It was particularly concerned that professional bodies should be assisted to attend Commonwealth ministerial meetings, and collaborate with professional associations in similar fields, with the Secretariat and with NGOs in other civil society categories. The message, then, was that to have real impact, the professional bodies should collaborate and focus their efforts particularly in the pursuit of Commonwealth values such as good governance. In this respect three important developments deserve comment. They concern human rights, parliamentary supremacy and HIV/AIDS.

One of the most notable of the collaborative professional groupings is the **Commonwealth Human Rights Initiative** (CHRI). It was formed in 1987 by five pan-Commonwealth organisations – the Journalists Association (CJA), the Trades Union Council (CTUC), the Lawyers Association (CLA), the Legal Education Association (CLEA) and the Medical Association (CMA). Each was concerned to protect the welfare and rights of its members and had an interest in promoting human rights generally. They were later joined by the Parliamentary Association (CPA) and the Press Union (CPU) and in 1993 transferred the headquarters to New Delhi, in the most populous member country.

In 1989 they appointed an advisory group to report on how the Commonwealth could contribute to human rights. For the Harare Chogm in 1991 their first 232-page report, *Put Our World to Rights*, was signed by the group's convenor, Flora MacDonald, a former Canadian External Affairs Minister. The report accorded great importance to the role of NGOs. 'The Commonwealth would be meaningless if it were just a Governmental Club; it is the Commonwealth of Nations, and this means ultimately the Commonwealth of People.' It called on individuals, communities, the voluntary sector and governments to 'make human rights more than a slogan, much more than a battle-ground, but a reality'.[12] It called for a Commonwealth human rights declaration, for member governments to adopt implementation procedures and provide education in the matter; that there should be a commission to study the causes of ethnic violence and that a human rights fund should be established. **Member governments that violated the**

principles should be denied aid. A standing commission on Human Rights was advocated with machinery for investigation and adjudication. CHRI called on the Secretariat to strengthen its Human Rights Unit; for the CFTC and the COL to foster human rights education; and for professional associations and the other NGOs to adopt human rights codes. CHRI's study paralleled the work of an Inter-governmental Working Group of Experts on Human Rights, who were responsible for a section of the 1991 Communiqué and the Harare Declaration's generalised pledge to protect 'fundamental human rights' including equal opportunities.

For the 1993 Chogm a further Advisory Commission chaired by Dr Kamal Hossain, former Foreign Affairs Minister of Bangladesh, produced a report *Act Right Now* which welcomed the Harare Declaration but called for a move from rhetoric to reality. CHRI called again for an independent Commonwealth body to investigate violations of human rights and a Commonwealth Action Plan for Human Rights. Moving from human rights in general, CHRI began to focus on regional and national problems. A workshop held in New Delhi in 1994 on 'Police, Prisons, and Human Rights' focused on violations of the rights of prisoners in the four South Asian member states.

Before the Auckland Chogm in 1995 the chief concern was the military dictatorship in Nigeria, where the presidential elections of 1993 (which followed nine years of military rule) had been annulled. The winning Social Democratic candidate, Chief Moshood Abiola, had been subsequently imprisoned, along with some 40 leaders including the former Head of State, Olusegum Obasanjo. Prior to the Chogm CHRI sent a fact-finding mission to Nigeria and published its findings in *Nigeria: Stolen by Generals*. CHRI called on the Commonwealth to give leadership on Nigeria, which was in clear breach of the Harare Declaration. It argued that '25 years of military rule in Nigeria have shown how, in the absence of a democracy, in a country rich in talents and resources, the whole framework of human rights gets subverted, and how development itself becomes a casualty'.[13] In the event, Auckland became a turning point. Summary executions, at the very moment the Chogm opened left Heads of Government with no alternative. **Nigeria was suspended.** The Millbrook Action Programme went some way to meeting CHRI's call for enforcement mechanisms. The C-Mag became the Commonwealth's watchdog in the matter of violations of Harare principles.

In 1999, CHRI held a 'Dialogue on Indigenous Rights' which led to the creation of the Commonwealth Association of Indigenous Peoples

(CAIP), which had a stand at the People's Centre in Durban. In the run-up to Durban, CHRI turned to the problem of the proliferation of small arms and the spread of violence. A report entitled *Over a Barrel*, signed by Margaret Reynolds (a former Australian Senator from Queensland), called for a Commonwealth Consensus on Light Weapons; it called on the C-Mag to take responsibility for the human rights agenda and for a Commonwealth High Commissioner for Human Rights. The Durban Chogm, however, could not agree on a new mandate for the C-Mag and also looked to further efficiencies in the Secretariat that affected its Human Rights Unit. Anxious that the C-Mag's powers might not be sufficiently enhanced and that the Human Rights Unit would lose staff, CHRI began the new century with a report *Rights Must Come First*, pleading, again, for a stand-alone Human Rights Unit within the Secretariat.[14]

In its endeavours CHRI has received funding from the Foundation, from the Canadian International Development Agency and the Ford Foundation. The University of London Institute of Commonwealth Studies hosted CHRI's Trust Fund Office. The Secretariat has been cooperative with documentation. The CHRI reports are always well referenced. CHRI is nevertheless critical of the reluctance of governments to grapple with human rights abuses. For more than a decade it has demonstrated the way professional organisations, while remaining loyal and cooperative to inter-governmental bodies and to the political Commonwealth, can be severely critical and can perform the role of educator of public opinion and goad of governments.

While CHRI has taken on the role of a watchdog on behalf of human rights, a second professional grouping came together in 1998 to draw up guidelines on relations between the Executive, Parliament and the Judiciary for fulfilling the values of the Harare Declaration. Fifty representatives from 20 countries were sponsored by the Commonwealth associations of Lawyers (CLA), Legal Education (CLEA), Magistrates and Judges (CMJA) and Parliamentarians (CPA), supported by the Secretariat, the Foundation and the FCO. Meeting at Latimer House in Buckinghamshire, 15–19 June 1998, they drew up guidelines for meeting the principles of good governance, human rights and the rule of law. The '**Latimer House Guidelines**', as they are termed, enjoined responsibility and restraint in the exercise of power. The supremacy of Parliament in law-making was affirmed. Judges interpret legislation, but must not usurp Parliament's power to make it. The judiciary's independence was essential; appointments to the bench being made on merit and a culture of judicial education striven for. The freedom of speech within, and the independence of, Parliament, embodied in the British Bill of Rights of 1689, was reaffirmed. There was a call for more gender balance and an enhancement of the role of women in political parties. The accountability of the Executive to Parliament was restated along with the importance of Public Accounts Committees, Ombudsmen, Human Rights Commissions and Access to Information Commissioners. The colloquium also produced a draft statement on Freedom of Expression, re-emphasising the importance of a free press.[15]

The third group of professionals – this time in the health field – combined at the 1999 Chogm to highlight the Commonwealth's most urgent problem – the devastating impact of the HIV/AIDS epidemic. Statistics assembled by the International AIDS Vaccine Initiative (IAVI), indicate the disproportionate extent of the crisis for the Commonwealth. Containing about 30 per cent of the world's population, Commonwealth countries account for 60 per cent of global AIDS infections. In sub-Sahara Africa it was estimated in 1997 that over 14,000,000 people were infected and in one country there were 1,500 new infections *daily*. Southern Africa was particularly affected, with life expectancy falling from 60 to 40. Elsewhere, Tanzania expected that 27,000 teachers would die of AIDS by 2020; Kenya expected a 15 per cent fall in GDP because of the effects on the workforce; Uganda spent 79 per cent of its health budget on AIDS treatment. India, with the highest number of HIV-infected people in the world, estimated that 20,000,000 would be infected at the start of the twenty-first century.

To highlight the problem and make a submission to the Chogm in Durban, the ACU and the CMA combined with the University of Natal and six other health professionals' organisations. These were the Commonwealth associations concerned with Mental Handicap and Developmental Disabilities (CAMHADD), Paediatric Gastroenterology and Nutrition (CAPGAN), Dentists (CDA), Nurses (CNF), Social Workers (COSW) and Pharmacists (CPA). The university and health professionals committed themselves to integrating HIV/AIDS work into all their operations. They called for much more effort towards educational campaigns to change behaviour in order to stop the spread of infection and enable infected people to work productively and avoid too much social collapse. It also called for new efforts in care for those infected; for appropriate and affordable drugs; and research on the development of affordable vaccines.[16] The Durban meetings praised the initiative of the British government, which announced a £14,000,000 grant for vaccine research. IAVI announced vaccine development partnerships to deal with regional virus types.

The ACU, BMA and health professionals' coalition 'implored' Heads of Government to take a lead and call for a global state of emergency on HIV/AIDS. The Durban Communiqué records agreement that the AIDS epidemic 'constituted a Global Emergency' and Heads of Government pledged themselves to lead the fight in their own countries. They urged governments, international agencies and the private sector to give priority to preventative measures, vaccines and affordable drugs.[17] In this way the academic and health professionals brought their unmatched professional authority to bear on an urgent issue. Representative, as it is, of the countries worst afflicted by the epidemic, the Commonwealth is an appropriate organisation to give a lead. At the same time, this professional group used its advocacy and practical expertise to highlight the needs of the disabled and disadvantaged in a manner akin to the philanthropic role of many other NGOs which are the subject of the next chapter.

20
Philanthropic Organisations

After concentrating for over a decade on fostering professional inter-changes, the Foundation was given a vastly enlarged mandate in 1980. From being a charity in law, it became an international organisation with eight areas of interest. The list – food production, health, education, social welfare, science and technology, culture, the media, and public administration – was a dauntingly comprehensive one. After nearly two decades of fulfilling this role, the Foundation, in its report for 1996–9, had refined its mission down to support for three general areas: 1) NGOs, 2) professional associations, and 3) cultural activities. Priority for its grants was given to South/South cooperation, poverty eradication and sustainable development.

Central to this refinement of role in relation to the voluntary sector stands the 1995 study by Ball and Dunn, *Non-Governmental Organisations: Guidelines for Good Policy and Practice*. Written in the context of the explosion of voluntary organisations during the previous 20 years and the ease of air travel, which made pan-Commonwealth organisations possible, the *Guidelines* brought, for the first time, some clarity to this burgeoning area. It was estimated that in Britain there were 500,000 organisations with a combined turnover of some £17 billion. Canada had 2,000 environmental organisations alone. In India there were 100,000 organisations. The *Guidelines* placed this movement, first of all, in an historical context that revealed a circular evolutionary cycle. From the charitable and philanthropic organisations in the first industrialised economies that pioneered welfare provision (and which, in colonies, were for many years the sole providers of health and education), there had grown organisations to advocate public action and reform. Gradually, governments were alerted to needs, built welfare bureaucracies and created expectations that there would be public service delivery of welfare. From the 1960s, however, increasing disillusionment about the newly entrenched 'welfare state' arose over such concepts as dependency traps, and there was growing dislike of bureaucratic power and discretion. There was also advance from the concept of 'care and welfare' to one of 'change and development' – to **'working with people, rather than institutionally doing unto them'.**[1] With the economic crises of the 1970s induced by the oil price hikes, and the marginalisation of many groups by the globalised economy of the 1980s and 1990s, governments found themselves constrained in their powers of action. At the same time, a new breed of voluntary organisations arose concerned about environmental threats, globalisation and marginalisation, human rights, gender and AIDS. With the almost universal triumph of free market economics, governments attempted to confine themselves to policy-making, leaving service delivery to others. In this climate huge areas of welfare and development came to rely, once again, on private enterprise, voluntary initiative or charity.

Most usefully, the *Guidelines* defined, first of all, the multifarious varieties of voluntary organisation. Their sole unifying characteristic is that they are not part of government – hence the unsatisfactory label 'NGO'. They are voluntary, independent, not-for-profit and not self-serving. Their prime role is to **'improve the circumstances and prospects of disadvantaged people'.**[2] Many professional associations and inter-governmental organisations do the same, but that was not their original *raison d'être*. Having reached this definition, the *Guidelines* made detailed recommendations over the management, transparency, ethics and accountability of the voluntary bodies working in the broadly philanthropic area.

If the *Guidelines'* spectrum – running from the 'care and welfare' tradition to the 'change and development' phase – is taken as a framework, a few examples may be given of how pan-Commonwealth organisations fulfil the various roles. These were defined as: 1) service delivery, 2) mobilising resources, 3) research and innovation, 4) human resource development, and 5) public information, education and advocacy.[3]

Long-established examples of **charities providing 'service delivery'** are those that assist the blind and deaf. Sight-Savers International began as the Royal Commonwealth Society for the Blind in 1950. It arose from the Royal National Institute for the Blind in Britain working along with the British and Commonwealth governments. Concentrating its work in 20 developing countries, Sight-Savers

International works to prevent and cure blindness and provide rehabilitation for the incurably blind. Nearly 4,000,000 people have been
cured and 35,000,000 treated. Sound Seekers – the Commonwealth
Society for the Deaf – dates from 1959. It works in developing countries, especially among children, to assist in the prevention and treatment of deafness and in providing audiology equipment and training.
Equipment and hearing aids are supplied to schools. An appeal for the
provision of Land Rover field ambulances fitted with audiology equipment for Africa was launched in 1997 with Nelson Mandela as president.[4]

An interesting example of the second category – an association for
'mobilising resources' – is provided by the Commonwealth Countries'
League (CCL), the pioneer pan-Commonwealth women's organisation.
It was also the first voluntary organisation to adopt the label
'Commonwealth' in its title. Founded back in 1925 and arising from
the Women's suffrage movement and the quest for women's input in
international affairs, it evolved in recent times into an organisation to
provide funds to enable young women to stay at school in their own
countries.

Originally the League was a wide-ranging women's rights movement
which was influenced by the pioneering success in winning the right
to vote by women in New Zealand and Australia. In London, representatives of the suffrage movements from these Dominions, who urged
the need for a union of empire suffragist movements, succeeded in creating the British Dominions Suffrage Union in 1914. It later became
the British Overseas Committee of the International Women's Suffrage
Alliance, but in 1924 it was felt that a separate organisation should be
re-established. Thus at an inaugural meeting in 1925 representatives of
women's organisations from Australia, Bermuda, Britain, Canada,
India, New Zealand and South Africa met to form the British
Commonwealth Women's Equality League – a title amended to simply
British Commonwealth League. Its aim was 'To Secure Equality of
Liberties, Status, and Opportunities between Men and Women in the
British Commonwealth of Nations'.[5]

Each year the League's annual conference considered a comprehensive range of legal, moral and international issues. First on the agenda
were voting rights, citizenship and legal inequalities. These were followed by the question of getting women's voices heard at the Imperial
Conferences and at the League of Nations. Economic issues such as
women in industry and the professions and equal pay were discussed,
as were the problems of Aboriginal women, equal moral standards,

health, education, motherhood and, increasingly, problems of war and peace. After a period of suspension during the Second World War, the League revived in 1947 and changed its name to Commonwealth Countries League in 1964. With many of its original issues either met or taken up by other pressure groups, the League moved into specialising in women's education and evolved into a fund-raising body for this purpose.[6] Its suffrage origins were symbolised, however, in 1993 – the centenary of the first achievement of the female franchise in a Commonwealth country (indeed in any nation state) – by its election as Vice-President of Christina, Lady McCombs, daughter-in-law of New Zealand's first woman MP.

In the third category, one of the **organisations for 'research and innovation'** is the Commonwealth Council for Educational Administration and Management (CCEAM) formed in 1970 at Armidale, New South Wales, as the Council for Educational Administration. The Council grew in response to the development of the study of educational leadership as an academic discipline in an age when educational restructuring was placing ever-growing demands on leaders. To reflect some of these new demands, 'management' was added to its title in 1996. Its objectives are to foster linkages with national associations and debate and disseminate knowledge about research into educational leadership and to foster high standards of management. International conferences are held on a quadrennial basis. The 1996 conference in Kuala Lumpur on 'Indigenous Perspectives in Education Management' examined the implications of indigenous theories and practice for education administrators generally.

CCEAM is one of the handful of decentralised voluntary organisations. After having its office in Armidale, Australia, it shifted it to England with a new president located first at Luton University and then the School of Management at the University of Humberside and Lincolnshire in Lincoln. Its professional journal *International Studies in Educational Administration* switched its editorial office in 1999 from the University of Tasmania to the University of Hong Kong – another example of Hong Kong keeping non-official linkages with the Commonwealth. In 1998 its newsletter was converted into the glossy magazine *Managing Education Matters*, which combines general Commonwealth issues with news of national associations. The importance of the research role was highlighted in 1999 by the president, Angela Thody, after its sponsor the Commonwealth Foundation, asked for a report on how it had been able to improve the life of people in developing countries. She commented:

We write books, we read books, we teach people who teach others to read ... we produce articles for journals and edit Newsletters and share ideas at conferences ... None of this 'hands on', visible impact stuff. We don't go out and build schools for communities that don't have them. We don't pay children's school fees. We don't even worry too much at globalisation, rain forests, ecological disasters.

But, she pleaded, 'don't dismiss our efforts ... We're a multiplier organ- isation ... We're ideas people ... So we'll keep on writing our books and the papers and keep on exchanging opinions.' She referred to some practical cases where innovations could be seen at work around the Commonwealth and invited observers to ask 'whose idea was it?'[7] For the 2000 conference in Hobart, Tasmania, CCEAM joined the rest of the Commonwealth in tackling 'The Global Challenge'.

Another organisation which had its genesis in Australia is the Commonwealth Association for Local Action and Economic Development (COMMACT). Sporting the Gandhian motto 'Think Global, Act Local', COMMACT falls within the *Guidelines'* fourth cate- gory of a '**human resource development**' body and is another of the voluntary organisations to maintain its headquarters outside Britain. The idea arose in 1987 when half a dozen people from the ABC countries – Australia, Britain, Canada – involved in the fields of unemployment, job creation and local development had a evening discussion in York, Western Australia. They considered the possibility (already raised by the Director of the Foundation, Inoke Faletau) for a conference of local economic development practitioners from both developed and developing countries. With assistance from the Foundation, the Government of Western Australia, and some 20 private and public sponsors, the first of a series of 'Working for Common Wealth' Conferences (WCW1) was held at Goa, India, in September 1988. Both in the organisation of the conference and the approach to local develop- ment the group broke new ground. There was 'a gradual transition from structure to flexibility', so that participants in the conference could have input as to how their time would be best spent. Similarly, the general philosophy was: 'Organisers have to let go'. Projects needed to involve those who were supposed to benefit. 'If people don't have ownership, they do not develop responsibility and realise their potential.'[8]

The rapporteur of the Goa gathering was Colin Ball, later to co- author the NGO *Guidelines* and, in 2000, to become the Director of the Foundation. At Goa he regretted the appellation NGO or voluntary agency as hangovers from the days of 'charity and institutionalised forms of care and welfare'. He coined the label Local Development Organisation (LDO), the principles of which were: an **integrated** approach to social and economic development, **empowering** of people rather than setting up services or activities by 'imperialist professionals or outsiders however well-meaning', and playing roles that were **supportive, facilitative and catalytic**. 'The LDO creates opportunities, space, choices; it makes it possible for things to happen, rather than creating the "happenings" itself.'[9]

The Goa Conference produced a declaration on 'Working for Common Wealth' which might be taken as a manifesto for the new-style philanthropic organisation which would increasingly become the aspiration of the greater part of the People's Commonwealth. In the pursuit of excellence, efficiency and achievement in development it was recognised that:

- We must ensure that in our quest for efficiency, it is not at the expense and alienation of the disadvantaged.
- The pursuit of excellence must not result in someone's gain being someone's loss.
- Good economic development should aim to enhance social, ecological and environmental conditions.[10]

A committee was set up to draft a constitution embodying this philosophy. A permanent secretariat was established in Kuala Lumpur, Malaysia, in 1989.

The constitution of COMMACT was developed at the WCW2 conference in Christchurch, New Zealand, in 1990. Representatives of the association then attended the inaugural NGO Forum in Harare in 1991. In common with virtually all voluntary organisations, COMMACT developed regional arrangements. By the end of the 1990s, as all sectors in the Commonwealth became preoccupied with tempering the adverse effects of globalisation, COMMACT's philosophy of local action well accorded with the desires of ordinary people as expressed in the *Civil Society* report.

The fifth category enumerated in the *Guidelines* was voluntary bodies devoted to '**public information, education and advocacy**'. In this area an organisation which endeavours to fulfil all three of these roles is the Council for Education in the Commonwealth (CEC). Formed in 1959 at the time of the first Commonwealth Education Conference, the CEC applied for charitable status in Britain in 1999. It started as a parliamentary discussion group and meets in the Houses of Parliament in

Westminster. The purpose is to provide a forum where members of both Houses and other interested people may exchange views and it offers a platform for experts to air educational issues. The Council's comparatively small membership is mainly made up of parliamentarians, but includes other interested individual and corporate members. Close relations are maintained with the FCO, the British Council, the BBC, the ACU and the Commonwealth Secretariat. As well as holding meetings, conferences and workshops, the Council makes submissions to ministries, parliamentary committees, Commonwealth Education Conferences, and it sponsors parliamentary questions. In 1995 and 1997 Secretary-General Anyaoku was invited to report to CEC after the Chogms.

At the time of the FAC enquiry into the 'Future of the Commonwealth' in 1995–6, the CEC's submission regretted that successive British governments had been 'so careless of Commonwealth sentiment and Commonwealth infrastructure'. It stressed the need for education and training to have a higher profile in Commonwealth cooperation. It deplored recent changes in the administration of the scholarships scheme. It concluded: 'We visualise the Commonwealth of the future as being in essence itself a "Commonwealth of learning", an international community for sharing experiences and ideas, transferring technologies for the common benefit, and learning to appreciate the values and cultures of other societies.'[11] Consistent with this vision of the Commonwealth, the CEC made another submission to the FAC in 1999 in response to the announcement that British aid to developing countries would be focused on poverty alleviation in fulfilment of the 1997 Chogm pledge.

While welcoming the poverty elimination focus in general, the CEC argued that British relations with member countries went wider than aid donation; that concentration on the poor could damage cooperation and dialogue with the most creative classes. Broad areas of educational, scientific and cultural cooperation should not be allowed to suffer. If scholarships for training in Britain were reduced because they were deemed to be not cost-effective in poverty alleviation, this might mean that such training would become the privilege only of the wealthy élite that could afford it. Focus on basic education should not be at the expense of secondary and higher education. Funds devoted to poverty alleviation channelled through the British Department For International Development (DfID) should not mean starving FCO scholarships, the British Council and the BBC World Service. Any appearance of a 'new neo-colonialism' should be avoided.

Professor Peter Williams, executive vice-chairman of CEC, posed the question in an article titled 'Can we avoid a poverty-focused aid programme impoverishing North–South relations?'. He pointed to the danger of institutionalising status differences between countries – division into those treated as equals, with which 'we cooperate' and those who are not equals and which 'we assist'. If, under the scholarships plan, students from Australia and Canada are funded by the FCO while those from India and South Africa come under the DfID, the impression is given that Britain 'cooperates' with some countries and 'assists' others. Taken to its logical conclusion, the poverty alleviation focus could divide the Commonwealth into 'co-operable' and 'assistable' elements and create a new form of apartheid. Instead, Professor Williams argued, it should be recognised that the mission should be not just to eliminate poverty (which none would gainsay) but to develop broad-based relations including alliance-forging activity and cultural diplomacy.[12]

Another advocacy organisation, with an integrated approach somewhat akin to COMMACT's, is the Commonwealth Human Ecology Council (CHEC), one of the most persistent of the expert pressure groups. CHEC came into being in 1969 to argue for an inter-disciplinary approach to improving quality of life. It was the work of an enthusiastic New Zealander, Zena Daysh, who, while working in Britain in the Second World War, had made studies for the Ministry of Supply concerned with the connexion between punctuality and worker health, which, in turn, could not be separated from malnutrition, housing and the work environment. After the war, pilot studies of the concept of human ecology – the relation of the individual, society and the environment – were conducted in Malta culminating in the first CHEC conference there in 1970.

Mrs Daysh argues that the Commonwealth with its cross-cultural, multi-regional span, is an ideal type of association for pursuing CHEC's philosophy. She wrote that: 'Human ecology is an integrating concept whose holistic, inclusive approach has been applied successfully at scales from villages to multi-million cities and is now guiding development. The key to human ecology is valuing the individual and nature equally.'[13] In association with the UN Centre for Human Settlement (Habitat), CHEC organised a pre-Chogm conference in Edinburgh in 1997 also bringing together a group styled the 'Built-Environment Professionals in the Commonwealth'. These included architects, engineers, planners and surveyors. In Edinburgh they petitioned the Heads of Government to implement the UN's 'Habitat Agenda' – a blueprint of sustainable urban development that highlights poor shelter as the biggest contributor to poverty. In 1998 Secretary-General Anyaoku asked CHEC to coordinate a Commonwealth Consultative Group on Human Settlement (CCGHS). CHEC also cooperated with the Commonwealth Business Council over private sector involvement in the commitment to 'Adequate Shelter for All' to ensure 'a holistic approach to shelter provision incorporating secure tenure, primary health care, education, and youth programmes ... '.[14]

Further examples of voluntary organisations for public information, education, and advocacy are discussed in the next chapter.

21
Educational and Cultural Endeavours

Pious invocations of the importance of education are frequent in Commonwealth conclaves, but education has not generally been given a high priority. Yet educational cooperation and dissemination of knowledge about the association remain vital elements of the People's Commonwealth. It is true that some of the longest-established institutions in the Vippso world have broad educational purposes, but there has rarely been any systematic educational endeavour. Instead, there has been a lot of enthusiastic, but disparate, activity. It does, however, warrant discussion since education is one of the areas where the intergovernmental organisations – Secretariat, Foundation and COL – increasingly interact with the People's Commonwealth.

The provision of schools in colonies was usually pioneered by missionary societies rather than governments. The first generation of nationalist leaders in the New Commonwealth were often educated in British colleges and universities. Professional practitioners sought British qualifications. Thus education gave rise to widespread linkages at the personal level. The first attempt to create a Commonwealth-wide scheme arose from Canadian Prime Minister Diefenbaker's enthusiasm during the post-Suez period. At the Commonwealth Economic Conference in Montreal in 1958 there were calls for a scholarship scheme. This was taken up at the first Commonwealth Education Conference held in Oxford in July 1959, by delegates from ten independent countries, plus the Central African Federation, and representatives from 16 colonies or groups of colonies.[1]

The Oxford Conference had four outcomes. First, the Commonwealth Scholarship and Fellowship Plan (CSFP) was approved whereby up to 1,000 scholarships would be made available annually on a bilateral basis. Britain agreed to provide half; Canada offered 250, and India and

Australia 100 each. The plan was based on 'mutual co-operation and sharing of educational experience among all the countries of the Commonwealth'. By 1995, over 28,000 awards had been made and from the recipients some 30 vice-chancellors or principals had emerged.[2] Second, there was a realisation of urgent needs in teacher training, teacher supply, technical training and interchanges among scientists and technicians. Third, an administrative infrastructure was created in London to implement the conference's recommendations. This involved the creation of the Commonwealth Education Liaison Committee with its secretariat – the Commonwealth Education Liaison Unit. Both were housed, along with the ACU, in Marlborough House, which became the Commonwealth Centre at this time, the by-product of another recommendation of the Montreal Economic Conference. Fourth, the Council for Education in the Commonwealth [CEC] (discussed in the previous chapter) was created at Westminster as a forum for discussion among members of both houses of Parliament and other interested parties.

Soon after its creation in 1965 the Secretariat absorbed the Commonwealth Education Liaison Committee and the Liaison Unit as its Education Division. The Commonwealth Foundation, in fostering professional linkages from 1966, assisted new pan-Commonwealth associations concerned with literature and language studies; education administration; legal education; science, technology and maths education; journalism and communications education; and adult education. After the 1980 restructuring, a wide mandate for fostering education, community development, women, youth, science, technology and culture was adopted. In the tertiary education sector the ACU is one of the oldest professional bodies; the COL the newest IGO, and various scholarship schemes have provided continuous linkages. The Symons Report on Commonwealth Studies in 1996 arose from the Secretary-General's initiative following the Education Ministers' Conference in 1994. In spite of the spotty nature of Commonwealth educational and cultural endeavours, then, they provide material of rich interest, some of the variety and flavour of which is depicted below.

*

Education about the Commonwealth may be considered first. The two oldest organisations for fostering knowledge about the Commonwealth – the Royal Commonwealth Society and the Commonwealth Institute – both went through crises in the 1990s. The former closed its club premises for six years and operated from temporary offices in New Zealand House. The latter – for long the only permanent Commonwealth exhibition in Britain – closed its galleries. However, both, along with the Commonwealth as a whole, enjoyed a renaissance at the end of the century that left them better fitted to fulfil their educational and social roles.

The Royal Commonwealth Society (RCS) originated in 1868 as a response to the worst crisis in relations between Britain and the self-governing colonies. Variously titled Royal Colonial Institute and Royal Empire Society, it became the Royal Commonwealth Society in 1958. A grand and dignified building, designed by Sir Herbert Baker and opened in 1936, stood on Northumberland Avenue, close to Trafalgar Square and the offices of several Dominion High Commissions. It provided a meeting place, residential club facilities and a library that became a major research base for postgraduate students, interested scholars and aficionados. Many of the building's interior furnishings were in fine Commonwealth timbers. Numerous distinguished British and Dominions citizens were members and officers. Prize essays and a monograph series led to publications by distinguished scholars. Some of the seminal meetings in the growth of the 'People's Commonwealth' were convened by the RCS, and it was the first formally to publicise that title and concept.

As the empire that gave birth to the RCS reached its dénouement in face of rapid decolonisation, the Society mirrored the ambiguities of attitude that characterised the rest of Britain between the 1960s and 1980s. Its club premises, which had been seriously damaged by bombs in 1941, were increasingly expensive to maintain by the ageing and declining membership. The imperial grandeur of the club appeared dated, especially the cavernously impressive cloakrooms and lavatories. A Society that, on the one hand, was adapting imaginatively in its educational work to the challenges of the post-imperial Commonwealth, was, on the other hand, increasingly hampered by financial constraints imposed by maintaining its premises.

Concluding a centennial history in 1968, Trevor Reese suggested that the Society's contribution in the post-imperial age might be to focus on the library as the premier international Commonwealth research centre.[3] However, management consultants, brought in during the 1980s, targeted the library as a liability. Taking up 13 per cent of the building space and 24 per cent of the Society's costs, it was, they suggested, hard to justify. They said it was a 'tired inert collection ... a piece of history ... a dead thing'.[4] Would disposing of the library with its ongoing cost solve the financial problem? The basic problem was that the Society had major assets – the centrally located freehold premises, and the historic library – but inadequate income.

It was decided to redevelop the building in association with the Victoria League, for which it had for some time provided office accommodation. The Victoria League for Commonwealth Friendship had been founded in 1901 to foster friendship and arrange hospitality for colonial visitors. It had 55 branches worldwide. It ran a 60-bed students hostel in London, 'Victoria League House'. It formed a charity, in association with the FCO and the British Council in 1980, called 'Hosting for Overseas Students' (HOST) to arrange contacts with British families.

On 1 January 1989 the RCS and the League joined together to create The Commonwealth Trust. In association with a developer, the Trust planned to rebuild behind the fine Baker façade, as an office block, within which a thoroughly modern 'Commonwealth House' would be revived as an educational and social centre. The library would be retained, with a reading room containing a reference collection of about 20,000 volumes and the balance of the materials stored off-site, available by a call system. Income from the redevelopment would secure the Trust's finances and charitable work.

The collapse of the London property boom in the early 1990s scuppered this plan after considerable expense had been incurred in consultants' fees and feasibility studies. The Trust was left with an overdraft of £3,000,000 and the banks pressing for settlement. Therefore, the decision was taken in May 1991 to sell the moveable portion of the assets – the library. If a benefactor could be found to match its value – put at £2,800,000 – it might be possible to keep it together in London. If not, it would have to be sold piecemeal. Eager buyers began to make enquiries. The premises closed at the end of 1991 and some of the library collection was packed in boxes to go for auction.

Then, over the next two years a remarkable rescue operation was mounted. Representatives of Cambridge University met with the Director of the Trust, Sir David Thorne, to discuss how the collection could be maintained as a national asset, preferably in London, but in the last resort, at Cambridge. A letter to *The Independent* by Jan Morris, author of *Pax Britannica,* the most popular multi-volume history of Empire/Commonwealth, excited considerable media interest. This was fed by exploitation of the Library's visual collection – the 'royalty and dead tigers' motif becoming a major drawcard. An influential fundraising committee volunteered its services, with Prince Charles as patron. The overseas branches of the RCS made collections. By May 1993 the committee was able to hand over a cheque for £3,000,000 to pay off the banks. In July–August 1993 the collections were transferred to the Cambridge University Library, into a newly erected stack area, where it became the library's largest special collection.[5]

Meanwhile, under the vigorous leadership of General Thorne, the Commonwealth Trust worked to secure its future. The merger ended with the Victoria League, which was concerned to secure the integrity of its own hostel property. Commonwealth Trust was disbanded and the old name Royal Commonwealth Society (which had been retained by some overseas branches) was resumed in 1996. In fulfilling the function of the British NGO Liaison Unit (or Clu), the Society was extremely active in the run-up to the Edinburgh Chogm. It persuaded the British government to designate 1997 as the 'Year of the Commonwealth'. It also helped to organise the first NGO 'Commonwealth Centre' in the wings of the Chogm. This was done in association with the Scottish Council for Voluntary Organisations, the Commonwealth Foundation and the FCO. From late 1996 the RCS convened planning meetings with the numerous NGOs that participated. It also published a colourful up-to-date booklet by Richard Bourne on *Britain in the Commonwealth.*

A new partner was found to develop the Northumberland Avenue site as a 186-suite apartment hotel and premises for a new 'Commonwealth Club'. The new logo, of entwined strands of green, red, orange and blue, symbolised vibrancy and the members of the Commonwealth entwined in friendship, was also adopted for the Chogm décor in Edinburgh. This colour scheme also suffused the Club's furnishings. The new Club facilities – with airy dining room, bars, function rooms, relaxation areas and private meeting spaces – was opened at the time of the Commonwealth Day observance in 1997. The first function was a lunch for a London meeting of the C-Mag. Formal opening was by the Queen in June 1998. Discounted rates for the adjacent Orion Apartments were available for members.[6] A new membership drive; hirings by corporate clients for functions; a variety of prominent Commonwealth speakers; and cultural evenings, secured more stable income and continuance of the RCS's charitable and educational work. The library remained open to members and outside scholars, who could travel to Cambridge. In these ways the RCS re-established itself as a premier forum for discussion about the Commonwealth.

*

In the original charter of the Royal Colonial Institute a museum had been envisaged as well as the club facilities and library. The museum function, however, was left to the Imperial Institute founded as part of Queen Victoria's Golden Jubilee in 1887 and following the Colonial and Indian Exhibition of the previous year. Opening its doors in 1893, in an impressive French Renaissance-style building, with three towers, in South Kensington, the Institute was designed to foster science, trade and industry within the Empire. It built up a large permanent exhibition of colonial products and raw materials, concentrating on minerals and scientific and technical information. The British government undertook financial responsibility from 1899. Between the wars, the Institute reached out to schools and had an innovative part in the development of film documentaries. After the 1939–45 war, however, its exhibits seemed dated. A review in 1950 suggested shifting the focus from 'products to people'. Also, the site was needed for university expansion, thus the splendid, if somewhat impractical, buildings were razed to the ground except for the central tower.[7]

By Act of Parliament in 1958 it was reconstituted as the **Commonwealth Institute**, funded by the British government, and charged with projecting the Commonwealth in Britain. It re-opened in 1962 at the corner of Holland Park, fronting Kensington High Street, in a strikingly modern building, whose hyperbolic, paraboloid roof enclosed the largest single covered public space in London until the Millennium Dome of the 1990s. In the multi-tiered exhibition galleries Commonwealth countries mounted permanent exhibits. The library was built up, with particular attention to Commonwealth literatures. The premises were available for conferences and meetings. Perhaps the Institute's most valued role was as the leading resource centre for schools on Commonwealth matters. Information packs were available, visiting lecturers were sent out and school parties welcomed. The Institute was host to Commonwealth arts and cultural events and gave support to the nearby cultural carnivals. Student essay contests were organised and a number of Student Chogms arranged around Britain, where communiqués (usually anticipating those of the Heads of Government) were forwarded to the full Chogms. Prize-winning students were even taken in to observe a Chogm executive session – something no NGO or media representative was able to do![8] A regional centre was opened in Bradford and an autonomous Scottish Institute was organised in Edinburgh. In its centennial year, 1993, the Commonwealth Institute's mission was described as: 'to increase throughout Britain, knowledge and understanding of the Commonwealth, its nations and peoples and the principles upon which it is based and to further educational and cultural co-operation and understanding within the Commonwealth'.[9] The centennial celebrations included a visit by the Queen.

There hovered, however, a major shadow over the future. From the mid-1980s restructuring of Whitehall pointed to funding cuts. The Institute, as a non-departmental body under FCO oversight, was costing £2,500,000 per year of public money. There were hints that the Institute's support for boisterous cultural festivals was subversive of the quiet of the neighbourhood. The building, listed for its architectural merit, had been economically built and was in need of structural attention. The exhibition galleries were dated and losing their appeal. A review in 1993 reported that the Institute did a worthwhile educational job consistent with government policy, but the FCO decided that it could not find the extra funds for refurbishment and upgrading and announced that the grant would cease in 1996. Through the second half of the 1990s, the Institute's future was in doubt. Those who believed the FCO wanted to close it, fought to preserve the uniquely valuable schools' service. The FCO certainly wished to terminate its responsibility for funding, but gave a stay of execution. It agreed to continue funding the library and educational services – to pay £2,700,000 for 1995–6; £1,000,000 in 1996–7, but to end grants by 1999/2000. It was for the Institute and its advocates to make economies and seek private sponsors or alternative sources of income.

There were drastic staff cuts (from 96 to 27). The Director's salary was funded for a time from an outside source. The Scottish Institute and Bradford branch were closed, as were the Kensington exhibition galleries. The role as conference and events centre was promoted as a major income earner. The Foreign Affairs Committee, in its 'Future Role of the Commonwealth' report, insisted that there must be no proposal for closure without a debate in Parliament.[10] New exhibits were planned. In May 1997 'The Commonwealth Experience', with interactive exhibits was opened, but did not last a year.

Finally, at the Durban Chogm on 13 November 1999, the Foreign Secretary, Robin Cook, announced a permanent settlement. The Institute was made an independent, pan-Commonwealth agency for 'promoting and celebrating' the Commonwealth through programmes in education, arts and culture, business and public affairs. An £8,000,000 final grant was made to ensure full restoration of the 1960s landmark building. Otherwise the Institute was to be self-funding from the income of the conference and function centre, charges for admission and sponsorships.

In the prospectus for 2000 the priorities were stated as the development of a multi-media resource and training centre for schools; the development of the conference and events centre in association with the Commonwealth Business Council; the refurbishing of the building as an up-to-date centre for visual and performing arts, and becoming a provider of internet services. A start was made in April 2000 with 'eCommonwealth', connecting 10,000 Commonwealth websites. Don McKinnon, the Secretary-General, said this gave the Commonwealth 'a virtual meeting place where individuals, communities and business can come together'. Like the RCS, the Institute entered the new century better fitted to promote interest in the Commonwealth and with the independence to do this in innovative ways.[11]

*

While the newly autonomous Institute projected and celebrated the contemporary Commonwealth, the historic heritage was preserved and presented more permanently by the new **British Empire & Commonwealth Museum** opened in Bristol in 2000. As the port from which John Cabot sailed to the New World in 1497, Bristol has claims to be regarded as Britain's birthplace of empire. Five hundred years later, the museum opened its first temporary exhibits, while work proceeded in restoring the building to house it, fund raising, and assembling the collections. The Museum Trust started in 1986. Distinguished patrons included former Secretary-General Ramphal and ex-Australian Prime Minister Malcolm Fraser, and the Board of Trustees included Jan Morris and Sir David Thorne of the RCS.

The Museum is housed in Brunel's original Temple Meads Railway Station, built between 1839 and 1847 – the oldest remaining purpose-built railway terminus in the world, including a splendid space provided by the train shed with its hammer-beam roof, sporting the largest single wooden span ever built in Europe. Exhibits depict the rise, development and legacy of empire. The library received collections of parliamentary papers from the former Colonial and Foreign Offices, the archives of the Crown Agents, and the National Railway Museum's archive of empire railway expansion. Rich varieties of film, video and photograph collections were acquired, and an oral history project began to record the memories of hundreds of people who had served the Empire/Commonwealth. Annual lectures started in 1996. Jan Morris explained the purpose of the Museum as to exhibit for post-imperial generations 'this astonishing phenomenon – neither to justify it nor to condemn it, but to present it dispassionately in all the diversity of its merits and its failings'.[12]

Also to serve schools and young people there gradually gathered a clutch of voluntary bodies, to constitute an informal educational secretariat in '**Commonwealth House**', **Lion Yard, Clapham**, the headquarters, since 1989, of the League for the Exchange of Commonwealth Teachers (LECT). Originating in 1901 as the 'League of the Empire' for organising correspondence between schoolchildren and arranging hospitality for Dominion teachers in Britain, LECT began teacher exchanges between the ABC countries in 1919. The name changed to 'League of the British Commonwealth and Empire' in 1949 and to the current name in 1963. Teacher exchanges between Britain and the Dominions expanded, from the 1960s, to include exchanges with the newly independent countries. As LECT approached its centennial, a total of over 17,000 exchanges had been arranged. During the 1990s, between 700 and 800 teachers would be involved in exchanges with 20 countries in some years. One returned exchangee commented: 'It should be made compulsory for all teachers in their 40s!'[13]

A different type of exchange – this time of educational materials – is organised by the Commonwealth Linking Trust (CLT) which also operates from 'Commonwealth House'. Founded originally as the 'Commonwealth Youth Movement Affiliation Scheme' in 1974, the Trust became a charity to arrange links between schools for sharing ideas and educational aids and for promoting interest among pupils in other parts of the Commonwealth. More than 3,000 schools in 40 countries have been put in touch with each other by the Trust. In the words of Jill Dilks, who chaired CLT for 25 years: 'We in the ... Trust want to bring the concept of the Commonwealth alive in the minds of the young ...'[14]

The third, more recent, co-tenant in 'Commonwealth House' is the Commonwealth Youth Exchange Council (CYEC) which dates from 1968. The initial meetings were held at the RCS and the Council was launched at a large meeting there in 1970 of representatives from Local Education Authorities, British Ministries and Commonwealth High Commissions. The chairman, Professor David Dilks, described the purpose as to 'bring into harmony the resources of government, the expertise of voluntary organisations and the enthusiasm of individuals'.[15] The British government made some funds available through the British Council, and the Rhodes Trust made a grant. Group visits of people aged between 16 and 25 have to be planned round some common interest and visits can be for between ten days and ten months. The participants organise the visits themselves and raise 70 per cent of the funds. CYEC grants are to kick-start the exchange and are less than £5,000. As one British youth officer put it: 'The exchanges are really helping young people to live in a diminishing world.'[16] CYEC puts youth groups in touch with each other, helps organise exchanges and arranges forums for participants to share their experiences afterwards. Over 30,000 people from 40 countries have engaged in these exchanges. In preparation for the first 'Commonwealth Youth Forum' in 1997, CYEC, along with the Scottish Community Education Council, facilitated prior visits with British youth organisations for the Commonwealth youth delegates. The Forum was attended by delegations from 46 independent countries and ten dependencies and the communiqué was sent to Heads of Government.

A fourth co-tenant joined 'Commonwealth House' in 1999 when LECT undertook the administrative services of CEC – the parliamentary educational forum discussed above – which transferred its administrative base from Westminster to Clapham.

*

Some of the same voluntary impulses that lay behind the educational NGOs had a role in formulating the Secretariat's move towards a youth programme. After British Prime Minister Harold Wilson in 1969 suggested Commonwealth cooperation to deal with the needs of out-of-school youth, David Dilks, as well as organising CYEC, put some ideas to Arnold Smith, who consulted regional forums in 1969–70 and proposed a scheme for a joint youth programme to the 1971 Chogm. The proposal was discussed by a meeting of ministers responsible for youth affairs at Lusaka in 1973. **The Commonwealth Youth Programme** (CYP) was launched in 1974 with separate funding based on voluntary contributions from member states. The focus in the first decade was building up regional Youth Centres for the training of leaders. Residential diploma courses on 'Youth and Development' were offered at Georgetown in Guyana, Lusaka in Zambia, Chandigarh in India, and Suva in Fiji (later transferred to Honiara in the Solomons). Oversight was provided by a Commonwealth Youth Affairs Council meeting biennially, with a Committee of Management for more regular control. After a review in 1990 called for greater youth involvement, a 'Youth Caucus' was called at the time of Council meetings. The Secretariat focused in the early 1990s on youth employment, young women's role in development, health issues, literacy and youth policy. In his review of ecosoc activities in 1995, Professor Toye singled out the CYP as 'the clearest case of those reviewed in which the Commonwealth enjoys an absolute advantage'.[17] With its separate funding and four regional centres the CYP had few competitors.

From 1992 the CYP was reviewed on a regular basis by triennial Youth Ministers' Meetings. The 1995 meeting urged member countries to formulate national youth policies by the end of the decade. For this the CYP developed a technical assistance package called 'NYP2000 Tool Kit'. As well as policy formulation, the meeting called for more focus on Youth Empowerment and Human Resource Development. To meet the latter need the regional diploma courses were widened to include diplomas available by distance learning through cooperation with the COL and a number of tertiary institutions. The CYP also developed a Commonwealth Youth Credit Initiative (CYCI) to assist budding entrepreneurs. This was tested in regional pilot projects based in the four CYP centres.

Youth Empowerment, however, proved to be a more contentious issue. The project for a 'Commonwealth Plan of Action for Youth Empowerment to the Year 2005' met reservations at the third meeting of Youth Ministers in 1998. In some traditional societies, where wisdom was equated with age, the whole concept of empowerment required caution. There were calls for cultural sensitivity. Gender awareness, too, had its paradoxical aspects. A Caribbean delegate pointed out that in their region girls dominated at secondary school and university, while males 'dominated in prisons, street gangs, drug users, and other fora of under-achievers'. This was supported by a New Zealand delegate who spoke of young men featuring prominently in educational failure, youth suicide, road accidents and drug abuse.[18] It was, therefore, emphasised that there must be equal gender empowerment. In some regions there were particular problems in rehabilitating former 'child soldiers'.

By the end of the century, Youth Ministers' Meetings were attended by over 30 ministers, were addressed by the Secretary-General and included participation by the Foundation, the COL and the Committee on Co-operation Through Sport, whose representative always alerted delegates to the unique value of sport in attracting the enthusiasm of young people.

*

While the promotional and youth aspects of Commonwealth educational endeavours were reviewed and revised in the 1990s, the scrutineer's spotlight was also turned on higher education. Here was the oldest area of Commonwealth educational cooperation, the ACU being one of the oldest NGOs. Many of the political leaders who had become the founding fathers of the new nations had been educated in British universities or colonial institutions established on British models.

New efforts for cooperation were made after the Second World War by the Inter-University Council for Higher Education Overseas founded in 1946. Support for existing universities in Hong Kong, Malaya, Malta and Sudan was organised and new institutions were founded in Botswana, Ghana, Lesotho, Nigeria, Uganda, Rhodesia, Swaziland and the West Indies initially as University Colleges in special relation to the University of London.[19] These 'Oxbridges in the bush' all became autonomous national institutions and the committee was wound up in 1970.

After decolonisation, universities proliferated in many countries and membership of the ACU burgeoned. For its fiftieth anniversary in 1963 Sir Eric Ashby, in *Community of Universities*, suggested that the 'four substantial assets' in the balance sheets of British colonialism were Christianity, representative government, educational institutions and the English language. He believed that 'the most universally accepted and the least changed by the indigenous cultural environment were the educational institutions'. But he concluded: 'If we allow this society to lose its cohesion it will disintegrate, and if it disintegrates we shall have lost one of the most powerful forces uniting the countries of the Commonwealth; for Commonwealth leadership is largely in the hands of its graduates ... '[20] Nearly 40 years later, the ACU remained to grapple with the problems of a vastly increased membership. University institutions – often quite different from the Oxbridge model attempted in the university colleges of the 1950s – proliferated. These, however, were designed to produce the professional, business and technical élites for their developing nations and they often paid little attention to the Commonwealth as an association. The same was true for most of the new universities of the old Dominions and Britain.

Increasingly aware of the yawning generation gap in knowledge and experience of the Commonwealth, the Education Ministers' Meeting at Islamabad in 1994 endorsed the Secretary-General's suggestion that a commission should report on the subject of '**Commonwealth Studies**' in tertiary institutions. The findings of this commission, chaired by Professor Tom Symons, of Trent University, Ontario, were presented in draft to the 1995 Chogm and published in June 1996. They were as alarming as Derek Ingram's contemporaneous report on the Commonwealth's information services. The stark conclusion was clear: 'Present levels of awareness and understanding of the Commonwealth can only be described as truly appalling.'[21] There were no full degrees in the subject, only optional courses within subjects. The most common frameworks of study were in history and literature, the former mainly in the guise of 'imperial history' and the latter as 'post-colonial literatures'. Such studies, in the view of the Commission, paid insufficient attention to contemporary developments and failed to do justice to the Commonwealth as a 'truly polycentric association'.

In spite of these pessimistic conclusions, the report, *Learning From Each Other,* made a strong plea for action. 'What has struck us most forcefully is the extraordinary and unprecedented opportunity that exists today for Commonwealth countries to learn from the rich experience of their Commonwealth partners in many fields.' It provided a working definition of Commonwealth Studies: 'They concern inter-relationships between and among Commonwealth countries (including their collective institutional endeavours) and comparative study of their experiences.'[22] Arguments in favour of the academic study of the Commonwealth included: understanding the evolution of the Commonwealth as background to the history of each member; as a context for the study of parliamentary institutions; as a convenient frame for comparative studies; to assist decision-making by revealing ranges of options; and service to the global community as an example of a multilateral association operating by consensus.

In its 43 practical proposals the commission did not espouse grandiose or expensive remedies. Among many ideas, it pointed to ways of building on existing arrangements. Some scholarships might be targeted towards Commonwealth Studies. Universities should produce handbooks indicating what Commonwealth-related courses and study facilities were on offer. An Association for Commonwealth Studies should be formed. The Secretariat should deposit its publications with tertiary institutions. A new *Survey of Commonwealth Affairs* should be commissioned as successor to the influential 'Chatham House Surveys' of W. K. Hancock, N. Mansergh and J. D. B. Miller. The COL offered many possibilities and might also create a 'bulletin board' for Commonwealth Studies. The most urgent recommendation was that there should be focus on school-level study of the Commonwealth. Perhaps the most surprising idea was that attention to the 'cultural Commonwealth' might be facilitated by a foundation, fund or arts council to mark the Millennium or the Queen's Golden Jubilee.[23]

The Symons Commission had discovered much high quality study and research going on, but remarked on its 'invisibility and latency'. It found that Commonwealth studies were largely confined to Britain, and there to the 'Golden triangle' of Cambridge–London–Oxford, all three of which had professors in the subject.

Oxford had, in the past, played a notable part in the evolution of Commonwealth idealism as represented by the Beit Professors and Beit Lecturers of Commonwealth History, who included some of the most notable advocates of the old 'Commonwealth of Nations'.[24] There was also the Rhodes House Library and the Rhodes Scholarships. However, the Oxford Institute of Commonwealth Studies, which had existed from 1947 to 1982, came to an end when its programmes were merged to form the Centre for International and Development studies. Commonwealth advocacy gave way in the 1960s to more dispassionate scholarship, exemplified, in the 1990s, by the five-volume multi-authored *Oxford History of the British Empire*. Of the works' 125 contributors (affiliated to institutions in 11 countries) 60 per cent had research degrees from the golden triangle – 31 at Oxford and 22 each at Cambridge and London.[25]

Cambridge responded quickly to the Symons Report by producing in 1997 *The Cambridge Compendium of Commonwealth Studies* edited by Bill Kirkman, who ran courses for Commonwealth Press Fellows at Wolfson College. Teaching and research in many fields connected with the Commonwealth were tabulated in convenient form. Cambridge has the Smuts Memorial Fund, the Smuts Professorship and Readership and also the Vere Harmsworth Professorship. Scholarships are awarded by the Cambridge Commonwealth Trust, established in 1982 in response to the Thatcher government's imposition of a cost-recovery fee regime for overseas students. Associated trusts were set up in a number of Commonwealth countries: more than 100 jointly funded schemes were created and, after a decade, some 700 Commonwealth scholars were in residence at the university. As the university's representatives told the FAC, this was three-and-a-half times the number of Rhodes Scholars at Oxford.[26] To cater for the inrush, the Cambridge Commonwealth Society was established. The Cambridge University Library provided the new home for the Royal Commonwealth Society Library. In 1995 the Malaysian-funded Commonwealth Policy Studies Centre was established, not as part of the university, but linked to it. The University also has centres for South Asian and African Studies.

In London there is the Rhodes Professor at King's College and a Professor of Imperial and Commonwealth History at the Institute of Commonwealth Studies (ICS) – the only postgraduate centre in the field. Celebrating its fiftieth anniversary in 1999 – also marked by the Secretariat as the jubilee of the modern Commonwealth – the ICS was founded in 1949 under the directorship of Sir Keith Hancock, the distinguished Australian historian. The Institute maintains the best specialist library on the Commonwealth; awards research fellowships, and runs a comprehensive seminar programme for MA and PhD students. In 1994 it became a research institute in the University of London's School of Advanced Studies. Between 1982 and 1999 it was also host to the 'Sir Robert Menzies Centre for Australian Studies' endowed by the Australian Government. Relocated in 1999 to Kings College, the Menzies Centre retains its seminar links with the ICS. The inaugural meeting of an Association for Commonwealth Studies was called by the ICS in 1998. For its fiftieth anniversary the Institute hosted a conference on 'Cultures of Democracy', which was addressed by, among many others, outgoing Secretary-General Anyaoku and former Secretary-General Ramphal. A new venture, in the same year, was the creation within the ICS of a 'Commonwealth Policy Studies Unit', which facilitated discussion on the first draft of the Foreign Policy Centre's *Re-inventing* paper. Headed by Richard Bourne, the Unit embarked on studies of the role of universities in socio-economic development and civil oversight of security services.[27]

Lying at the interstices of the golden triangle, the Vippso world, and the official and business Commonwealths is a unique institution – the **King George VI and Queen Elizabeth Foundation of St. Catherine's at Cumberland Lodge**. It was the brainchild of South African-educated Amy Buller, a graduate of Birkbeck College, who, as an annual visitor to Germany between the wars, had been horrified by the rise of Nazism. Especially perturbed by the spectre of graduates from ancient German universities uncritically accepting the fascist doctrine, and fearful that a similar phenomenon might afflict Britain, she conceived the idea of a residential college where students, teachers and experts could discuss issues in a relaxed and dispassionate atmosphere. Although the outbreak of war in 1939 postponed her scheme, the book she wrote of her 1930s experiences, *Darkness over Germany*, attracted the interest of the Queen. When invited to Buckingham Palace in 1944, Amy Buller explained her idea to the King and Queen, who, in 1947, granted Cumberland Lodge in Windsor Great Park to found such a residential study centre.

Over the years thousands of students, mainly from London University, but also members of non-governmental organisations like the RCS and the ICS, have gathered for short conferences at Cumberland Lodge. Special emphasis is given to the Commonwealth, the theme of an annual conference since 1987. Many of the current problems of the Commonwealth – the British government's lack of interest; the role of the NGO networks; higher education cooperation;

the IT revolution; the generation gap; the role of business – have been aired by influential panels of the Commonwealth *cognoscenti*. The Cumberland Lodge conferences had a major role in the rediscovery of the Commonwealth in Britain in the 1990s. It was at the 1995 conference on 'The Commonwealth into the 21st Century' that (as Prunella Scarlett told the FAC) the young leaders present were 'appalled by their own lack of knowledge ...'.[28]

Outside the golden triangle, the content of Commonwealth Studies was usually subsumed within national histories or area studies. Centres for Commonwealth Studies existed at Exeter and Stirling and at Liège; Nottingham hosts the Cust Memorial Lectures; Commonwealth literatures were more widely represented.

The biggest surprise from the Symons Commission was the suggestion of a cultural foundation or arts council, since, in a small way, such bodies already exist. The Commonwealth Institute has long been a centre for arts and cultural festivals. The Commonwealth Foundation promotes arts and culture as a significant part of its mandate. The RCS intersperses cultural events with its political-discussion meetings.

The Foundation's funds are, however, extremely limited and are largely devoted to three types of competition. First are the writer's prizes – one for best book and another for best first book. Prizes are awarded, first, in four regional competitions and, then, in an overall Commonwealth competition. Second, there is a short story competition, the winning entries from which are broadcast on the BBC World Service. Third, there are Arts and Crafts Awards, which provide ten annual travel and study grants. Another way the Foundation promotes Commonwealth understanding is through a Fellowship Scheme which brings a dozen selected professionals to visit London and other Commonwealth centres. It also runs an induction course for London or Europe-based Commonwealth diplomats.[29] In 1998 an annual Commonwealth Lecture was inaugurated – the first given by Professor Amartya Sen, the Nobel Prize-winning economist and Master of Trinity College, Cambridge. The 1999 lecture was by former Australian Prime Minister Malcolm Fraser and that for 2000 was by Kofi Annan, the Ghanaian Secretary-General of the United Nations.

The Foundation also gives financial support to the Arts and Cultural Festivals at the time of the Commonwealth Games. Here, the arts gain considerable profile and exposure by their association with the Commonwealth's most popular event.

22
Sport and the Commonwealth Games

'The future of the Commonwealth will not rest on economic factors alone. It is vitally important for the continual relevance and strength of the association that the meaning and spirit of Commonwealth reaches the grassroots, particularly young people. Sport can serve the Commonwealth well in this regard, becoming a first point of information about the Commonwealth for young people.'[1] These evangelistic words from the 1993 report by the Chogm Committee on Co-operation Through Sport (CCCS) highlight the significance of the Commonwealth's most popular activities.

We have seen how knowledge about the Commonwealth is found by many commentators to be abysmally low – confined mainly to a few political leaders and some professional Vippso élites. Even among university graduates the level of information is poor because the Commonwealth hardly figures in today's curricula. There is, however, one great popular occasion when the Commonwealth hits the news, fills television screens day after day for over a week, and generates excitement and passion among people of all ages and that is **the Commonwealth Games**. In the four-year interval between the Games, passions are undoubtedly kindled by other international sporting contests, especially the Olympic Games, and the great soccer, cricket and rugby fixtures. In the last two, Commonwealth members provide most of the leading practitioners and most of the winners. But only the Games are an *exclusively* Commonwealth occasion; **indeed, the Games are often the only point of popular identification with the Commonwealth for most of its peoples.**

One billion people, out of the 1.7 billion total population of the Commonwealth, are under the age of 16. A first priority for the Sports Committee was finding ways to connect with these young people and help them develop their potential. Sport, by its universality and popularity, attracts, inspires and motivates. Sports heroes become role models. 'Sport and physical activity', say the CCCS, 'are among the best ways of empowering young people – of building self-confidence, self-respect, and, most importantly, the conviction that they can make a difference in their own lives and the lives of others.'[2] The playing field is seen as important as the classroom in forging value systems and codes of conduct.

Many of the popular team sports that excite interest and passion around the world were codified in industrial Britain during the nineteenth century. In place of 'folk football', which was a traditional ritualised brand of inter-village warfare in rural England, a football game was codified with rules at Cambridge University and largely became the basis of the game played by the Football Association founded in 1863. 'Soccer' remained a kick-and-dribble game. Other versions of football, which allowed handling and running with the ball, developed and another code of rules was drawn up at Rugby School in 1845. The Rugby Football Union was formed in 1871. In the north of England, where working men needed payment to compensate for loss of wages while playing, a separate game (permitting such 'professionalism') came under the Rugby League in the 1890s. While football games were variously codified in this way, stick-and-ball games were also systematised. Cricket, which had developed in the eighteenth century, established a county championship in 1873. Some cricket clubs played hockey (using a cricket ball) as a winter sport and the Hockey Association was founded in 1886. All these and other games were spread around the Empire by soldiers, missionaries, administrators, teachers and traders – partly for their own recreation, partly to spread British cultural values. Soon the colonial pupils were out-matching their imperial tutors.[3]

Sports emerged, indeed, as powerful elements in the rise of nationalism and they played an important part in the growing national identities of the Dominions, later of other dependencies. Cricket was the great game in Australia, the West Indies and India. In rugby football the South African Springboks, the New Zealand All Blacks and Australian Wallabies became the leaders. For many years India or Pakistan were the Olympic hockey champions. In recent times, Pakistan, Sri Lanka and Zimbabwe have entered the cricketing limelight, and Fiji, Tonga and Samoa have produced very formidable rugby players.

These games call for teamwork and loyalty, obedience to the rules, respect for umpires and referees; they are meant to foster strength, agility, courage in adversity, magnanimity in victory, sportsmanship and sportswomanship. The ethics and argot of sport has enriched the English language with many moralising slogans. There are the positive injunctions like 'play the game', 'toe the line', 'play to the rules', 'fair play', 'up with the play', 'on the ball', 'go in to bat', 'hit for six', 'pull together', 'may the best man win', 'crack the whip' and that recent cliché, the 'level playing field'. There are also the pejoratives like 'caught out', 'off side', 'out for a duck', 'throw in the towel', 'foul play', 'bowled out' and the ultimately devastating – 'it's not cricket'!

Unlike the great imperial team sports of cricket and rugby, which became established in the nineteenth century, the Commonwealth Games – focusing originally around individual events in track, field and swimming – did not start until 1930. Ideas for a Pan-Britannic Contest mooted in the 1890s were overtaken by the modern Olympic movement, the founder of which, Baron Coubertin, had been inspired by the British games revolution. But in the Olympic Games the medal winners tended to be Americans. Ideas about fielding a British Empire joint team to match the Americans came to nothing. In the 1920s, special United States versus the British Empire events, following the Olympics, still saw higher American medal tallies. Thus, largely to have a contest without American competitors, the first British Empire Games were held in Hamilton, Ontario, in 1930. The British Empire Games Federation was founded in 1932 and four-yearly contests, between Olympics, were commenced. There were Empire Games in 1934 and 1938 and then an interval of 12 years because of the Second World War before the next Games in 1950. In 1954 the name changed to British Empire and Commonwealth Games. As the first of the series to be televised, these Vancouver Games attracted world-wide attention, and had the added attraction of the 'mile-of-the-century' race between Roger Bannister (England) and John Landy (Australia), both of whom had recently broken the four-minute mile barrier.

With the growth of air travel, the acceleration of decolonisation and a wider spread of sporting expertise, the Games got bigger and more events were added to the core track, field and swimming events. At Swansea in 1958, a peak of relative sporting success was reached when ten world records fell. For these Games the Queen inaugurated the baton relay. At Christchurch, New Zealand, in 1974 it was agreed that the title should become simply Commonwealth Games. By now, African sporting prowess was in evidence, especially from Kenyan long-distance runners. But the Games also reflected the tensions within the Commonwealth especially in respect of racial discrimination.[4]

Sporting boycotts began to be used as a stick to combat South Africa's apartheid. Thus countries or individuals who played with South Africa gave rise to controversies. The South Africa tour by New Zealand's All Blacks in 1976 led to an almost complete African boycott of the Montreal Olympics in that year. Mrs Thatcher's attitude to sanctions against South Africa, as well as the activities of a few South African athletes, led to so many pull-outs from the 1986 Edinburgh Games that, in the end, more countries boycotted them than competed. At the same time the question of the uneven spread of sporting facilities, medal winning and even the hosting of the Games excited political comment. The venue for the XVth Games in 1994 was up for decision at a Commonwealth Games Federation (CGF) meeting during the Seoul Olympics in 1988. At that date, all the Games had been held in Australia, Britain, Canada or New Zealand, except once at Kingston, Jamaica in 1966.

In bidding for New Delhi as the next venue, India's Minister of Sport asked: 'Are you permanently going to keep us in Asia and Africa away from the pride and pleasure of hosting the Games for the Commonwealth family ... are we permanently going to be guests at the table of the affluent, ... Do we not have the right to participate as equal members of the Commonwealth family?'[5] The choice went to Victoria, BC. The Canadian government was, however, so worried about the implications of this debate, and about a growing shadow over the future arising from the sheer expense of mounting the Games, that in 1986, they proposed that the future of the Games should be discussed by the Heads of Government. Thus, the Kuala Lumpur Chogm in 1989 requested the Secretary-General to form a Working Party made up of sports administrators, governments and the Games Federation to consider the problems raised by the Canadians.[6] Ramphal chose Roy McMurtry, a former Canadian High Commissioner in London, and then Associate Chief Justice of Ontario, to convene the group, with Anne Hillmer, of the Canadian Olympic Association, as Executive Secretary. This group reported to the SOM in 1990 and to the Harare Chogm in 1991, where it was constituted the 'Chogm Committee on Co-operation Through Sport' as a 'forum for consultation and co-ordination' for a period of four years.[7] After eloquent reports from the CCCS, largely drafted by Anne Hillmer, in 1993, 1995, 1997 and 1999, Heads of Government renewed its mandate for another four years in Durban.

The CCCS, with representatives from Australia, Barbados, Britain, Hong Kong, Jamaica, Malaysia, Nigeria and Zimbabwe, and David Dixon, then Honorary Secretary of the CGF, preached a philosophy as visionary in its way as that of Asa Briggs for the COL. The committee's cumulative four-fold message was that sport could contribute to individual development, national identity, economic development and Commonwealth cohesion. At the individual level, the Committee cited inspiring examples of how community-driven grassroots youth programmes, incorporating sport, helped to:

- build trust and self-confidence;
- encourage self-sufficiency, personal empowerment and independence;
- open doors to education and literacy;
- address health issues;
- offer employment opportunities;
- build community cohesion;
- fight environmental degradation;
- combat juvenile delinquency; and
- break down ethnic, cultural and racial barriers.[8]

Sports activities gave young people goals, self-respect and engaged them in community concerns.

At the national level, sport created national unity and pride. It was a passion shared by presidents, prime ministers and peoples. It could transcend cultural, linguistic and racial barriers. The social benefits include improved health and productivity, and mental and moral well-being. Sport projected Samoa into the international spotlight, when a rugby team, helping to attract disaster relief after a hurricane, unexpectedly won the Middlesex Sevens tournament in Britain. In Malaysia, the 'Raku Muda' (Young Partners) programme, including sport, was adopted as a way of fostering patriotism and good behaviour among young people. In South Africa, sport was given a major role in healing scars after apartheid. When recently released Nelson Mandela met Jim Bolger, the New Zealand prime minister, during the Secretary-General's reception in Harare in 1991, one of the first things he said was that he hoped soon to welcome the All Blacks back to South Africa.

By 1997 sport was also seen as good business. Hosting major sporting events is a major incentive for infrastructure improvements. Sports-based community endeavours have contributed to slum clearance, urban hygiene and schooling improvements. Thus a major thrust of the CCCS philosophy at the end of the 1990s was that sport should be given an integral part in Official Development Assistance programmes. Sport began to be included in the aid programmes of the ABC donors – Australia, Britain and Canada. The Australian Sports Commission supported sports development in South Africa and the Pacific Islands. Britain helped with sports management training in Malaysia, Mauritius and Namibia. The Canadian International Development Agency (Cida) funded programmes in Southern Africa and the Caribbean. A regional forum on sport and development at Harare in 1997, included participants from ten Southern Africa countries. In its 1999 report the CCCS argued:

> Sport is an essential investment for governments and all agencies seeking to address youth at risk. In the short term it offers an alternative to the streets. In the medium term it reclaims lives that might be lost or spent in prison, hospitals or rehabilitation. In the longer term it helps form the basis of a healthy, productive society.[9]

The committee's expansive views (reminiscent, as they were, of the moral imperatives of the Victorian sports revolution) were the subject of presentations to the ministerial meetings on health, education, youth affairs and gender development.

Because of the amazingly all-embracing popularity of sport, it has probably become the most effective and accessible means of fostering Commonwealth solidarity. In 1993, when the NGO Liaison Officer was appointed in the Secretary-General's Office, strengthening links with sporting organisations, along with the other voluntary bodies, was part of his role. In 1994, the Secretariat included sport in its Human Resources Development programme and sponsored studies into two particular problems – gender equality in sport and the link between national sports policies and development. In 1995 a £50,000 grant was provided by the Secretariat for a five-year period. The importance of sport was re-emphasised by the inaugural Commonwealth Youth Games held in Edinburgh in August 2000. Over 600 athletes from 14 countries competed and a second such event was planned for Australia in 2004.

As well as enunciating a philosophy embracing the social, national and intra-Commonwealth significance of sport, the CCCS and the ABC governments and others have given support to the Games Federation. The Queen, as the Head of the Commonwealth, is the patron of the Games Federation and Prince Edward succeeded the Duke of Edinburgh as president in 1990. The Federation is made up of representatives of the Olympic and Commonwealth Games associations or committees in 72 countries. The CGF membership far exceeds the Commonwealth's 54, because (as with the Parliamentary Association) the component nations of Britain and its off-shore islands compete separately and the remaining colonial dependencies and associated states also send their teams.

The CGF, as a voluntary organisation, was always run on a shoe-string and faced financial and administrative strain as the size of the Games, the controversies they engendered and the sheer costs of running them grew. There were real fears for their continuance when, in 1989, the Canadians put the Games on the Chogm agenda. Heads of Government, however, pledged their support for the Games and urged member governments to help the CGF. By 1992 the Federation felt it had passed the turning-point. Temporary financial support from the ABC members, along with Malaysia, Namibia and New Zealand, enabled the Federation to acquire new office accommodation in London, two professional officers, in marketing and sports develop-ment, and secretarial staff. But the CGF still relies on the services of volunteers, who provide its main officials and committee members. In order to increase the appeal and participation in the Games, the core track, field and swimming events were joined, over the years, by rowing, boxing, weight lifting, cycling, gymnastics, badminton, bowls, shooting and squash. For the XVIth Games in Kuala Lumpur in 1998, the first to be staged in Asia, popular team sports were included experi-mentally for the first time. These were limited-over cricket, seven-a-side rugby, netball and field hockey (both men's and women's).

Since the Vancouver Games in 1954, a scientific congress has also been held at the same time as the Games. The initiative came from the Canadian Association for Health, Physical Education and Recreation, who organised the first Commonwealth Conference on Physical Education. Subsequent Games (except those in 1966 and 1998) were preceded by such congresses. The IXth at Auckland in 1990 was widened to embrace Physical Education, Sport, Health, Dance, Recreation and Leisure. It attracted over 1,000 participants to discuss the theme 'Creative Interaction'. It was also in Canada that the first Arts Festival, in association with the Games was held, starting in Edmonton in 1978.

The Commonwealth Games with their more than 3,000 competitors, colourful opening and closing ceremonies in stadia seating from 50,000 to 100,000 spectators, and hundreds of millions of television viewers, are brief moments when the Commonwealth comes alive for ordinary people. In her Commonwealth Day message on 9 March 1998, the Queen, as Head of the Commonwealth, had this to say:

> I believe that sport will always play a very important part in the social welfare of all generations. Sport – and team games in particular – teaches young people many valuable social lessons. It demonstrates the value of cooperation, teamwork and team spirit; it teaches the need to abide by rules and regulations; it emphasises the importance of self control and how to take victory and defeat with good grace.
>
> Sport is a great leveller. The same rules apply to all; there are no age, racial or cultural barriers to participation. Indeed, enthusiasm for sport brings together people from every background.[10]

The CCCS insists sport is 'an integral part of the Commonwealth identity .... Ask a person in the streets of Karachi or Bridgetown or London and he or she is likely to associate the Commonwealth with sport.'[11] The Commonwealth is also the only international association with 'this unique sports dimension'.

This dimension can be seen in providing constructive relationships in unexpected places. For example, in Uganda, during the 1980 elections, which followed the toppling of the Idi Amin regime by the Tanzanian Army, two diplomats sent to observe the election in the West Nile Province encountered hostility from the soldiers. One of them, Chris Laidlaw, a former Rhodes Scholar and member of the New Zealand All Blacks, records their interrogation by a Tanzanian brigadier:

> 'I can see you are not a Ugandan,' he said with menacing irony. I told him I was a New Zealander and his eyebrow lifted ever so lightly. He peered at me more closely. 'What's your name?' The relevance of this seemed a little remote to me but I told him. 'Not the chap who captained Oxford against the Springboks that time at Twickenham?' he said to my astonishment. When I nodded he burst into a brilliant smile and said, 'I was there. I loved seeing those bloody Boers being taken apart by a bunch of students. I was on a staff course at Cambridge at the time ... I never forgot it. Well, well, well. You certainly are welcome. What can I do to help you?'[12]

Similarly, although soccer is not a sport where Commonwealth countries dominate as in rugby and cricket, the British soccer leagues are avidly followed in Commonwealth countries. Thus keen supporters of 'Spurs' and 'United' can be encountered in unlikely places.

Moving beyond personal contacts, sport has also led on to new forms of community development. In 1999 the CCCS report gave particular attention to the work of the largest youth sport and community service in Africa. This was the Mathare Youth Sports Association covering a 30-square mile area of slum communities on the outskirts of Nairobi, Kenya. It began with a group of boys kicking around a home-made football. Under voluntary coaching, their game improved, became a local passion and led on to a 10,000-member association with 80 soccer leagues. After success in a national tournament, one of the Mathare teams went to compete in an international contest in Norway, where they were deeply impressed by the cleanliness of the towns. They determined to clean up their own home towns. Thus, from soccer, a community organisation evolved which encouraged youngsters to stay at school, gain qualifications, help clear up the garbage and unblock the drains near their homes, and to work in the campaign against HIV/AIDS. Passion for soccer led to self-discipline, organisational skills, educational improvement and even moved on to gender equality, as girls were helped to take up soccer. Some of the 'Norway graduates' went on to higher education and became community leaders. These endeavours attracted some outside funding and became a model for youth community service.[13]

*

In the 'People's Commonwealth' sports are the people's events. They are also seen as the exemplar of Commonwealth values. To fulfil the principles enunciated in Chogm declarations, the CCCS has pictured an ideal of civil society for the twenty-first century:

> Societies which are tolerant, democratic, and accountable; which are participatory and transparent and where the rule of law is not abused, biased, or abrogated. Where the aspirations of young women and men can be achieved with a minimum of obstacles. And where people are empowered with the skills and tools they need to remove themselves from social and economic hardship.[14]

Sport, it argues, has a big role in helping to build such societies. At the individual, national, and Commonwealth-wide levels sport gets people involved as players, organisers and supporters. Sport provides excitement, enjoyment, interest, community spirit and, above all, moments of colour and high achievement. Sport promotes in the Games, the Commonwealth's chief piece of pageantry.

In these respects sport emerges as the most tangible element of the 'People's Commonwealth'. It has genuine popular appeal, it engages people in ways that transcend age, gender, class and ethnicity, and the Commonwealth Games (and perhaps in future the new Youth Games) give a brief public institutional event. By contrast, the professional associations, care and welfare organisations, and educational endeavours, cover such a wide range that they lack focus and for them 'People's Commonwealth' is little more than an overall label indicating an aspiration rather than an achievement. Many of them look to the Foundation for support and they participate in the NGO forums. Others help the Secretariat to fulfil its programmes. The events now associated with Chogms become a focus of collaborative efforts and attempts to get viewpoints across to Heads of Government. But it is significant that attempts at umbrella organisations like CPAs and OCA did not succeed because of the very disparate nature and specialist focus of the many bodies which are being subsumed under the 'People's Commonwealth' label.

23
Public–Private Partnerships and a Commonwealth Business Culture

The most striking example of non-governmental contributions at the start of the new century was the new-found role expected of the private business sector. In the emerging new balance within the Commonwealth, private investment and private management expertise were extolled as never before. **Public–private partnerships – 'smart partnerships' as they were dubbed – became the new panacea.** If the first half of the 1990s had seen the fleshing out of Commonwealth political values, culminating in the suspension of Nigeria and the creation of the C-Mag in 1995, the second half of the decade was time for the clarification of the economic tenets of the Harare Declaration. The creation of the Commonwealth Private Investment Initiative and the Commonwealth Business Council signified deepening faith in market forces, free trade, and the ability of private business enterprise to solve the problems of economic inequality. In this new climate, the private sector, the inter-governmental agencies, NGOs and governments faced the new millennium with astonishing, possibly quixotic, optimism.

*

Trade and finance had always featured in Commonwealth councils. In the 1950s the management of the Sterling Area was a key issue, followed in the 1960s by debates about Britain's impending entry into the EEC. In the 1971 Declaration of Principles the Heads of Government condemned 'wide disparities of wealth' among peoples as 'too great to be tolerated'. Arnold Smith's parting words, at the end of his Secretary-Generalship in 1975, were that the growing gap in living standards between the developed and developing countries was 'neither decent nor sane'.[1] Ramphal's years were those of the North/South Dialogue in which the Commonwealth's contribution was embodied in the reports of the 13 Groups of Experts that reported on global economic issues. Yet at the end of it all this endeavour, when he summarised the findings in the book *International Economic Issues: Contributions by the Commonwealth 1975–1990,* Ramphal confessed to 'less than encouraging progress in some areas'. His conclusion by 1990 was that the 'disparities which Commonwealth leaders found to be too great to be tolerated in 1971 have now become greater and less tolerable'.[2]

In pursuing the concept of sustainable development, interest increasingly focused on the **three-fold elements of private investment, technology transfer, and information technology**. In the immediate aftermath of the 1991 Declaration attention focused on the first group of Harare tenets – 'fundamental political values' – democracy, the rule of law, good governance and human rights. But the second group, 'sustainable development and the alleviation of poverty', were always seen as essential concomitants. They demanded a stable international framework; sound management of the economy and of technical change; the central role of market forces; the freest possible flow of multilateral trade; debt reduction; and human resource development.

By the end of the 1980s, with the sudden thaw in the Cold War and the demise of apartheid, there was time for closer attention to problems of under-development and poverty. But the colossal tasks of rehabilitation in Eastern Europe, capitalisation in China and reconstruction in Southern Africa created fears that the needs of smaller Commonwealth countries would be consigned to the sidelines. Commonwealth Finance Ministers became increasingly preoccupied with the debt levels of the weaker economies and uncertainty in capital flows. Private investment was looked to more and more, and the Secretariat enjoined to encourage such investment. The 1989 Finance Ministers Meeting supported the idea of a Commonwealth Equity Fund. This plan was approved by the Kuala Lumpur Chogm, where Ramphal heralded the 'Hibiscus Issue'.[3] The Equity Fund was launched in 1990, with initial subscriptions of US$56,600,000. The main targets for investment were in South Asia; soon Caricom was calling for a Caribbean Fund. In 1993 the Finance Ministers considered the whole matter of privatisation and discussed the running of the Equity Fund with Britain's Commonwealth Development Corporation (CDC). The proposal was now that a new series of regional funds should be created, managed by the CDC on a commercial basis. Thus the 1995 Auckland Chogm approved the **Commonwealth Private Investment Initiative** (CPII), with the CDC appointed as the fund manager. In this way the CDC, a British development finance house, was, for the first time, brought into the mainstream of multilateral Commonwealth endeavours.

Founded in 1948 by the postwar British Labour government as the Colonial Development Corporation, its initial role had been to borrow long-term from mainly Exchequer sources, in order to invest in development projects, chiefly public utilities, agriculture and manufacturing. In 1963 it marked the rising pace of decolonisation with a title change to Commonwealth Development Corporation and in 1969 the field of operation was widened to embrace some non-Commonwealth countries.

CDC had started, then, as a purely British statutory corporation for channelling government funds into colonial infrastructure development. From the 1950s, when it began to favour investment in private businesses, it pioneered a more commercial approach to development.[4] As decolonisation accelerated, the CDC became the lender-of-last-resort for the poorer countries. Thus its portfolio of investments (valued in 1981 at £385,000,000) was, in the words of John Majoribanks, 'exposed to downside risk more than upside potential'.[5] Yet, as the British and other governments looked in the 1990s to view private sector investment as the key to development and poverty alleviation, they turned to the revamped CDC Capital Partners as an in-house specialist to advise and manage the funds of the CPII. The first of the new funds was the Commonwealth Africa Investment Fund Ltd (COMAFIN CPII) formed in 1996 and incorporated in the Virgin Islands. This was followed in 1997 by the Kula Fund Ltd (KULA CPII) for investments in the Pacific and incorporated in Vanuatu, and the South Asia Regional Fund Ltd (SARF CPII) incorporated in Mauritius. In 1999 the Tiona Fund Ltd (TIONA CPII) was incorporated in Barbados for investment in the Caribbean. On the last day of the old century commitments to these funds were, respectively, COMAFIN – US$63,500,000, KULA – $16,800,000, SARF – $108,200,000, and TIONA – $21,500,000.[6]

*

After private investment, the second area of concern was the rapidity of technical change, the problems of technology transfer and the vast possibilities of the new information and communications technologies (ICT). In these fields the task of forging new public–private partnerships fell to the **Commonwealth Science Council** (CSC).

The Council, whose Secretariat constitutes the Science and Technology Division of the Commonwealth Secretariat, is financed by separate, assessed, member contributions, the total being under

£1,000,000. The CSC dates from 1975 when it became the successor to the Standing Committee of the British Commonwealth Scientific Officials Conference started in 1946. After 1975 the liaison role performed by earlier committees was expanded to include specialisation on the transferring of technology that was freely available but not yet adequately applied to development. Early successes in the new role were in the fields of rural technology, energy, mineral resources and standardisation. A review conducted by an expert group under Sir John Kendrew FRS in 1984 called for the incorporation of more basic science into technology and emphasised the vital role of technology and innovation for development.[7] In 1995 the CSC outlined three areas of priority – protecting biodiversity and genetic resources, water and energy. To share up-to-date developments in water resources it sponsored the Small Island Water Information Networks (SI-WIN). For energy, it promoted the use of solar power for lighting and crop drying. It sponsored seminars in Remote Sensing and Geographical Information Systems. To protect water, air and land from industrial pollution the CSC participated in a project on Chemical Research and Environmental Needs (CREN). After five years under a Consultative Group on Technology Management, a public–private sector partnership was created in 1993. This work bore fruit at the 1995 Auckland Chogm in the launching of the Commonwealth Partnership for Technology Management Ltd (CPTM), a not-for-profit company for promoting government/business cooperation. The initial participants were 13 Commonwealth governments, and 16 blue chip international corporations, and three universities. CPTM promotes best practice in technology management, attempts to mobilise the skills of the private sector to assist governments, and sponsors 'smart partnership dialogues', regionally, between governments, businesses, trade unions and other interested groups.

The third area of public–private partnership is in the field of ICT. As governments, IGOs and NGOs established their websites on the Internet, the Secretariat looked to exploit the possibilities of the World Wide Web for multilateral Commonwealth networking. In 1990 it created the Commonwealth Network of Information Technology for Development (COMNET-IT). After five years of development by the Secretariat, COMNET-IT was transferred to an international foundation hosted by the government of Malta. The foundation has both institutional and individual members and holds seminars and workshops to advance expertise in the use of the Internet. COMNET-IT was followed in 1979 by the Commonwealth Business Network (COMBINET) to link up Chambers of Commerce, stock exchanges, manufacturers' associations and individual businesses to capitalise further on the Internet. A review of the CSC in 1998 entitled *Knowledge Networking for Development* suggested that ICT should become the Council's chief focus. A new Vision Statement was proposed:

> CSC in the new millennium will be an innovative, creative and proactive organisation that will overlap the S&T capability in the public and industry domain within the Commonwealth through networking of both knowledge and finance using modern information technologies to facilitate the application of S&T by member countries for sustainable economic, environmental, social and cultural development.[8]

The Durban Chogm in 1999 approved the Commonwealth Knowledge Network (CKN) to assist in the use of science and technology for development. In the words of the CKN Task Force: 'Tomorrow's societies will be knowledge societies. Tomorrow's workers will be knowledge workers. Tomorrow's world will be dominated by the economics and transfer of knowledge.'[9]

*

The public–private partnerships in investment, technology transfer and ICT represent the practical results of the Secretariat's joint explorations with the private sector dating from the late 1980s. In Commonwealth councils they tended to be overshadowed, at first, by preoccupation with the political aspects of the Harare Declaration. Popular memories of the 1995 Auckland Chogm tend to focus on the debates about 'Nukes and Nigeria', the suspension of the latter's membership, and the creation of C-Mag, rather than on CPII, CPTM and COMNET-IT. By the second half of the 1990s, however, the climate of opinion had changed dramatically and the role of private business and, especially, private investment, more openly discussed in the ongoing crusade for good governance.

An important reason for the changed climate was Britain's 'rediscovery' of the Commonwealth in the post-Thatcher, post-apartheid, years. The House of Commons Foreign Affairs Select Committee's enquiry into the future role of the Commonwealth straddled the 1995 Chogm. Starting its Westminster hearings in June 1995, making Commonwealth tours in June and October, resuming London hearings in November and December, the FAC completed its report in March 1996. Two things had particularly impressed the members: first, the value of Commonwealth networks and, second, emerging possibilities for trade and investment. Shortly before the FAC got to work Professor David Dilks, who had been a pioneer in Commonwealth youth organisations, wrote an 'Outside Voice' contribution for *Commonwealth Currents* on the value of Commonwealth connections. He wrote of the 'unsung Commonwealth' the principal characteristic of which was to him, that 'the people in a room often know each other well, want to get on and generally do'. He went on: '**I have never met a European colleague in politics, business or academic life who would not give his eyes to have the range of contacts and ease of entry all over the world which we take for granted, nor one who understands why we do not make more of that priceless asset.**'[10]

Later in 1995, in her Chatham House discussion paper *Economic Opportunities for Britain and the Commonwealth*, Katherine West coined the phrase '**Commonwealth Business Culture**'. Use of the English language; shared legal, commercial, accounting, financial practices and procedures, and administrative heritage, all added up to a 'bonus' for business transactions.[11] This concept was taken up eagerly by the FAC, which saw the advantages for trade and investment. This perception was re-enforced by the figures it received indicating a trend in trade and investment to the Asia-Pacific region, and the fact that British trade with the Commonwealth was in favourable balance, while the larger-volume trades with the rest of the world were in deficit.[12] David Howell, the FAC Chairman, emphasised both the network and the Asia-Pacific aspects during the House of Commons debate on the report on 27 June 1996. 'There suddenly seems to be a new awareness of the value of the club of Commonwealth nations ... Britain's trade and capital investment is noticeably tilting away exclusively from Europe towards Asia, which happens to include several of the major Commonwealth countries.'[13] He drove home the message more succinctly to the ICS seminar on the report, where he admitted the FAC members had come to educate themselves and had realised that 'capital and investment drove trade and that the former went where there was a common culture and good governance'.[14] Howell's words were, in a sense, a vindication of the two prime tenets of the Harare Declaration.

The British government, as host to the 1997 Chogm, responded positively to this new mood. The FCO, having been rapped over the knuckles for its initial 'downbeat' submission to the FAC, went along with the RCS idea for declaring 1997 as the 'Year of the Commonwealth' and co-sponsoring the first NGO or People's Forum in the wings of the Chogm. More importantly the British government chose 'Trade, Investment and Development' as the Chogm theme. This in itself was a new departure and was accompanied by plans for new institutional arrangements in pursuing the theme. Before the Chogm two preliminary forums met that gave firm endorsement to the philosophy of the free market and the role of private investment in development. First, the British Council held a conference, with meetings in London and Edinburgh in association with the Secretariat, the European Commission and three major companies, on *The Commonwealth and Europe*. Eighty participants, from 36 Commonwealth and EU countries viewed the potential of the Commonwealth for economic good. The conference summary recorded that participants were 'almost unanimous about three propositions which, a handful of years ago, could have been expected to provoke fierce disagreement'. They were:

- Foreign capital investment is not re-colonisation in disguise.
- Aid budgets have shrunk, are shrinking, and can be left to go on shrinking without protest because – outside the important areas of physical infrastructure and skills transfer – aid does not contribute to economic growth.
- Tariff protection and subsidies, of whatever kind and however temporarily useful, are in the new global marketplace not merely ineffective but actively damaging to the economies which use them.[15]

These starkly expressed tenets, untempered by the usual Commonwealth ameliorative genuflections in the direction of small states, set the tone, philosophically, for the second pre-Chogm meeting, the First **Commonwealth Business Forum**, held in London 22–23 October 1997 on the immediate eve of the Chogm.

The Forum was jointly organised by the Secretariat, the British government and the Financial Times Conferences Ltd. Three hundred delegates from 47 Commonwealth and six non-Commonwealth countries attended. Six Heads of Government spoke – from Australia, Britain, Canada, Singapore, Sri Lanka and Uganda – as did ministers from Barbados, Bangladesh, South Africa and Zimbabwe. Business leaders also addressed the forum. It identified a need for special attention to poor physical infrastructure in many countries and for codes of good practice in government, business and finance, to ensure transparency and reduce corruption. It was also proposed that a Commonwealth Business Council (CBC) would be established as an ongoing private sector voice on trade and industry. The creation of the CBC was approved by the Edinburgh Chogm and Lord Cairns, chairman of the CDC – the Commonwealth's new fund manager – was chosen as first chairman. The Council was made up of 12 business leaders at the level of chief executives from major companies working in Commonwealth countries. Its task was to provide public sector–private sector dialogue, business-to-business networking, encourage best practice, enhance the role of poorer countries in the WTO and provide reliable information by publishing investment almanacs.

The views of the Business Forum were reflected in the *Edinburgh Commonwealth Economic Declaration – Promoting Shared Prosperity* which was hailed in the Chogm Communiqué as 'a fitting complement to the Harare Commonwealth Declaration of 1991'.[16] Trade, investment, new technologies and market forces were depicted as the 'engines of growth'. As not all countries had benefited equally, globalisation needed to be 'carefully managed'. Market principles, open international trade and investment, the development of human and physical resources, gender equality, good governance and political stability were declared as 'major components of economic and social progress'. Wealth creation was seen as requiring 'partnerships between governments and the private sector'.[17] These principles were qualified by the need for codes of good practice in order to eliminate corruption and attract investment; special attention to the problems of small states and the indebtedness of poorer countries; protection of the environment; and the overall goal of halving the proportion of people living in extreme poverty in less than two decades.

In Edinburgh, then, the political and economic tenets of the Harare Declaration finally came together. The message was clearly proclaimed that the alleviation of poverty and the promotion of prosperity and sustainable development depended on open trade and investment, the application of new technology, the development of human resources and the operation of market forces. These, in turn, required good governance, the rule of law and political stability, which depended on democracy, human rights and honest administration. As the Edinburgh Communiqué emphasised – democracy, good governance, sustainable development and respect for human rights and fundamental freedoms – were 'interdependent and mutually reinforcing'.

The Forum and the Edinburgh Declaration were full of generalities. How far would action follow the talk-fest? In addressing the vital background question of how to make countries attractive to investors, the

Secretariat turned, once again, to the voluntary sector. To emphasise the vital role of Boards of Directors, the Commonwealth Association for Corporate Governance (CACG) was formed in April 1998 to pursue excellence in corporate governance. With support from the Secretariat, the World Bank, the New Zealand government, several international corporations and the Institute of Chartered Secretaries it participated in a Technical Policy Workshop at Sandridge Park in Britain to produce guidelines for best practice. The first of the *CACG Guidelines, 'Principles for Corporate Governance'* was seen as a 'living document' to be updated in response to developments. They were reviewed by an International Corporate Governance Seminar and the second Commonwealth Business Forum in Johannesburg in November 1999. The development of these *Guidelines* was welcomed by the Durban Chogm. CACG went on to conduct workshops in Africa, Asia, the Pacific and Caribbean on best practice for Boards of Directors. Help was provided in creating national institutes of directors and creating regional centres of excellence. Another example of decentralisation, CACG was incorporated in New Zealand, and its chief executive, Geoffrey Bowes, of the New Zealand Institute of Directors, toured the Commonwealth to run the corporate governance workshops to train directors.[18]

On the wider question of corruption, the Secretary-General set up an Expert Group on Good Governance and the Elimination of Corruption in Economic Management. In its report of October 1999 the group endorsed the inter-dependence of the two main tenets of the Harare Declaration in these words:

> Smaller and more efficient government, fewer discretionary powers in administration, greater reliance on diversity and private initiative, a free press and other media, well-paid civil servants appointed by merit, democratic processes in political parties, and supremacy of the rule of law, are all important factors that serve to promote good governance and reduce corruption.[19]

The Group looked to international action in the long run and to create global legally binding inter-governmental compacts. Meanwhile, it suggested that the Commonwealth tradition of operating by consensus should be utilised to adopt Codes for Good Conduct on Integrity in Public Office and Good Corporate Governance. This report was received by the Durban Chogm, which endorsed a 'Framework for Commonwealth Principles on Promoting Good Governance and Combating Corruption'.

In the *Fancourt Commonwealth Declaration* the Heads of Government reiterated the link between good governance and economic progress: 'we affirm our commitment to the pursuit of greater transparency, accountability, the rule of law, and the elimination of corruption in all spheres of public life and in the private sector'.[20] Governments, intergovernmental organisations, public–private partnerships and all manner of Vippsos entered the new century collaborating closely and more freely than ever before. They do so with an openness and optimism, which deserves to be better known. But how far will they deliver practical results in the direction of poverty alleviation? Hard evidence of positive trends will be eagerly awaited.

Conclusion: The Commonwealth and the New Century

The Commonwealth embarked on the new century nursing considerable satisfaction about the renaissance of the 1990s, while facing some urgent issues about the association's future. Through all the activities, innovations, declarations and reassessments of the final decade of the twentieth century, a new balance has been emerging that is little understood and is, as yet, uncertain of outcome. As the new Secretary-General entered his suite in Marlborough House and the High-Level Review Group of Heads of Government under the new Chairperson-in-being considered the challenges of the new century, the issues needing their attention may be summarised, baldly, under four headings – credibility, focus, mechanisms, and balance.

*

Credibility is a problem the modern Commonwealth has always had. At the start of the new century it was manifested in two ways. First, the question of relevance: 'What's in it for us?' is the question most frequently asked. It has to be addressed. The big members use the Commonwealth to gain understanding of their causes; sometimes even to gather votes in the United Nations. The small states cherish the one major forum in which they can have a large role. They gain assistance from the Commonwealth's flexible arrangements for sharing technical assistance, specialist advice and expertise. The multiplicity and informality of the Commonwealth's inter-governmental agencies and Vippso associations are major strengths that need to be trumpeted.

Second, there is the problem of the critical 'generation gap' in knowledge, experience and regard for the Commonwealth. The young journalist, who told the RCS meeting in Durban, that she had no sentimental attachment to the Commonwealth and that young people in the new South Africa did not feel they needed to know about the

Commonwealth, could have been speaking for members of their generation anywhere. But if people want to overcome their ignorance, how and where can they learn? The Australian Federal Foreign Affairs Committee seminar in 1997 was told of a pupil who went to the school library to get information for a project on the Commonwealth, only to be told by the librarian that it had been abolished and superseded by the United Nations! Young leaders in Britain attending the Cumberland Lodge conferences expressed themselves appalled by their own lack of knowledge on the Commonwealth. Third – and underlining the two previous points – there is the problem of public relations. Derek Ingram's 1997 report on the Commonwealth information programmes exposed serious deficiencies. He particularly regretted the lost opportunities for portraying success stories.

Addressing the credibility gap – especially among the younger generations – is therefore a priority task for the new Secretary-General and the High Level Review Group. Maybe Marlborough House, as the association's headquarters, sends the wrong signals. The Secretary-General seems holed up in a gracious ivory tower in a former royal boudoir. The building, hidden behind high walls, on Pall Mall, seems shrouded in security, secrecy and splendour. The supreme irony is that it is within a stone's throw of one of the most intensively crowded tourist haunts in Europe. Do the tourists even notice the sign telling them the Secretariat is there? The Ingram Report's proposal of a 'shop window' for the Commonwealth in Quadrant House, the overflow building across the road, was followed up, but does not really meet the need for eye-catching public presentation.

Why not a fine Commonwealth Visitor Centre in the garden of Marlborough House, with an entrance from The Mall? Many institutions around the world display themselves informally and even elegantly in visitor centres. On Parliament Hill in Ottawa, beside the historic gothic revival federal buildings, a tent-like visitor centre has been added where guided tours assemble and are briefed. A visitor centre for the Commonwealth would have to be securely separated from the Secretariat (though full views of Marlborough House across the lawn would be desirable). Well-chosen and regularly updated exhibits could depict the structure, meaning and activities of the Commonwealth. Pamphlets and pictures should be readily available, along with more serious publications for purchase. Doorway attractions of a Commonwealth cultural nature (for example, a steel band, even Sierra Leonean dancers) would attract notice. Possibly there could be a well-designed coffee bar. If it is desirable to present pictorially and graphically the existence and purposes of the Commonwealth for a general public, there is hardly a more propitious spot for getting a message across to people from all over the world. When American visitors can tell their friends that the Commonwealth Visitor Centre is a 'must', some measure that a mark had been made would be gained.

To make a start in closing the generation gap, the prime target area should be schools. The Secretary-General, Secretariat staff, Commonwealth diplomats, Vippso enthusiasts, even private sector leaders, should all be enlisted to interact with school pupils about the Commonwealth and its relevance to their lives, hopefully getting as much local media coverage as possible. Efforts are needed to ensure some coverage in national school curricula. Well-written textbooks are needed and should be kept up-to-date. The proposals of the Ingram Report on the association's information services and image and the Symons Report on tertiary education need further follow-up. Such attention to the credibility problem becomes all the more urgent now that the Commonwealth has a Chairperson-in-being to speak for it in international forums. In such forums, how are, say, Americans, Europeans or North Asians to know what the Commonwealth so represented, is about, if the citizens and youth of the member countries remain in ignorance?

*

The second problem, which also bears on the question of credibility, is the matter of **focus**. Critics, both inside and outside, complain that the Commonwealth is too all-over-the-place in its endeavours. It tries to cover too much with minuscule resources. Yet, as we have seen, in the 1990s, the Commonwealth *did begin* to focus, even if the final balance of that focus is, as yet, to be determined.

The Harare Declaration and the Millbrook Action Programme were very clear as far as they went. The two prime tenets are **political values** – democracy, the rule of law, good governance and human rights – and **sustainable development** – requiring free trade, the market economy, equal opportunities, and special support for small states. The third tenet, **consensus building** is the Commonwealth's missionary role – as the bridge between regions and cultures. To repeat Ramphal's famous phrase: it cannot negotiate for the world, but can help the world to negotiate.

All this raises the critical chicken-and-egg question. Some will argue that you cannot achieve the luxury of democracy and human rights without development. People need to eat and read and work computers if they are truly to participate. Others will say that prosperity cannot be achieved without good governance, the rule of law and the sort of infrastructure that only honest administrators and legitimately elected rulers can give. Resolving this question is probably the Commonwealth's most fundamental intellectual problem. As the *Civil Society* report puts it clearly: 'Good governance is an essential requisite for the eradication of poverty, just as the absence of poverty is essential to ensure good governance.' These are two very legitimate goals – but where lie the priorities for collective action?

Heads of Government pledged themselves to halving gross poverty by 2015 – a very specific and ambitious goal since starvation and malnutrition hamper any progress. On the other hand, real development and prosperity will surely depend on *values* – honest structures, obedience to rules, the work ethic, freedom of choice, freedom to innovate, freedom from corruption and community spirit. There is, of course, a link between the two – education – which obviously becomes another major priority. It is, therefore, significant that the COL has moved away from its original tertiary emphasis to concentrate its distance education expertise on basic and vocational education and women's education. Other Commonwealth educational initiatives may also need similar adjustments. New ones may be called for, since countries that score highly in 'physical quality of life' and 'human development' indices are those that spend generously on public education. In this respect the old members are ranked: Canada, Australia, Britain, New Zealand. Of the New Commonwealth, only Singapore, Trinidad and Barbados approach comparable levels. **Education for young women cannot be overemphasised as the quickest way to tackle overpopulation as a source of poverty.**

We come back always to the two prime tenets – fundamental political values and sustainable development. Neither can exist without the other, but intensive debate is required as to where first, and how best, to proceed.

On the third Harare/Millbrook tenet – consensus building and assisting the international community in bridge building – is it worth resurrecting the idea of a 'Global Humanitarian Order' mooted by Anyaoku in the early 1990s? In spite of the end of the Cold War and salutary reductions in weaponry and armed forces in some quarters, the world is still afflicted by numberless vicious conflicts, massacres and human rights violations. It is clear that the role of armed force cannot be neglected. It must not be wielded by the type of untrained 'militias' so often seen wasting their ammunition in front of TV cameras. Intensively trained, well-educated, disciplined, properly equipped and clearly mandated professional forces are still needed. Should there be reconsideration of Commonwealth cooperation in this area? Could the sort of cooperation seen in East Timor in 1999 be made available **as a deterrent** for conflict prevention, rather than simply as an *ad hoc* stop-gap arriving too late?

The one thing that well-meaning consensus and idealistic declarations cannot anticipate is the unexpected. The new Secretary-General took over in 2000 prepared to tackle the general issues that had become evident, but within days his energies were diverted to fire-fighting operations. The first months of the new century were marked by vicious armed confrontations amounting to civil war in Sierra Leone and Sri Lanka, continuing military rule in Pakistan and intimidation by armed mobs in Fiji, Solomon Islands and Zimbabwe. It was supremely ironical that less than ten years after the Harare Declaration, the country of its birth should flagrantly negate its principles. In the interests of human rights and the sanctity of life, ordinary citizens crave more potent mechanisms for curbing unconstitutional usurpation of agreed political systems by armed minorities. But solutions seem nowhere in sight. The Commonwealth needs to reconsider the question of deterrence against anti-democratic tendencies.

*

The third matter to be addressed is a review of **consultative mechanisms** at all levels – at the summit, between summits and at the grass-roots. At the top stand the Secretariat and the Chogms. To help resolve the questions of focus and balance; to service the enhanced role of the C-Mag; and to fulfil the aspirations so eloquently voiced in the Foundation's *Civil Society* report – the Secretariat needs strengthening. Yet over the 1990s it has been slimmed down. Indeed, it was reported to be suffering from 'review fatigue'! In support of Commonwealth values more emphasis should be given to its political and economic divisions, its youth and education divisions, its attention to sport and to human rights. The latter issue should surely have a stand-alone division.

Turning to the Chogms, a frank look would suggest that the three-and-a-half-day format is too short and should go to at least four, preferably five days, with two full nights on Retreat. Longer meetings would permit the revival of more private audiences for Heads of Government with the Head of the Commonwealth. The difficulty, of course, is to persuade the 'heavies', from Australia, Britain, Canada and India, to give the time. If they were willing, the small state leaders would surely want to stay. Greater informality might be induced by experimenting with different seating arrangements. The vast round, or oblong, table layouts mean that the delegates peer at each other across vast spaces filled by veritable botanical gardens. Voice enhancement becomes a requirement. A jumble of small tables, as for some Head of the Commonwealth dinners, might be tried to create less rigidity, more compactness and conviviality.

The leaders need to pay more attention to the media. This is not to suggest that executive sessions should be broadcast – this would destroy the intimate purpose of the gatherings. But more needs to be divulged afterwards about the themes debated, the outcomes decided, and the on-going activities of the officials and inter-governmental agencies. As well as briefings about the executive sessions, there should be briefings (as there once were) about the Committee of the Whole. **Knowledge and commentary about all the on-going work of the Commonwealth is vital in the education process and for raising awareness about the association.**

Between summits there is now the Chairperson to speak for the Commonwealth in international forums. How will he or she be briefed? What impact will this new role have on the status of the Secretary-General? There needs, surely, to be some continuous network of consultation – now possible through ICT – by which a variety of specialist professional, academic and technical skills, as well as business and administrative expertise, can be tapped.

The new communications technologies also raise possibilities for decentralisation. There have been suggestions that the Secretariat itself should be moved out of London or should move around like the Chogms and the ministerial meetings. This would probably be impractical and expensive (and consensus about a new venue hard to achieve). But some grassroots regional presence for the Commonwealth is desirable. Possible embryos exist in the Regional Youth Centres, the Commonwealth of Learning, the Small Missions Office for the United Nations in New York, and in the headquarters of some of the professional and voluntary bodies. The new ICT makes the idea of some further decentralisation worth exploring. The idea of Commonwealth honorary consuls in each member state might also be revisited and the idea reconsidered of a roving commissioner or special ambassador for the Secretariat. A Commonwealth presence at the grassroots should also help to overcome the problem of the credibility and the generation gap previously mentioned.

*

Finally, the most interesting, and least understood, question relates to the **emerging new balance** in the functioning of the Commonwealth.

Until comparatively recently there were interactions at the Heads of Government, ministerial and official agency levels on the one hand, and, on the other, among numerous voluntary organisations, some of them historically well established, others very new. Since the creation of the Foundation and the burgeoning of new professional and welfare organisations, many efforts have been made to link the official and non-official sectors. The Secretariat itself has sponsored new professional organisations involving specialist officials. It could be argued that the Vippso world really held the Commonwealth together in the lean years of the 1970s and 1980s. But in the 1990s the pace of change was remarkable. NGO Forums began in 1991, NGO accreditation started in 1993, and a 'People's Centre', in the wings of the Chogm, was first tried in 1997. More significantly, in the last decade of the century, the private sector was increasingly courted. The Regional Investment Funds, the Partnership for Technology Management, the ICT networks, the Business Forum and Business Council all mark the waxing faith in the private business sector.

In which direction will the long-term balance tilt – public sector, voluntary sector, private sector – IGOs, civil society, business? What are the implications of private–public partnership? The voluntary sector has experienced an explosion of interest and attempts have been made to define, and even regulate, these activities. Distinctions have been drawn between the professional organisations and the care and welfare organisations. Sometimes there are territorial rivalries; sometimes tensions with governments; sometimes questions of accountability. The idea of the 'People's Commonwealth' seems well established in rhetoric and it is clear that the official Commonwealth (with its extremely slender resources) has come to rely on voluntary expertise. As we have seen, where the Vippsos team up they *can make a mark*. The Commonwealth Human Rights Initiative has been dubbed the 'conscience of the Commonwealth'. The built environment professionals pressed the shelter priority in Edinburgh. The educational and health professionals in Durban persuaded the Chogm to recognise the Global Emergency presented by HIV/AIDS. A new association of Commonwealth NGOs is planned, but will it go the way of the Organisation of Commonwealth Associations, which lapsed through lack of focus? For, of course, all is not sweetness and light in the voluntary, civil society sector. Passionate enthusiasms, heartfelt concerns and devoted voluntary service, unaccompanied by administrative and diplomatic skill can make the Vippso world a contentious, struggling and, in some cases, inward-looking world. Some NGOs are so single-minded that they ride roughshod over rivals and even spurn legal process. Signs of an anti-NGO backlash are already evident, especially in the United States, after the disruption of the World Trade Organisation in 1999.

Similarly, the private business sector must always be in an ambivalent position. Business directors, bankers, chief executives and corporate managers are appointed to make profits and satisfy investors. They are, in the long run, out to compete with rivals. Where government regulations are supported this must be because they are in the interest of the business world. An investment conference jointly organised by the Commonwealth Business Council and the Nigerian Government in March 2000 identified the chief deterrent to investment as corruption. A fruitful environment for investment depended on vigorous reform by the recently elected government.

Compared with the voluntary civil society world and the private business, corporate realms, the traditional arenas of political dialogue, diplomatic interchange and bureaucratic cooperation may, in the end, seem havens of calm and efficiency. The question remains, however, how far member governments are willing to devote resources to these traditional modes of interaction? Or are they simply opting out? As the new century opened, the Vippso and business sectors were being given an ever-increasing role, and 'private–public partnership' had become the panacea for the future. But whether their success in fulfilling Commonwealth values, sustainable development and alleviation of poverty will be any greater than the older modes has yet to be proved. The fascinating, unanswered question remains as to the long-term nature and impact of the private–public partnership. Many look with anticipation for the appropriate balance between the political, voluntary and business sectors for securing the future success of the Commonwealth.

Until recently **the Political Commonwealth** was, for the most part, the main element, the visible part, of the association. **The People's Commonwealth**, under the new lexicon of 'civil society' has recently come into its own and is encouraged and increasingly used by the political Commonwealth because of its huge reservoirs of expertise and enthusiasm. For the moment the People's Commonwealth has great expectations. But the private business sector represents the new Star in the East and is more and more being sought after. It is almost as if **the Corporate Commonwealth is being elevated into a 'Credal Commonwealth'** by virtue if the astonishing faith being invested in it. The tenets of the new catechism are all too familiar – free trade, market forces, public–private partnership, good governance and equality of opportunity. The irony is that the respective values of the People's and Corporate Commonwealths seem at variance. The People's Commonwealth, as recorded in the *Civil Society* report, expects the state to play a major role in providing for a secure future. Yet the state expects private investment and private business, and the voluntary associations, to solve many of the people's problems. And business expects the state to create an environment for fair competition and secure investment.

Here, then, is the question of balance at its simplest. The Commonwealth seems uncertain of the exact balance of influences that will best fulfil its newly refined goals. Resolving this question is the most urgent task facing the new Secretary-General, the first Chairperson-in-being, and, indeed, all the many Commonwealth conclaves.

How to Keep up with the Commonwealth

The most useful tool is *The Round Table: The Commonwealth Journal of International Affairs*. Founded in 1910 by the 'Round Table Moot', this quarterly journal published anonymous reports until 1966. It ceased publication briefly between 1981 and 1983. Publishing five issues a year from 2000, its regular features include 'Commonwealth Update' by Derek Ingram and 'Documentation', which provides the full texts of such material as Chogm Communiqués and C-Mag reports. Leading Commonwealth figures, as well as commentators and academics, contribute signed articles. *The Round Table* is available on line at <www.carfax.co.uk >.

The official reference book is *The Commonwealth Yearbook* (produced since 1996 by Hanson Cooke for the Commonwealth Secretariat). It is the successor to *The Colonial Office List* and *The Commonwealth Relations Office List,* which were followed by *The Commonwealth Office Year Book* in 1967 after the CO and CRO had merged. The Foreign & Commonwealth Office (created by a further merger in 1968) changed the title to *The Commonwealth Yearbook* in 1987, and in 1993 transferred the title and responsibility to the Commonwealth Secretariat. The format was changed from 1996 in association with the new publishing partner.

The other important official reference book is *Commonwealth at the Summit,* vol. 1 *Communiqués of Commonwealth Heads of Government Meetings 1944–1986* (1987) and vol. 2 *Communiqués of Commonwealth Heads of Government Meetings 1987–1995* (1997). The texts from the 1997 and subsequent Chogms were published by the Secretariat in separate pamphlets. Other useful reference works include: *The*

Commonwealth Minister's Reference Book (from 1989/90 by Kensington Publications); Alan Palmer, *Dictionary of the British Empire and Commonwealth* (1996), and House of Commons, Session 1995–6, Foreign Affairs Committee First Report *The Future Role of the Commonwealth,* vol. 1, *Report, together with the Proceedings of the Committee,* vol. 2, *Minutes of Evidence and Appendices* (1996), which includes numerous very informative submissions from NGOs.

Academic study of the Commonwealth is catered for by *The Journal of Imperial and Commonwealth History* (thrice yearly since 1972) and *The Journal of Commonwealth and Comparative Politics* (thrice yearly since 1974 as the successor of *The Journal of Commonwealth Political Studies,* started in 1961). Content details of both journals are available at <www.frankcass.com/jnls>. For the literary approach, *Commonwealth: Essays and Studies* (twice-yearly critical studies of the New Literatures in English) is published by the Société d'Etude des Pays du Commonwealth at the Languages Faculty, Dijon.

The main inter-governmental organisations each produce magazines and periodic reports. The Commonwealth Secretariat issues the bi-monthly illustrated magazine *Commonwealth Currents* and the biennial *Report of the Secretary-General.* The Secretariat maintains a website, which includes the texts of news releases and speeches as well as descriptive material on the structure and membership of the association: <www.thecommonwealth.org>. The CFTC produces biennial reports entitled *Skills for Development.*
The Commonwealth Foundation has an illustrated news magazine *Common Path*; presents biennial reports for the Chogm; and maintains the website: <www.commonwealthfoundation.org>.
The Commonwealth of Learning has two news publications, *Connections* and *EdTech News.* The COL reports biennially to the Chogm and has the websites <www.col.org> and <www.col.org/colint>.
CAB-International (the former Commonwealth Agricultural Bureaux until 1986) publishes each year a report, such as *99 In Review: Presenting CAB International* and also *Reports of Proceedings* of its triennial Review Conferences. The component divisions maintain eight websites, which can all be accessed via the home site <www.cabi.org>.

For the work of the Secretary-General during the first 35 years of the Secretariat see: Arnold Smith, with Clyde Sanger, *Stitches in Time: the*

Commonwealth in World Politics (1981); Shridath Ramphal, *One World To Share: Selected Speeches of the Commonwealth Secretary-General, 1975–9* (1979); Ron Sanders (ed.). *Inseparable Humanity: An Anthology of Reflections of Shridath Ramphal* (1988); Shridath Ramphal (ed.), *International Economic Issues: Contributions of the Commonwealth 1975–1990* (1990); Emeka Anyaoku, *The Missing Headlines: Selected Speeches* (1997); Phyllis Johnson, *Eye of Fire: A biography of Chief Emeka Anyaoku, The Man and His Work* (2000).

Information on the People's Commonwealth is available from the regular Newsletters and Annual Reports of the numerous NGOs.

A selection of pan-Commonwealth websites is included below. Others are available at <www.thecommonwealth.org>:

Commonwealth Business Council – <www.cbc.to/>
Commonwealth Business Network – <www.combinet.net> and <www.combinet.org>
Commonwealth Association for Corporate Governance – <www.cbc.to > [governance]
Commonwealth Association for Public Action and Management – <www.capam.comnet.mt>
Commonwealth Electronic Network for Schools and Education – <www.col.org/cense/>
Commonwealth Games 2002 (Manchester) – <www.commonwealth-games2002.org.uk>
Commonwealth Human Ecology Council – <www.tcol.co.uk\comorg\CHEC.htm>
Commonwealth Institute <www.commonwealth.org.uk> and <www.eCommonwealth.net>
Commonwealth Lawyers Association – <www.oneworld.net>
Commonwealth Press Union – <www.compressu.uk>
Commonwealth Youth Exchange Council, – <www.britcoun.org>
Institute of Commonwealth Studies, London – <www.ihr.sas.ac.uk/ics/>
Museum of the Empire & Commonwealth – <www.empiremuseum.co.uk>
Royal Commonwealth Society – <www.rcsint.org>

For historical background, the classic works are the 'Chatham House surveys' by Hancock, Mansergh and Miller. W. K. Hancock, *Survey of British Commonwealth Affairs*, vol. I, *Problems of Nationality, 1918–1936* (1937); vol. II, *Problems of Economic Policy 1918–1939*, Part 1 (1940),

Part 2 (1942); Nicholas Mansergh, *Survey of British Commonwealth Affairs: Problems of External Policy, 1931–1932*, 2 vols. (1952, 1958) and see the same author's *The Commonwealth Experience* (1969); J. D. B. Miller, *Survey of Commonwealth Affairs: Problems of Expansion and Attrition, 1953–1969* (1974) and see the same author's *The Commonwealth and the World* (1965). See also H. Duncan Hall, *The British Commonwealth of Nations: A Study of its Past and Future Development* (1920) and the same author's *Commonwealth: A History of the British Commonwealth of Nations* (1970).

Studies of the Commonwealth have been sparse since the last 'Chatham House survey' in 1974. The chief published works were: W. David McIntyre, *The Commonwealth of Nations: Origins and Impact 1869–1971* (1977): D. Judd and P. Slinn, *The Evolution of the Modern Commonwealth, 1920–80* (1982); A. J. R. Groom and Paul Taylor (eds.), *The Commonwealth in the 1980s* (1984); Dennis Austin, *The Commonwealth and Britain* (1988); Stephen Chan, *The Commonwealth in World Politics: A Study of International Action 1965 to 1985* (1988) and *Twelve Years of Commonwealth Diplomatic History: Commonwealth Summit Meetings 1979–1991* (1992); Margaret Doxey, *The Commonwealth Secretariat and the Contemporary Commonwealth* (1989); D. A. Low (ed.), *Constitutional Heads and Political Crises: Commonwealth Episodes, 1945–85* (1988); D. Butler and D. A. Low (eds.), *Sovereigns and Surrogates: Constitutional Heads of State in the Commonwealth* (1990); W. David McIntyre, *The Significance of the Commonwealth, 1965–90* (1991); Leslie Zines, *Constitutional Change in the Commonwealth* (1991); R. Bourne, *Britain in the Commonwealth* (1997); I. M. Cumpston, *The Evolution of the Commonwealth of Nations, 1900–1980* (1997); D. Mansergh (ed.), *Nationalism and Independence: Selected Irish Papers by Nicholas Mansergh* (1997); W. David McIntyre, *British Decolonization 1946–1997: Why, When, and How did the British Empire Fall?* (1998); G. Mills and J. Stremlau (eds.), *The Commonwealth in the 21st Century* (1999).

Notes

1 Origins and Meanings

1. Speech by British Prime Minister, Mr Tony Blair, at the Chogm Opening Ceremony, 24 October 1997, p. 2.
2. S. R. Mehrotra, 'On the use of the Term "Commonwealth"', *Journal of Commonwealth Political Studies [JCPS]* (1963) 2(1): 1–16.
3. R. Jebb, *Studies in Colonial Nationalism* (London, 1905), pp. 272–80.
4. *Dictionary of Canadian Biography, XII, 1891 to 1900* (Toronto, 1990), p. 1055.
5. British Parliamentary Papers: 1907, *Accounts and Papers*, IX, 61, Cd 3523, pp. 80–1; K. C. Wheare, *The Constitutional Structure of the Commonwealth* (Oxford, 1960), pp. 7–9.
6. See L. Curtis, *The Problem of the Commonwealth* (London, 1915) and *The Commonwealth of Nations* (London, 1916).
7. N. Mansergh, *Survey of British Commonwealth Affairs: Problems of External Policy 1931–1939* (London, 1952), p. 270.

2 Dominion Status and the 1926 Declaration

1. H. D. Hall, 'The Genesis of the Balfour Declaration of 1926', *JCPS* (1962) 1(3): 169–93; P. Wigley and N. Hillmer, 'Defining the First British Commonwealth: the Hankey Memorandum on the 1926 Imperial Conference', *Journal of Imperial and Commonwealth History [JICH]* (1979) 8(1): 105–16.
2. L. S. Amery, *My Political Life*, 3 vols. (London, 1953–5), II, pp. 390–5.
3. Joe [Sir Saville] Garner, *The Commonwealth Office 1925–68* (London, 1978), p. 51.
4. *The Commonwealth at the Summit: Communiqués of Commonwealth Heads of Government Meetings 1944–86 [Cwlth. Summit, I]* (London, 1987), p. 295.
5. Amery, *My Political Life*, II, p. 395.
6. 'Document Number Two', in D. Macardle, *The Irish Republic* (Dublin, 1951), p. 960. See also N. Mansergh, 'The implications of Éire's relationship with the British Commonwealth of Nations', in *Nationalism and Independence: Selected Irish Papers*, ed. by D. Mansergh (Cork, 1997), pp. 148–68.
7. For Ireland under Dominion status, see D. W. Harkness, *The Restless Dominion: The Irish Free State and the British Commonwealth of Nations 1921–31* (London, 1969).
8. Professor Nicholas Mansergh was told that the affirmative answer about leaving the Commonwealth was elicited by the *Tass* correspondent. 'Irish Foreign Policy, 1945–51' in *Ireland in the War Years and After 1939–51*, ed. by K. B. Nowlan and T. D. Williams (Dublin, 1969), p. 140.
9. In his 1948 press conference in Ottawa Costello was quoted as implying that: 'Once partition was ended, the way would be clear for complete and friendly association of the republic of Ireland with Britain in a

Commonwealth of Nations.' *Winnipeg Free Press* (9 September 1948), p. 17. col. 7.

10. See J. M. Ward, *Colonial Self-Government: The British Experience 1759–1856* (London, 1976).

11. McIntyre, 'The Strange Death of Dominion Status', *JICH* (1999), 27(2): 193–212.

12. 'Canada, the Commonwealth and the World', address to Canadian Universities Society of Great Britain, 22 March 1965. Arnold Smith Papers, N[ational] A[rchives of] C[anada], MG 31/E47, vol. 81, file 24; address to editors of Christian newspapers of North America, Ottawa, 5 May 1965. MG 31/E47, vol. 72, file 8.

3 Republic Status and the 1949 Declaration

1. P. J. H. Stent, 'The British Commonwealth and Asia', January 1948. Copy in P[ublic] R[ecord] O[ffice]: PREM[IER] 8/735, pp. 25–33.

2. N. Mansergh *et al.* (eds.), *Constitutional Relations Between Britain and India: The Transfer of Power, 1942–1947*, 12 vols. [*TOPI*] (London: 1970–83), vol. X, pp. 609–10.

3. Governor-General of Malaya to Secretary of State for the Colonies (183) 27 June 1947 in CR(47)3, 15 September 1947. PRO: CAB[INET] 134/117.

4. CR(48)2, 21 May 1948; CR(48) 2nd.mtg., 31 May 1948. CAB 134/118.

5. Memo of 31 December 1948, with CR(49)1, 3 January 1949. CAB 134/119.

6. 2nd.mtg. between Fraser and Listowel, 22 March 1949, N[ew] Z[ealand] A[rchives] PM 205/3/4 Part 10, pp. 1–11 in series AAEG 950/3436; mtg. in McIntosh's room, 22 March 1949, p. 8.

7. Notes on a visit to London, 19–30 April 1949. Lester Pearson Papers, NAC: MG 26, N1, box 34, file India–Canadian Relations 1947–57, p. 5.

8. Mtg. on 22 April 1949. PMM (UK) (49)1, 25 April 1949. CAB 133/91.

9. The best account is in R. J. Moore, *Making the New Commonwealth* (Oxford, 1987).

10. PMM(49)5, 26 April 1949 and PMM(49) 6th. mtg. 27 April 1949. NAC: MG/26, N1, vol. 23, file Prime Ministers' Meeting – April 1949. The text of the London Declaration is in *Cwlth. Summit, I*, p. 29.

4 The Secretariat and the 1971 Declaration

1. McIntyre, 'Canada and the Creation of the Commonwealth Secretariat, 1965', *International Journal* [Toronto] (1998) 53(4): 753–77; 'Britain and the Creation of the Commonwealth Secretariat', *JICH* (2000), (28): 135–58. On earlier proposals, see B. Vivekanandan, 'The Commonwealth Secretariat', *International Studies* [New Delhi], 1968 9(3): 302–8.

2. R. Hyam, 'Bureaucracy and "Trusteeship" in the Colonial Empire', in J. M. Brown and W. R. Louis (eds.), *The Oxford History of the British Empire [OHBE]*, vol. 4, *The Twentieth Century* (Oxford, 1999), pp. 255–65.

3. H. D. Hall, *Commonwealth* (London, 1971), p. 588.

4. Phrase used by Sir Charles Jeffries. Jeffries to Sedgwick, 31 March 1953. PRO: Commonwealth Relations Office records, DO 35/5056.

5. McIntyre, 'The Admission of Small States to the Commonwealth', *JICH*, 1996 (24)2: 244–77.
6. 'Patriotism Based on Reality, Not on Dreams?', *The Times*, 2 April 1964, p. 13. Powell finally admitted to the authorship in 1997. S. Heffer, *Like The Roman: The Life of Enoch Powell* (London, 1998), pp. 350–1.
7. D-Home to Pearson, Menzies and Holyoake, 3 June 1964. Canadian External Affairs archives, NAC: RG 25, box 10662, part 2.
8. Holmes, 'The Commonwealth Faces 1964', *The Times* (7 January 1964), p. 9; 'Statement on the Commonwealth issued by the Royal Commonwealth Society on the eve of the Prime Minister's Conference', embargoed to 2 July 1964.
9. PMM(64) 3rd. mtg., 8 July, 4th. and 5th. mtgs., 9 July, 6th. mtg., 10 July 1964, consulted in series ABHS 950, PM 153/50/4 Part II in NZA and MG 26, N3, box 320, file 812.3 – 1964 in NAC. (CAB 133/253–255 in PRO are inexplicably closed for 50 years).
10. Trend for PM, 11 July 1964. PRO: PREM 11/4637.
11. The Agreed Memorandum, 25 June 1965 in *Cwlth. Summit, I,* pp. 105–11; see also Garner, *Commonwealth Office*, p. 352.
12. Text of the 1971 Declaration in *Cwlth. Summit, I,* pp. 156–7.

5 Rhodesia' UDI and the Crisis of the 1960s

1. A. A. Mazrui, *The Anglo-African Commonwealth: Political Friction and Cultural Fusion*, (Oxford, 1967), pp. 1–2.
2. Commonwealth Prime Ministers' Meeting, September 1966. Record of Restricted Session: 2nd. Mtg., 12 September 1966, Secretary-General 131/66/3. Arnold Smith boxes in ComSec Archives, Marlborough House Library.
3. McIntyre, 'End of an Era for the Commonwealth: Thoughts on the Hibiscus Summit', *N[ew] Z[ealand] I[nternational] R[eview]* (1990) 15(1): 6.
4. For the background, see A. Verrier, *The Road to Zimbabwe 1890–1980* (London, 1986); C. Palley, *The Constitutional History and Law of Southern Rhodesia 1880–1965* (Oxford, 1966).
5. Discussion on 'Progress of British Territories towards Independent Membership of the Commonwealth' 10 July 1964, as reported by Arnold Smith in *Stitches in Time: The Commonwealth in World Politics* (London, 1981), p. 2. He told his ghost-writer that Pearson's breaking the ice was a 'lovely moment'. Record of conversation with Clyde Sanger, 17 October 1979. NAC: MG31/E47, vol. 88, file 23. He also recounted the Banda story, as 'a healthy breath of fresh air … an intervention I shall never forget', in his address to the Canadian Universities Society of Great Britain, 22 March 1965. MG 31/E47, vol. 81, file 24, p. 32. The official British record merely summarised Banda as saying: 'He and Mr Sandys were good friends. Many of the things Mr Sandys had said about the development of the Commonwealth were very true. But he must question Mr Sandys' claim that Britain had given her colonies independence entirely of their own free will and without pressure. If Britain had indeed done so, he and some of his fellow Prime Ministers would not have spent time in British gaols.' Meeting

of Commonwealth Prime Ministers, July 1964, Minutes. NAC: MG226, N3, file 812.3–1964.

6. Communiqué, 12 January 1966. *Cwlth. Summit, I*, p. 119.

7. Ibid., pp. 124–6. The caucus's views in record of Restricted Session, 1st. mtg., 12 September 1966. Secretary-General 131/66/3 in Arnold Smith boxes, Marlborough House Library.

8. J. Davidow, *A Peace in Southern Africa: The Lancaster House Conference on Rhodesia, 1979* (Boulder and London, 1989); S. Chan, *The Commonwealth Observer Group in Zimbabwe; A Personal Memoir* (Gwelo, 1985).

6   Apartheid and the Crisis of the 1980s

1. D. Austin, *The Commonwealth and Britain*, Chatham House Papers, 41 (London, 1988), p. 15.

2. *The Round Table* (1987), 304: 431.

3. A. Sampson, *Black and Gold: Tycoons, Revolutionaries and Apartheid* (London, 1987), p. 218.

4. See Okanagan Statement and Programme of action in Southern Africa, 16 October 1987 and Southern Africa: The Way Ahead, the Kuala Lumpur Statement, 22 October 1989. *The Commonwealth at the Summit*, vol. 2, *Communiqués of the Commonwealth Heads of Government Meetings 1987–1995 [Cwlth. Summit, II]* (London, 1997), pp. 8–11, 46–50.

5. J. D. Omer-Cooper, 'Apartheid', in *Africa South of the Sahara* (London, 1987), pp. 916–29; T. R. H. Davenport, *South Africa: A Modern History* (London, 1977), pp. 257–327; *The Oxford History of South Africa*, ed. by M. Wilson and C. Thompson (Oxford, 1971), vol. II, pp. 459–70; S. Dubow, *Scientific Racism in South Africa* (Cambridge, 1995).

6. A. Sampson, *Mandela: The Authorised Biography* (London, 1999), pp. 192–4; N. Mandela, *Long Walk to Freedom: The Autobiography of Nelson Mandela* (Boston, 1994), pp. 303–69.

7. 'A Testing Time', introductory pamphlet to Secretary-General's Report, 1985, p. 15.

8. *Cwlth. Summit I*, p. 267.

9. *Mission to South Africa: The Commonwealth Report* (London, 1986), pp. 23, 103–4.

10. McIntyre, 'End of an Era', *NZIR* (1990) 15(1): 5.

11. P. Johnson, *Eye of Fire: Emeka Anyaoku* (Trenton, 2000), pp. 50–1.

12. T. Richards, *Dancing on Our Bones: New Zealand, South Africa, Rugby and Racism* (Wellington, 1999), p. 251.

13. Johnson, *Eye of Fire*, pp. 53–99.

7   The Head of the Commonwealth

1. See T. McDonald, *The Queen and the Commonwealth* (London, 1986); McIntyre, *The Significance of the Commonwealth 1965–90* (London, 1991), pp. 244–61.

2. W. Dale, *The Modern Commonwealth* (London, 1983), p. 35.

3. Text in *Cwlth. Summit , I*, p. 29.

4. Dale, *Modern Commonwealth*, p. 35.
5. Nehru's telegram in *The Times* (9 February 1952).
6. Pearson to Sir Alan Lascelles, 3 January 1952. Pearson Papers, NAC: MG 26, N1, vol. 34, Gov-Gen Appt.
7. Ibid., Pearson to J. W. Pickersgill, 12 February 1952.
8. Minute by Churchill, 4 Feb. 1955, submitting Pakistan application to HM Queen as Head of the Commonwealth. PRO: DO35/5134.
9. Ibid., Adeane to Clutterbuck, 26 September 1959 and 3 November 1959.
10. Table of visits in McIntyre, *Significance of the Commonwealth*, pp. 252–3.
11. Lester Pearson's report of meeting in No. 10 Downing St., 2 February 1955: 'This is a silly idea ... We must stop this proposal, which no one really wants but the "old man" ... ' Pearson Papers, NAC: MG 26, N1, vol. 23, Commonwealth PMM 1955.
12. *Commonwealth* (1986), 28(5): 177.
13. *The Times*, 2 April 1964, p. 13, cols. 5–7.
14. Text in *C[ommon]w[ea]lth Currents*, February 1984, p. 9.
15. *Daily Express*, 30 December 1983.
16. *The Times*, 21 January 1984.
17. Ibid., 26 January 1984 and 6 February 1984.
18. Ibid., letters of 20 February, and 24 February 1984.
19. Ibid., 17 July 1986.
20. Ibid., 21 and 22 July 1986.
21. H. V. Hodson, 'Crown and Commonwealth', *Round Table* (1995), 333: 89–95.
22. Ibid. (1996), 339: 279–86. J. Collinge, 'Criteria for Commonwealth Membership'.
23. HGM (97)7, Report of the Intergovernmental Group on Criteria for Commonwealth Membership, September 1997.
24. Quoted in V. Bogdanor, *The Monarchy and the Constitution* (Oxford, 1995), p. 269.
25. Only two other reporters picked up the significance of this move: John Hibbs: 'Mr Blair ducked awkward questions about the future role of the Queen as Head of the Commonwealth', *Daily Telegraph* (28 October 1997), p. 10, and Derek Ingram: 'The change in terminology from King (and now Queen) appeared to affirm that the Prince of Wales and his successors would automatically succeed as Head of the Commonwealth ... there appears to have been no discussion of the details of the report. It seems doubtful that many countries had understood the subtle but important change that had been quietly effected' (*Round Table* [1998], 345: 15).

8 The Logo, the Venue and the Argot

1. Smith, *Stitches in Time*, p. 18.
2. For Gemini's Commonwealth role, see R. Bourne, *News on a Knife-edge: Gemini Journalism and Global Agenda* (London, 1995), pp. 147–64.
3. RCS Newsletter, 1996, 1, pp. 1–2.
4. See McIntyre, 'Britain and the Creation of the Commonwealth Secretariat', *JICH* (2000) 28(1): 138–9.
5. Brook for PM, 29 January 1959. PRO: PREM 11/4102.

6. *Cwlth. Currents*, 1978, April p. 6.
7. Austin, *Commonwealth and Britain*, p. 60.
8. C. Ball and L. Dunn, *Non-Governmental Organisations: Guidelines for Good Policy and Practice [NGO Guidelines]* (London, 1995), pp. 29–30.
9. D. A. Low, 'Commonwealth Policy Studies: Is there a case for a centre?'. *Round Table* (1988), 308: 309.

9   Membership

1. D. M. Schreuder, *Gladstone and Kruger: Liberal Government and Colonial Home Rule 1880–85* (London, 1969), Foreword, p. vii.
2. On decolonisation, see W. R. Louis, 'The Dissolution of the British Empire', *OHBE, IV* (1999), pp. 329–56; J. Darwin, *British Decolonisation: The Retreat of Empire in the Post-War World* (London, 1988) and *The End of the British Empire: The Historical Debate* (Oxford, 1991); McIntyre, *British Decolonization 1946–1997: When, Why, and How did the British Empire Fall?* (London, 1998).
3. D. J. Morgan, *The Official History of Colonial Development*, vol. 5, *Guidance Towards Self-Government in British Colonies* (London, 1980), p. 43.
4. CPC(57)30 (Revise), 6 September 1957. PRO:CAB 134/1556. For a detailed analysis, see Tony Hopkins, 'Macmillan's Audit of Empire, 1957', in P. Clarke and C. Trebilcock (eds.), *Understanding Decline: Perceptions and Realities of British Economic Performance* (Cambridge, 1997), pp. 234–60.
5. See R. Holland, *Britain and the Revolt in Cyprus 1954–1959* (Oxford, 1998).
6. Note for the record by T. Bligh, 20 July 1960 about mtg. on 13 July 'No circulation' – as arranged by Sir N. Brook.' PRO: PREM 11/3649.
7. For the significance of the Cyprus decision see McIntyre, 'The Admission of Small States to the Commonwealth', *JICH* (1996) 24(2): 244–77.
8. Macmillan to Menzies (Secret & Confidential), 8 February 1962. PRO: PREM 11/3649.
9. PM's comments, 5 August 1964, on minute by Paul Martin, 4 August 1964. NAC: MG 26, N3, vol. 267, file 811/M261; Pearson memo. for Wilson, 25 March 1965. PRO: PREM 13/185.
10. *Cwlth. Summit, II,* pp. 160–9.
12. HGM(97), 7 Sep. 1997. Report of the Intergovernmental Group on Criteria for Commonwealth Membership, pp. 2–3; The Edinburgh Communiqué, 1997, pp. 3–4; preliminary explanation by Collinge, in 'Criteria for Commonwealth Membership', *Round Table* (1996), 339: 279–86.

10   At the Summit – Chogms

1. See J. E. Kendle, *The Colonial and Imperial Conferences 1887–1911: A Study in Imperial Organisation* (London, 1967).

11   Ethos, Values and the 1991 Declaration

1. *Cwlth. Summit , I,* pp. 156–7.
2. Ibid., pp. 198–9.

3. Dale, *Modern Commonwealth*, pp. 54–5.
4. S. Chan, *The Commonwealth in World Politics: A Study of International Action 1965 to 1985* (London, 1988), p. 50.
6. Chan with A. J. R. Groom, 'The Future', in S. Chan, *Twelve Years of Commonwealth Diplomatic History: Commonwealth Summit Meetings 1979–1991* (Lampeter, 1992), pp. 123–31.
7. Text dated 20 October 1991 in *Cwlth. Summit, II*, pp. 82–5.
8. McIntyre, 'The Mandela and Major CHOGM: consensus ninety per cent restored', *NZIR* (1992) 17(1): 7.
9. Ibid., p. 9, Chan, 'Action, issues and instruments in the post-Thatcher Commonwealth'.
10. Text dated 12 November 1995 in *Cwlth. Summit, II*, pp. 156–9.

12 Below the Summit

1. Report on the Commonwealth Ministerial Action group on the Harare Declaration (CMAG) to Heads of Government, September 1997, pp. 26–9; HGM(99)4 (Addendum), November 1999. Report of the Commonwealth Ministerial Action Group on the Harare Declaration (CMAG) Ministerial Mission to Pakistan, 28–9 October 1999, pp. 11–12.
2. The reports of Ramphal's expert groups are summarised in *International Economic Issues: Contributions by the Commonwealth 1975–1990* (London, 1990).
3. 1997 CMAG Report, pp. ix, x.
4. Ibid., p. xii.
5. J. Mayall, 'Democratizing the Commonwealth', *International Affairs* (1998), 74(2): 389.
6. HGM(99)4, 1 October 1999, 'The Future Role of CMAG', in CMAG Report, p. 25.
7. Durban Communiqué, November 1999, p. 11.

13 Rediscovery and the Generation Gap

1. House of Commons, Session 1995–6. Foreign Affairs Committee First Report 'The Future Role of the Commonwealth': vol. I, Report together with the Proceedings of the Committee, vol. II, Minutes of Evidence and Appendices (London, 1990) [FAC Report].
2. R. Jenkins, *Reassessing the Commonwealth*, Chatham House Discussion Paper 72 (London, 1997).
3. *Learning from Each Other: Commonwealth Studies for the 21st Century: Report of the Commission on Commonwealth Studies* (London, 1996) [Symons Report].
4. HGM (97) Commonwealth (2), 1 September 1997. Review of the Commonwealth Secretariat's Information Programme and Response by Commonwealth Agencies (London, 1997) [Ingram Report].
5. Parliament of the Commonwealth of Australia: Joint Standing Committee on Foreign Affairs, Defence and Trade. 'From Empire to Partnership: Report on a Seminar on the Commonwealth of Nations' (Canberra, 1997) [Canberra Seminar].

6. The Royal Commonwealth Society, Ottawa Branch. The Millennium Challenge – A Communiqué from the 'Commonwealth in the 3rd. Millennium Colloquium', 15 March 1998 [Ottawa Colloquium].
7. K. Ford and S. Katwala, *Reinventing the Commonwealth* (London, 1999).
8. FAC Report, I, pp. lx–lxii.
9. FAC Report, II, pp. 243–8.
10. Canberra Seminar: Fraser's address, 20 August 1997, pp. 5, 6, 8.
11. Ibid., Prof. Patience, pp. 66–7; Ruth Inall, p. 68.
12. Ottawa Colloquium Communiqué, p. 5.
13. FAC Report, II, pp. 237–9.
14. Ibid., p. 136.
15. Ibid., pp. 127–8.
16. West, *Economic Opportunities for Britain and the Commonwealth*, pp. 16, 26–9.
17. Canberra Seminar: West, 20 August 1997, pp. 75–9.
18. FAC Report, I, pp. xxi–xxiii.
19. Jenkins, *Reassessing the Commonwealth*, p. 56.
20. Ingram Report, p. 47.
21. FAC Report, II, p. 244.
22. Ibid., p. 47.
23. Canberra Seminar, pp. 28, 31.
24. Ingram Report, p. 64.
25. FAC Report, I, pp. xxxiv, lxiv.
26. FAC Report, II, pp. 94–5.
27. Ford and Katwala, *Reinventing the Commonwealth*, pp. 7, 19–20, 30–1, 60–3.

14 Globalisation, Small States and Regionalism

1. *New Zealand Foreign Policy: Statements and Documents 1943–1957* (Wellington, 1972), p. 93.
2. Smith, *Stitches in Time*, p. 18.
3. *Report of the Commonwealth Secretary-General 1977–1979* [*S-G Report*] (London, 1979), p. 6.
4. *Cwlth. Summit, II*, p. 159.
5. *A Future for Small States: Overcoming Vulnerability* [*Vulnerability II*] (London, 1997), pp. 3–4.
6. Promoting Shared Prosperity: Edinburgh Commonwealth Economic Declaration, 26 October 1997; pp. 1, 4, 5.
7. The Fancourt Commonwealth Declaration on Globalisation and People-Centred Development, 14 November 1999, pp. 3, 5.
8. Brook for PM, 26 April 1960. PRO: PREM 11/3220.
9. *Vulnerability: Small States in the Global Society* (London, 1985), p. vi.
10. Ibid., pp. 9–10.
11. *Vulnerability, II*, list on p. 10.
12. Ibid., pp. 9–13. See J. P. Atkins, S. Mazzi and C. D. Easter, *A Commonwealth Vulnerability Index for Developing Countries: The Position of Small States* (London, 2000).
13. Durban Communiqué, November 1999 (London, 1999), p. 17.
14. *Vulnerability, II*, pp. 41–2.

15. Pamphlet *The International Organisation of the Francophonie* (Paris, 2000).
16. *Cwlth. Currents,* 2000, 1, pp. 2–3.
17. C. van der Donckt, 'Examining the Commonwealth's Political Role: Constraints, Challenges, and Opportunities', in G. Mills and J. Stremlau, *The Commonwealth in the 21st Century* (Johannesburg, 1999), p. 33.

15   The Secretariat and the CFTC

1. *Report of the Review Committee on Inter-Commonwealth Organisations* (London, 1960).
2. *S-G Report, 1975,* p. 81. The best work on the Secretariat is M. P. Doxey, *The Commonwealth Secretariat and the Contemporary Commonwealth* (London, 1989).
3. Smith, *Stitches in Time,* pp. 108–20. The CFTC biennial reports were titled for many years *Commonwealth Skills for Commonwealth Needs,* later *Skills for Development.*
4. To Senior Officials, in Canberra, May 1976 quoted in *S-G Report, 1977,* p. 15.
5. *Introduction to S-G Report,* 1985, p. 21.
6. *S-G Report, 1979,* p. 6.
7. The scope of Ramphal's interests can be seen in his collections of speeches: S. Ramphal, *One World to Share* (London, 1979), and R. Sanders (ed.), *Inseparable Humanity* (London, 1988).
8. *S-G Report, 1999,* p. 19. For the range of his work, see E. Anyaoku, *The Missing Headlines: Selected Speeches* (Liverpool, 1997).
9. Report by M. Faber, '"Do Different": Review of the Commonwealth's "C" Programmes, Wholly or Partly Funded by the CFTC' (London, 1994), pp. 10, 16, 20.
10. Report by J. Toye, Review of the Economic and Social Programmes: Report to the Commonwealth Secretariat (London, 1995), pp. 25–6, 39, 154, 163, 167, 170.
11. *S-G Report, 1997,* p. 142.
12. Report by G. M. Draper, Change Management in the Commonwealth Secretariat 1998–1999: Report of the Change Management Officer (London), p. 55.
13. *Cwlth. Summit, II,* pp. 156–9.

16   The Commonwealth Foundation

1. J. Chadwick, *The Unofficial Commonwealth: The Story of the Commonwealth Foundation 1965–1980* (London, 1982), p. 67.
2. Ibid., pp. 53–4.
3. Ibid., p. 76.
4. E. Reid to C. S. A. Ritchie (Canadian High Commissioner in London), 6 February 1968. Arnold Smith Papers, NAC: MG31/E47, vol. 77, file 15.
5. Chadwick, *Unofficial Commonwealth,* p. 174.
6. *From Governments to Grassroots: Report of the advisory committee on relationships between the official and unofficial Commonwealth* (London, 1978); *Cwlth. Summit, I,* p. 215.

7. *The Commonwealth Foundation: Aims and Achievements 1966/1981* (London, 1981), p. 7.
8. *The Commonwealth Foundation: A Special Report 1966 to 1993* (London, 1993), pp. 5–10.
9. *Report of the First Commonwealth NGO Forum on Environmentally Sustainable Development and Collaboration in the Commonwealth, Harare, Zimbabwe 19–23 August 1991* (London, 1991), p. 110.
10. C. Ball and L. Dunn, *Non-Governmental Organisations: Guidelines for Good Policy and Practice [NGO Guidelines]* (London, 1995); media statement, 8 November 1995.
11. *NGO Guidelines*, p. 19.
12. Report by H. Acton, Reviewing the Commonwealth Foundation's Commonwealth Liaison Unit Programme, September 1997, pp. 27–9.
13. Strategic Plan of the Commonwealth Foundation 1997–2001 (London, 1997), p. 5.
14. The Commonwealth Foundation: *Citizens and Governance: Civil Society and the New Millennium* (London, 1999), p. 20.
15. Ibid., pp. 27–70.
16. Ibid., pp. 72, 92.
17. Outcomes of Durban: The Communiqué of the Third Commonwealth NGO Forum, November 1999, paras. 1–10.

17 The Commonwealth of Learning

1. *Cwlth. Summit, I*, pp. 285–6.
2. Report by A. Briggs, *Towards a Commonwealth of Learning: A Proposal to Create the University of the Commonwealth for Co-operation in Distance Education* (London, 1987), p. 2.
3. Ibid., p. 50.
4. Ibid., p. v. Foreword by Ramphal.
5. *The Commonwealth of Learning [COL]: Information Services Network [COLIS Network]* (Vancouver, 1989).
6. The COL: Annual Report 1990 – A Year of Consolidation (Vancouver, 1990), pp. 5–12.
7. The COL: Profile '95, p. 3.
8. The COL: Summary Report 1994–1996 (Vancouver, 1997), p. 2.
9. The COL: Report to the Commonwealth Heads of Government, 1997, p. 1.
10. Ibid., pp. 5–6.
11. The COL: Report from the Board of Governors to Commonwealth Heads of Government, (Durban, 1999), pp. 8–9, 16.

18 Outgrowing the Commonwealth – The Case of Cabi

1. For background, see McIntyre, *Significance of the Commonwealth*, pp. 174–8; T. Scrivenor, *CAB – The First 50 Years* (Farnham Royal, 1980); E. M. Aichison and D. L. Hawksworth, *IMI: Retrospect and Prospect* (Wallingford, 1993).
2. S-G interview with Sir Thomas Scrivenor, 16 March 1967; Scrivenor to Smith, 20 March 1967. Arnold Smith Papers: NAC, MG31/E47, vol. 2, file 7.

3. CAB International: Eleventh Review Conference, London, 1990, Report of Proceedings (Wallingford, 1990), pp. 40, 77–85; 1995 in *Review: Growing Globally* (Wallingford, 1995), p. 2.
4. Presenting CAB International: 96 in Review (Wallingford, 1990), p. 47.
5. CAB International: Eleventh Review Conference, 1990, p. 83.
6. CAB International: Twelfth Review Conference, London, 1993 Report of Proceedings (Wallingford, 1993), p. 71.
7. CAB International: Looking Today for Their Tomorrow – 94 in review (Wallingford, 1994), p. 1.
8. R. J. Williams 'New Strategies, Developments and Special Initiatives for the 2000–2002 Triennium'. CAB International: Fourteenth Review Conference, Report of Proceedings (Wallingford, 1999), p. 35.

19   Professional Associations

1. *S.-G. Report, 1999*, p. 21; *S.-G. Report, 1991*, p. 3; *S.-G. Report, 1993*, p. 10.
2. T. Dormer (Desk Officer for Non-governmental Organisations), 'Working with Non-governmental Organisations', February 2000.
3. H. Duncan Hall, *The British Commonwealth of Nations: A Study of its Past and Future Development* (London, 1920), pp. 372–8; [R. G.] Lord Casey, *The Future of the Commonwealth* (London, 1963), p. 114; RCS: 'A Statement of Faith', 22 June 1964, in 'How the Links in the Commonwealth May be Strengthened', *Commonwealth Journal* (1964) 7(4): 161.
4. M. M. Ball, *The 'Open' Commonwealth* (Durham, N.C., 1971), pp. vi, 201; J. D. B. Miller, *Survey of Commonwealth Affairs: Problems of Expansion and Attrition, 1953–1969* (London, 1974), p. xiii.
5. RCS: 'Towards a People's Commonwealth', 22 August 85, p. 1.
6. Dormer, 'Working with Non-governmental Organisations', pp. 1–2.
7. See H. Brittain, *Pilgrims and Pioneers* (London, n.d.).
8. See I. Grey, *The Parliamentarians: the History of the Commonwealth Parliamentary Association, 1911–1985* (London, 1986).
9. A. Donahoe, 'A Commonwealth of Parliaments', *The Parliamentarian*, October 1999: 359–64.
10. Chadwick, *Unofficial Commonwealth*, p. 16; see also E. Ashley, *Community of Universities: An Informal Portrait of the Association of Universities of the British Commonwealth 1913–1963* (Cambridge, 1963) and H. W. Springer, *The Commonwealth of Universities: The Story of the Association of Commonwealth Universities* (London, 1988).
11. Julius K. Nyerere, Keynote Speech, 16 August 1998, text in *ABCD – acu bulletin of current documentation* (1998), 135: 5–7.
12. *Put Our World to Rights: Towards a Commonwealth Human Rights Policy* (London, 1991), pp. 175–6.
13. *Nigeria – Stolen by Generals: Abuja after the Harare Commonwealth Declaration* (London, 1995), p. 28.
14. *Over a Barrel: Light Weapons & Human Rights in the Commonwealth* (New Delhi, 1999); *Rights Must Come First: The Commonwealth Human Rights Unit – A Chequered History* (New Delhi, 1999).
15. CPA, CMJA, CLEA and CLA: *Parliamentary Supremacy, Judicial Independence – Latimer House Guidelines for the Commonwealth*, 19 June 1998.

16. Prof. M. Gibbons (ACU), 'Submission to the Commonwealth Heads of Government Meeting in Durban, 12–15 November 1999, from 8 Commonwealth Professional Associations', Typescript 10 November 1999; Press Release, International AIDS Vaccine Initiative, 12 November 1999.
17. Durban Communiqué, 1999, p. 18.

20 Philanthropic Organisations

1. *NGO Guidelines*, p. 16.
2. Ibid., p. 19.
3. Ibid., p. 23.
4. Directory of Organisations, in *The Commonwealth Yearbook, 1999*, pp. 410–11, 422.
5. British Commonwealth League. Report of Conference, 'The Citizen Rights of Women Within the British Empire' 9–10 July 1925 (London, 1925), in the Sadd Brown Library, London Guildhall University; G. Davies, 'A Brief History of the League 1925–39' (typescript by courtesy of the author).
6. Commonwealth Countries League Education Fund, Annual Report 1998/1999.
7. *Managing Education Matters: The Professional Journal of the CCEAM*, 1999 (2)1: 10.
8. Working for Common Wealth Series No. WCW1: The International Commonwealth Conference on Local Economic Development, Goa, India, 21–28 September 1998, pp. 6, 7, 8.
9. Ibid., pp. 13–14.
10. Ibid., p. 19.
11. FAC Report, II, p. 219.
12. P. Williams, 'Can We Avoid a Poverty-focused Aid Programme Impoverishing North–South Relations?', in *Partnership and Poverty in Britain's and Sweden's New Aid Policies*, Occasional Paper 75, Centre of African Studies, University of Edinburgh, May 1998.
13. Z. Daysh, 'The Commonwealth – Globally to Centre Stage: The Human Ecology Route'. CHEC: *Human Ecology* (1999), 16/17, p. 6.
14. Ibid., p. 11, C. Liburd, 'Outcome of the First Meeting of the Commonwealth Consultative Group for Human Settlement (CCGHS)'.

21 Educational and Cultural Endeavours

1. *The Commonwealth Yearbook, 1959* (London: 1959), pp. 1099, 1105–6.
2. ACU: *Commonwealth Universities Yearbook, 2000*, 75th edn (London, 2000), II, pp. 1960–1.
3. T. R. Reese, *The History of the Royal Commonwealth Society, 1868–1968* (London, 1968), pp. 255–8.
4. T. A. Barringer, 'The Rise, Fall and Rise Again of the Royal Commonwealth Society Library', *African Research and Documentation* (1994), 64: 4.
5. Ibid., pp. 5–9.
6. Royal Commonwealth Society: Annual Report 1998–9.

7. See J. M. Mckenzie, 'The Imperial Institute' *Round Table* (1987), 302: 246–53.
8. 'British Teenagers Attend Commonwealth Summit'. Commonwealth Institute press release, Limassol, October 1993.
9. Commonwealth Institute – Centenary 1893–1993. Report to the Commonwealth Heads of Government Meeting, Limassol, 1993.
10. FAC Report, I, p. lxiv; II, pp. 272–8.
11. Commonwealth Institute: Review of 1999, Prospectus for 2000 (London, 1999).
12. The Empire & Commonwealth Museum, *Five Hundred Years in the Story of the English-speaking Peoples of the World* (Bristol, n.d.), p. 4.
13. Annual Report 96/97,'*Exchange Teacher*', p. 25; see also *LECT: The Story of the League, 1901–1991* (London, 1991).
14. Pamela Maryfield interview with Jill Dilks, *Overseas: Journal of the Royal Over-Seas League*, December 1996–February 1997, p. 20.
15. D. N. Dilks, 'Youth Exchanges in the Commonwealth', *Journal of the Royal Society of Arts,* August 1973: 4; see also, Dilks, 'Commonwealth Youth Exchange Council – A New Area at Work', *Commonwealth* (December 1971), 145–7.
16. L. J. Griffiths during discussion of Dilks' paper, *J. of R. Soc. of Arts,* August 1973: 10.
17. Toye, Review of Economic and Social Programmes, p. 163.
18. Youth Experience in the New Millennium: Report of the Third Meeting of Commonwealth Ministers Responsible for Youth Affairs, Kuala Lumpur, 27–30 May 1998 (London, 1998), pp. 11–12.
19. *The Commonwealth Office Year Book, 1968* (London, 1968), pp. 681–2.
20. Ashby, *Community of Universities,* pp. 92–5.
21. *Learning from Each Other*, p. 21.
22. Ibid., pp. 5, 17.
23. Ibid., pp. 39–43.
24. F. Madden, 'The Commonwealth, Commonwealth History, and Oxford, 1905–1971'; R. Robinson, 'Oxford in Imperial Historiography', in F. Madden and D. K. Fieldhouse, *Oxford and the Idea of the Commonwealth: Essays Presented to Sir Edgar Williams* (London, 1982), pp. 7–29, 30–48.
25. W. R. Louis (ed.), *The Oxford History of the British Empire,* 5 vols. (Oxford, 1998, 1999).
26. FAC Report, II, Memo. from University of Cambridge, pp. 224–7.
27. ICS Newsletter: '*1949–1999 50th. Anniversary*', 1990, issue 20.
28. FAC Report, II, p. 94; see also K. Bourne, 'Cumberland Lodge: The Influence of a Conference Centre', *Round Table* (1997), 342: 231–6.
29. *The Commonwealth Foundation, Report 1996–1999* (London, 1999), pp. 13–16.

22   Sport and the Commonwealth Games

1. *CHOGM Committee on Co-operation Through Sport* [*CCCS*], 1993 Report (London, 1993), p. 24.
2. Ibid., p. 2.

3. Sir Charles Tennyson, 'They Taught the World to Play', *Victorian Studies* (1959) 2(3): 211–22; J. Arlott (ed.), *The Oxford Companion to Sports and Games* (London, 1977); J. A. Mangan, *The Games Ethic and Imperialism: Aspects of the Diffusion of an Ideal* (London, 1986); McIntyre, *Significance of the Commonwealth*, pp. 224–43.
4. C. Dheensaw, *The Commonwealth Games: The First 60 Years, 1930–1990* (Auckland, 1994).
5. Commonwealth Games Federation General Assembly, 1988, Bids for 1994.
6. *Cwlth. Summit, II*, p. 76.
7. Ibid., p. 105.
8. *CCCS*, 1993 Report, p. 5.
9. HGM(99) (CW)5. October 1999, *CCCS*, 1999 Report, p. 1.
10. *The Commonwealth Yearbook, 1999* (London, 1999), p. 21.
11. *CCCS*, 1999 Report, p. 6.
12. Chris Laidlaw, *Rights of Passage*, (Auckland, 1999), pp. 86–7.
13. *CCCS*, 1999 Report, pp. 19–22.
14. Ibid., p. 3.

23 Public–Private Partnerships and a Commonwealth Business Culture

1. *Cwlth. Summit, I*, p. 157; *S-G Report, 1975*, p. 9.
2. *International Economic Issues: Contributions by the Commonwealth 1975–1990* (London, 1990), pp. 6–7.
3. *Cwlth. Summit, II*, pp. 66–7.
4. See W. Rendell, *The History of the Commonwealth Development Corporation 1948–1971* (London, 1976); Morgan, *Official History of Colonial Development*, II, pp. 320–82, IV, pp. 92–257.
5. J. Majoribanks, 'The Intellectual Case for the Public–Private Partnership as a Vehicle to Stimulate Investment in Poorer Countries; The Transformation of the Commonwealth Development Corporation into CDC Group plc', paper to OECD workshop, Paris, January 2000, p. 1.
6. CPII Financial Statements, xls, as at 31/12/99.
7. *Science for Technology for Development: An Expanded Programme of Scientific Co-operation in the Commonwealth* (London, 1984).
8. *Knowledge Networking for Development – Science and Technology for the Millennium: Report of the CSG Steering Group, Dec. 1998* (London, 1998), p. 15.
9. Ibid., p. 29.
10. *Cwlth. Currents*, March/April 1995, p. 4.
11. K. West, *Economic Opportunities for Britain and the Commonwealth* , Chatham House Discussion Paper 60 (London, 1995), pp. 26–9.
12. FAC Report, I, pp. xxii–xxiii.
13. *Parliamentary Debates (Hansard)*, 6th series, vol. 280, Session 1995–96, House of Commons, 27 June 1996, col. 479.
14. Jenkins, *Reassessing the Commonwealth*, p. 56.
15. *The Commonwealth and Europe: Investment and Trade – Opportunities for Partnership* (London and Edinburgh, 1997), p. 5.
16. The Edinburgh Communiqué, 1997, para. 6.

17. Promoting Shared Prosperity: Edinburgh Commonwealth Economic Declaration, 20 October 1997, paras. 1, 3.
18. CACG: Commonwealth Association for Corporate Governance (Inc.), 'Promoting Excellence in Corporate Governance in Commonwealth Countries' – An invitation to participate; CACG: 'Update on Activities', 1 May 2000.
19. HGM(99) (CW)1 (Supplement 3), October 1999. Report of the Commonwealth Expert Group on Good Governance and the Elimination of Corruption in Economic Management, para. 5.
20. The Fancourt Commonwealth Declaration on Globalisation, 1999, p. 5.

Index

.